What is unjust about Social Justice… according to some poor nobody.

By Edward Hall

Foreword

I hope to address those things I have observed to be unjust about the social justice movement in these pages. I have chapters for all of the big speaking points of said movement. I do not intend to comment exclusively on the failing of the left in these pages however nor is this a bait and switch to speak about what is wrong with the right as I see it. Instead I intend to speak on those speaking points in what I believe is an even-handed manner with observation on how I believe it should be done and my reasoning for my beliefs. You can call these pages philosophy if you like, I would go one or two steps further and call it natural philosophy or perhaps an excerpt on cycles and systems. Whatever you call it I hope you read it with an open but also critical mind. That is the spirit it was written in and the spirit with which I made the observations contained herein.

Chapter 1 Sexism

Let me start with a cautionary. I understand that there is sexism in our society. I understand that there is sexism from all people and that power has an effect on who can and does act in a sexist manner. On the other hand, I also understand power is very transitory and can be gained from victimhood as easily as from dominance. Indeed, most of the points to follow are both as victimhood has become the dominant narrative in the media and elsewhere. Worse, the single most stable form of power is the one the vast preponderance of coverage pointedly ignores but you will find little on that in this first chapter. This first chapter is instead dedicated to counterpoint of the most prolific of the largely one-sided narrative of social justice and some rather clear flaws inherent in it or so it seems to me.

<u>On Gender, Sex, and Sexuality</u>

As is consistently the case the left and the right are each half right and all wrong. The right says sex and gender are all nature and homosexuality is all nurture. Just as typical, the left says sex and gender are nonbinary social constructs (nurture) and homosexuality is genetic (nature). Come on people. Both are both. We aren't really surprised bible people want to stick to that silly homophobia thing though (no offense intended to the religious it is simply predictable that if you let a book dictate your views we already mostly know what you think, sometimes still very relevant today, sometimes a few thousand years wrong). The left though... come on folks, shame on you for real. Homosexuality is less mutable than your sex and gender... really? There is no way you don't know better than this? Well, there is one way. Your education has become indoctrination. You know, religion? And you let it happen, maybe even helped it to happen.

While I am upsetting people, I may as well speak the whole truth. Trans folks? You are conforming your body rather than conforming your mind to social expectation. Gender reassignment is seriously mentally unhealthy. If it wasn't so trendy this would absolutely fall under body dysmorphia and self-mutilation issues... and should. Psych gets a lot of things wrong… and well, body dysmorphia they had right, it is unhealthy. That they didn't apply them to people that legitimately need them… Guess what? They missed the bus... again. You can be gay and unashamed. You can defy gender conventions and be unashamed. That covers it. Yes, some will still judge you for either or both. You will never ever escape judgement and intolerance. Running to surgery is... at a minimum, not the answer. Are you proud of Michael Jackson or sad for him? You should be sad for him at least with respect to his plastic surgery and body image. I use the term unashamed intentionally rather than pride because being proud of any of your traits is unhealthy. I address that at other points here, but the gist is pride is elitism. Being unashamed is the neutral version of pride. It's what pride is, lacking arrogance and aggression.

Transgenderism is not brave, it is fearful. Let me take a moment to be clear here, when I say transgender in these pages I am referring to those people who wish to reassign their biological sex or suggest that there are more than two genders or that people with male bodies are actually female and vice versa. Your thoughts may well not be conventionally matching those of your gender, but your gender is physical and immutable. That your mind doesn't match the patterns implied by your body is precisely what gender roles are and why gender roles are a problem. Gender roles are generalizations, and again this is something that I will address in greater detail but the point is it is very easy to misuse generalizations. Make no mistake, I understand how much pressure can be found in our current society's press for conformity but altering your body so that your mind is now found to be appropriate for society is every bit as bad as the other way around, maybe worse. A transvestite is brave. They are actively fighting gender roles which have no place and should be eliminated. The argument is a very simple one. Transgenderism is comprised of 2 facets. The one facet is sexuality. The other facet is gender role. As a society we have overwhelmingly allowed for homosexuality. We recognize it as not a choice and completely natural. Not everyone does, but most do. That only leaves gender roles, which is where the dysfunction of transgenderism is likely to reside. Put simply, if it's okay to be gay and it's okay to defy gender roles, then the notion of redefining your gender or biological sex is an act of desperation due to fear of confronting either sexuality norms or gender roles. A person that would rather reassign their biological sex than confront gender roles or acknowledge homosexuality is not brave. I understand the feeling that people are judging unfairly and harshly. I understand wanting to fit in. I also understand that fitting in is not about becoming what others say you are. Our culture is extraordinarily divisive and it produces extraordinary adaptions and this is one such. But it is not this that should be adapted but society's unwillingness to accept differences. The answer is also not to be militant about these things. The answer is to be you as truly as you can be. We should get rid of gender role entrenchment, which is not to be confused with trying to alter basic realities that males and females are in fact, in general, different, with abundant exceptions. That said, transgenderism, meaning the belief that one is a gender other than that which one is born, whether it pursues surgery or not, accepts the gender roles society has placed upon them. No one can be considered reasonable and sane to surgically alter their body rather than deal with not being 100% accepted by society- a fictive position in itself. This is body dysmorphism and/or a deeply injured sense of self resulting in a radical need to assimilate and gain acceptance. In a nutshell, homosexuality is normal and healthy because it's natural. If we assigned people the trait of homosexuality culturally, it wouldn't be healthy, but we don't. By similar argument transgender people are born with a biological sex. We cannot change nature. These peoples' minds function in a manner that society wishes to suggest is other than their gender. This is nurture and it is flawed. That society doesn't allow room for their nature is the issue. But society is not correctly corrected with notions that there are more genders nor with the notion of surgical intervention. Society is correctly corrected with understanding that generalities have exceptions. The emphasis is important; indeed, it is crucial as peoples' understanding builds upon previous ideas, be they good or bad. Put simply, what makes one male or female is more anatomy and less thought pattern. That relates more to personality which, while it does lean in a direction, is far less clearly defined by sex.

To the psychologists out there… whether this is a bid for attention on the part of the affected as seen with much of plastic surgery or an issue of conforming one's flesh or mind to society's expectations it should be obvious that the mental state of people who use a knife to make themselves look acceptable is not a healthy state of mind. I do not believe that it is healthy for those affected to be treated thusly and it speaks poorly to the credibility of the profession to respond to something such as this with permissive indulgence. Your patients are greeted with the polar messages of permissive indulgence and rigid intolerance throughout society. It doesn't seem to me that this should be your position for this reason and also for the responsibilities of your profession. Mental health is about balance, is it not? Should it be the patient's choice? Yes. Should it be labelled brave or cowardly? No. That said I understand that as a rule psychology looks at the individual and sociology the society. The two are inseparable but treated separately. The result? If it is the environment that is broken and you "repair" the individual you, by necessity, have broken them. We need substantial reforms in this arena. We divorce cause and effect, nature and nurture, objectivism and relativism, and many more intrinsically linked things throughout our society to demonstrably poor effect.

The divisions produce nothing so much as they produce stagnation of progress and diminishment of understanding.

It doesn't help that the same block of professionals is responsible, in no small part, for the push of feminism, which heavily contributes to this issue, in the first place. Quite a few men would rather be women in the world you are making. Don't just look at the trans folks, check how many males are playing female characters, particularly on MMOs, a simple but not irrelevant point and one of many. Is this because those poor oppressed underrepresented females have it harder or maybe because they get stuff... for free... all the time... from males? The argument is rapidly losing the right to be approached in a dignified manner rather than a dismissive and caustic one though that would, of course, help no one. It is merely difficult for me to imagine that people that wish to speak of fairness could so completely fail to look objectively at both sides of any given situation.

There are not innumerable genders. There are two with a few known genetic disorders that only serve to prove that every rule has an exception, not that the rule does not exist or that it is incorrect. The source of the confusion is not anatomical but psychological. There may well be innumerable psychologies. Our experience possesses commonalities but also subtle differences in various ways. This does not mean there are innumerable genders but innumerable gender *roles* which is to say gender roles should not be used, as people are too individual for such. As to how such an error occurs perhaps psychology should seriously consider reducing their attention to gender as it seems to me they have attributed traits to genders both more and less than they actually occur depending on the gender in question, creating or reinforcing gender roles that happen to be gross misattributions and overgeneralizations. It is ironic that they characterize gender thus while also claiming it is heavily experiential. The claim that it is heavily experiential is found in developmental literature. That they reinforce the roles is demonstrated by two facts. Psychology is heavily feminist, feminism labels males all manner of predator, and disorders are heavily gendered. When two very similar behaviors are displayed, one from a male and one from a female, the female is far less likely to be called sociopath for instance, because women are nurturers of course, only plenty aren't and that's what a gender role looks like. Perhaps they know not what they do?

They want to celebrate culture, and not in the sense that all people blend to make one culture. Some people want to celebrate the tiny pockets of culture. They want foreigners(outsiders) but they don't want to call them foreigners. I wish that the kinds of things that are directed at me were only microaggressions. I watch a feminist smile at a woman as she walks by and scowl at me, not one second later. That's not a micro-aggression. That is flat out naked aggression, and I doubt they even realize they transmitted it on their face.

<u>Misappropriations of History</u>

Wealthy women like wealthy men, had. Poor women like poor men, did not. Then and now, money has been the determiner of how much power, influence and prestige a person receives and how many "rights" they have. I put rights in quotes here because in a situation where people, whatever their demographic, lack power their rights will be overlooked when and where possible by those who are immoral and/or utilitarian. Society might value rich men slightly higher than rich women but that is due to a preference of women themselves. Not many women date a man of lesser means than themselves, even today. At least as important for the justice and its lack is to look to the bottom and a look at the bottom shows that women have it better. They are typically given less demanding jobs for equal pay. Historically, in those situations in which a man was paid more it was so he could provide… for a woman and her children. I say her children because for many years now that has been the way it is, but more on that shortly. All of this sounds like him against her and vice versa though, and in no small part it is, so let me take a moment to make a grander point. What was the effect of adding women to the workforce in ever increasing numbers? The effect in simple economic terms was to substantially increase the labor pool. Can we agree on that? What is the effect of substantially increasing the labor pool on wages? It decreases wages, does it not? More competition for jobs, right? Women historically are even reputed to negotiate less aggressively for wages, meaning the standard wage drops even more, does it not? I could paint the picture more dire by several shades but let me bring this to its point, shall I? Do we believe that those who look at stocks and bonds daily, even hourly, that see labor as a cost to be reduced rather than an asset to be grown, that grow ever richer while the rest of the country grows ever poorer, are incapable of forecasting and even engineering such a fantastic boon to business and profit as that which comes from feminism? What I mean to say quite simply is, is it conceivable that this was engineered for nothing more than profit? Do not answer overly hastily. There is more to consider. Please read on. But do not forget that throughout the history of the west men have always been treated as expendable and women have always been protected. You may not like the reason as its practical position is predicated in essence on a womb but that is the fact history shows both in the distant and the very recent past. And speaking of expendable men that brings us to…

<u>The Draft</u>

There is nothing that proves the fact that society holds men expendable quite so much as the fact that they are the ones expected to lay down their lives for the interests of some rich lobbyist or another. It is by no means the only proof of expendability though. Look to all sorts of industry positively choking their rolls with female employees. Look to psychology essentially declaring the male mind to be abnormal, damaged, deleterious to society and then making it fundamentally so by creating an environment completely toxic to healthy development. But back to the point, as it pertains to the draft. First, poor men paid for the right to vote with their very lives. This meant that their vote considered the consequences of said lives, in general. Second it meant that when women marched for the right to vote, and yes everyone should have a right to vote if voting is how our society determines what rules its citizens are to follow, they paid very little for it. Much is said about the bravery of women marching and, yes occasionally being beaten in their pursuit of the right to vote but nothing about the elephant in the room. Did these feminists argue that the draft should be abolished? Did they argue that the draft should apply to them? Did they argue that the wealthy should have been conscripted as well? No, they simply wanted what they wanted for the least they could get it for and declared that just. Justice has the scales balance folks, and that is not what feminism is about nor what it was ever about. It broke the inertia of being at rest in an unjust place. It did not, nor does it now move toward justice. And before there was a draft, for generations and generations there were wars, basic tribalism, and the people who fought and died in these wars were men. That for a time society dictated men have higher positions was not an imbalance; it was a balance. It was the means by which they ensured men stayed relevant in societies that were predominantly female (because men absorbed all casualties). Those women did not object to not having to fight in the wars and they didn't object to the wars(because they too wanted the resources). Men's position on high in a society like that is not dictated by men thinking themselves superior. It is because they are extraordinarily outnumbered. That men also preferred to have sons in a society like that makes just as much basic, practical sense. Those are future protectors. And in times of peace, a hope of returning some balance to the population in terms of genders. Feminism doesn't care about this and makes the same mistakes absent the same stimuli. There is no war on women, and women don't bear the primary cost of a war for resources. The problem is the war for resources, whether it's waged with guns, laws or businesses. Feminism doesn't speak against these things but for the guns. Competition has casualties. I still have more case to make however. Let use segue from the topic of soldier and terrible environments into…

<u>Domestic Violence/Violence</u>

I want to start with soldier in this scenario because it is a too common issue and the link is obvious. I say it is obvious but frankly, people are ignoring half of it. People who see the wider world and/or open conflict have their eyes forced open, presuming they were shut, on the nature of humanity. At that point several things seen by many as innocuous are revealed for what they are. The sexism in this country against men is prolific. Soldier or not, being attacked upon the basis of your gender day in and day out has an effect on your state of mind. Men are spoken of collectively as rapists, murderers, ABUSERS (the topic at hand) of both physical and mental bent, liars, cheats, and villains of every magnitude. Women may be "slut shamed", but for practically all other behavior the comments to follow are near inevitably apologencia. In fact, more often than not it is, you guessed it, a man that made her that way, supposedly. Time to clarify a point, I do not excuse abuse, physical or mental, perpetrated on anyone. But the fact is men are presumed to be the aggressor of this behavior, both psychologically and physically. The psychological bit, meaning psychological abuse, incidentally, is blatantly dishonest. We all know which sex is more prone to that behavior but public opinion and the law both say, men, and treat them accordingly. It is worth noting that both good men and good women suffer from this. Good women are silent knowing the power they have with the system as damaged as it is. Good men are easily declared bad and, when the circumstances fall correctly, sooner or later, made bad, everyone has a breaking point, a fact well worth remembering in structuring one's justice. The charges should they be levied at all, are different. Punishments, should they actually be levied against both genders are also dramatically different. Removal of the male in such a call is all but assured as well. It is worth noting that these clearly sexist and institutional (doesn't get more institutional than the law) practices were pushed by feminists. To be clear, I am referring to policies that consistently, near uniformly, remove the male from the household in a domestic complaint. Speaking of institutional, the courts get to prosecute the man even if the supposed victim doesn't want to. Why did I say the man? Because that's who they arrest… by default. It is also worth noting that males are more frequently the victims of violence and perhaps more importantly, a male making a domestic violence call is simply not going to be taken seriously and will likely be the one removed in any case, much like how a male who was raped can still be accountable for child support but then that is another point for later. So a male can be removed from the home on an unfounded allegation of abuse and, still paying rent on said property while having no place to go which brings us to…

There are many more shelters for women than men. I find this to be a curious phenomenon for several reasons. First is the reason above. There are many domestic violence shelters for women but the man is the one removed from the home. I am not suggesting that some women do not have good reason to go to a shelter in some of these cases. I am suggesting that the man again has the greater need due to the way society handles it and less access for the same reason. Court ordered separation is common but he, assuming he is the provider, his expected role, is still obligated to pay said rent for her meaning he is without means. Remember most men, most people even, are poor or lower middle class. This gap too was pursued by feminism incidentally but we will address that. This seems a fair time to move on to the other kind of shelter, the homeless shelter. The vast majority of homeless people are men. The point for expendable males should be revisited here. And why are so many men homeless? I would suggest three reasons predominantly. The male is treated as expendable and the male psyche is treated as both impervious and pathological. This is a fantastic recipe for making a sociopath incidentally or so it seems to me, and one must wonder at cause vs effect for the quantity that we have in this country and the world at large. Since some people think cause and effect are dirty words we can use a couple that very nearly mean the same thing but suddenly I am virtuous instead of pathological (for implying an element of objectivity to the world, more on that later too) nature vs nurture. It is interesting how dramatic the difference in reaction from some crowds is between these very close synonyms, is it not? If you don't believe me try it yourself amongst the social sciences crowd. I did say three reasons though did I not? The third reason is that women do not need a shelter as much because…

Welfare

Welfare is a great idea and a I believe it is a step in the right direction to provide a safety net for our citizens. No one wants to be poor and the people on welfare are poor. The stories that get widespread attention and have been spread thousands of times are absurd edge case scenarios at best and outright lies at worst. The fact is our society needs an overflow for unneeded labor to continue to live until it is again needed, and if capitalism is to be used, so that labor be compensated adequately. Too many laborers mean not enough pay under our system as already stated. That said, this chapter is about sexism primarily and yes welfare is sexist and has been for some time. Welfare was and predominantly is for women and their children. Remember I said that the children in our society essentially belong to the women. Here again is your proof though there is ample more, if you desire it. Men are rarely if ever entitled to it and to make matters worse men might be asked to pay back welfare for a woman that he has no influence over whatsoever, who claims welfare on the grounds that she has a child in her custody that the man offered to take and support which brings us to…

<u>Abortion/Child Support</u>

In the event that both parents want the child, the customary legal outcome is that the woman gets majority contact and the man pays majority child support. In fact, for all practical purposes, our courts declare that the woman is more capable of physical care of the child regardless of circumstances lest they be truly extreme. The man is similarly viewed in a one-sided manner by the courts as overwhelmingly being capable of providing more financial support again, in all but the most extreme of circumstances. I know of a male who was working class who was expected to pay back welfare because the woman in question insisted on keeping custody of a child in spite of the fact that she had a drug habit and no income. She was neither caring for the child nor financially independent and he was predominantly providing care and basically at a subsistence wage, but the state wanted to collect the welfare she collected from him. Now this is an egregious example but it's not that uncommon. Family court is incredibly sexist and it is overwhelmingly pro-female and anti-male. Where is the feminist protest about this? They claim to be about equality, right? But we also have to look at the situation of unwanted children and the disparities we find in our system on this subject as well. Women have the right to an abortion in many states, most in fact, to my knowledge. It is her body and I can appreciate the argument that entitles her to abortion. It is in fact the essence of the gun rights, yes? I said right not control regarding guns to be clear.. The connection I am making between gun rights and abortion is the necessity of autonomy to freedom. Women would be able to obtain an abortion whether it is legal or illegal and have throughout history done so. You can't take away her ability to determine her course any more than you can take away gun owners'. Pandora's box cannot be closed. So, if women can obtain abortions, we must use that as the benchmark for the male side as well, of necessity, if we value justice. Here is what that looks like. The female can, if she so chooses, abandon the responsibilities of parenthood not once but twice, legally. She can abort and she can give the child up to adoption. The male must also have the ability to abandon responsibility of a child. This would be a simple issue of informing the female, upon notification of

pregnancy or before, that he does not consent to being a father, in which case he loses both financial responsibility and parental rights, exactly as she would should she choose to abandon. Rights and responsibilities must match and this is the only method that maintains autonomy for both parties and also gives
commensurate accountability, again to both parties. There are those that like to ignore justice and suggest that the man, having consented to sex has lost the right to choose, which ignores the fact that the
same exact argument could be applied to the woman who is still offered a choice and brings us rather
clearly to…

#MeToo movement/Sexual Assault/Sexual Harassment

The fact is men have long been disproportionately held accountable for sexual assault and sexual harassment. Why do we suppose that is? Let's start with statutory rape, shall we? An older gentleman has sex
with a teen and he is a creep, right? A sexual predator? A deviant? And what of our friendly neighborhood Ms. Robinson? Kindly? Sweet? Patient? Come on people. You can't have it both ways. We have
seen a small rise in females prosecuted and I don't consider that a win for several reasons, but we can
get into that more in a more appropriate section. The trend continues as we move on to sexual assault not
statutory in nature. Women are accused less. Women are punished less. Men are believed less. Men are
ridiculed more. But of course, women are ridiculed too much and questioned too harshly or so we are
supposed to believe. And this particular accusation carries, frankly, far too much faith from the public.
We live in a rape culture? Our society is not at all far from mob "justice" whenever there are allegations
of sexual misconduct, especially against a woman or child. Rape culture indeed. In an environment
where people treat the accusation of such a thing as synonymous with guilt, and such a thing has little to
no evidence used or sought, being ultimately a he said she said most of the time and in which males are
supposed to be exactly this vile loathsome creature, we do live in a rape culture. But it isn't prone to rap-
ing females. Again, it's males. The #MeTooMovement goes no small distance to prove my point on this
if you didn't already know from long exposure to the rest of the human race. I don't know if any of
those people accused are guilty. I don't know if the accusers were willing or duped. I do know that most
people declared the first many guilty if only in their minds immediately. Sexual harassment is even more
lopsided than sexual assault and directly because of the above plus the fact that even less proof is necessary often times. I have seen a man reprimanded for mentioning a smack on the bottom and a woman
high-fived for actually grabbing someone's bottom. Is it anecdotal? Sure it is. Is it isolated? Not hardly

and for the same reasons. The men report less than the women and are believed less and the women are punished less. Sex is a normal healthy thing and a lot of these problems can be eliminated if we stop treating it as some obscene taboo, presumably dating back to our puritanical roots. We both celebrate and shame it and neither is healthy. It is one more polarization among many. One thing that strikes me about this issue in particular is that the women, in many cases, who level these very damaging accusations would welcome the exact same behavior from someone else in exactly the same environment. Why is this noteworthy? Because women, in general, expect, no, demand that the male be the active pursuer or instigator, at least on the level that others would reasonably take note. Meaning that one must extend oneself for their pleasure but the men are supposedly the ones making a power play. This is not to say that women remain completely passive. They invite attention with subtle queues men, the supposedly oblivious ones, are meant to read, like little hints of clothing, and posture, and speech. In other words, they indicate their interest by sexualizing themselves, if only a little which brings us to…

Sexualization of Women

The infantile mentality that women not be viewed sexually is not realistic due to the very nature of humans, and it applies to both men and women. Humans are literally sexual by nature. It isn't a convention. I say infantile because that's what it is. This is like the notion that it's icky that your parents have sex, magnified by several degrees. It's simply immature.

Feminists ask for equal rights without equal accountability. Men do not walk around with their shirts off and say don't objectify me. And if they do, they are laughed at. If you want the gain, you have to pay the price. Do you think the price should be eliminated? Then you should have talked about that in the first place when it was happening to men. Feminists weren't saying that then. Why are they saying it now?

Arguing that women not be sexualized and arguing that women get to act like men who are in fact sexualized without arguing against the sexualization of men demonstrates unequivocally that one has not considered one's point. That is hypocrisy, that is bigotry and it has nothing to do with equality. The fact that women have to cover their breasts and specifically their nipples where men don't is indeed absurd. It comes from the same absurd place as the defined definition of rape in most states, which would have men necessarily be the rapist and women necessarily be the rapee. They removed those specific words from the definition, but functionally they did not. The penis is still the offending organ, while the vagina is, in most places, not. People want to complain about a law that says women can't show their sexualized organs but are okay with a law that says the owner of this organ is a rapist, not a rapee. Don't get me wrong, the law (on nipples) that people want abolished should be. That's not the point of my statement. But if we had to pick, the genital implications of rape should be getting a lot more attention.

Feminist objections, while correct, do not acknowledge the entirety of the facts of this situation. Women that want to walk about topless in public but also want to not be seen sexually are not being reasonable, rational, accountable adults. First, most obviously, humans are inherently sexual. It is the reason that we have reproduction. If you think that we need to stop seeing someone as a prospective mate for any reason, but particularly because it might make them uncomfortable, you aren't approaching the topic seriously. So, women want to be able to walk around topless outside because it's hot out and men can. That's fair. But then I already said that. The issue comes in in that some people also have an issue with the "sexualization" of women and that when they walk around topless, people will look at them and they will be uncomfortable with that because they're not "sex objects". No, they are not sex objects but then few if any people, male or female look at a person and see an object in the sense that is meant when one says objectification. Let's not pretend that the precise scale of aesthetic interest a person has with another person makes them immoral or moral. Put another way, young people and males, in general, are more body focused. This is by degree first, meaning women also hold the body in high regard, some more than others, and second is not remotely unnatural or wrong. In fact, it would be unnatural to pretend that physicality was unimportant and that bodies, those things we require for most, strike that, ALL tasks we perform, to be undertaken, are not essential. All of that said, we can see the problem is deep and long standing when entitlement and outrage even extend to what we do with our own eyes…

The Male Gaze

How on earth did anyone think it reasonable to seek to shame and or control where we direct our eyes? Seriously folks. There is nowhere that you can look at another human being that does them real harm. On the other side of this equation however we are looking at direct social control of where we, supposedly autonomous human beings are allowed to look and not look and for how long. I am not suggesting that it is not uncouth to stare overly long, especially at a person that clearly does not reciprocate. I am suggesting that uncouth is our right and indeed one more vehicle by which people can determine their compatibility with others. It is almost incidental to point out that females do this too albeit more subtly, in general. It is also definitely worth mentioning that should the gazer be one who is desired, there is really no degree to which the gaze is inappropriate, meaning it is just one more piece of the "if I desire you everything, if I do not nothing" equation. A gaze, no matter how uncomfortable, is not harassment. Get used to it and you will find it isn't even uncomfortable and they will find it isn't productive. Put another way, you do not get to decide what others do with their bodies (eyes) in order for you to feel more comfortable in your own skin. Imagine men judging women for where they look and don't. Whether the female gaze is subtle or unsubtle no one is shaming women for where they fix their gaze, nor should they. We can all be looked at in public. It is part of being in public… and existence. Some of us seem to think themselves royal that others must avert their eyes in their presence. This is the height of entitlement.

<u>A musing. (pun intended)</u>

I've grown up around a large body of women who call men superficial, who then "change" themselves with a bottle of hair dye and some makeup. Funnier still, they are surprised when the superficial method of acquisition only lasts… superficially.

<u>Openly Sexist Women Exclusive Establishments/Clearly Pro-woman Practices</u>

We have a fitness location called Curves in the U.S. It is exclusively female clientele… by policy. We aren't talking about a barber here who only knows how to cut men's hair because the barber only knows men's hairstyles. You are welcome to said barber cutting your hair. You just don't want them to. We have ladies' night and we wonder why some ladies think scamming drinks from guys is the way to go? We had a women's only screening of Wonder Woman not that long back. Are these big things? Not in their own right, no. They do show no regard for the fact that sexism is illegal in this country, however. They also show no empathy or self-awareness to talk about solidarity and exclude half the population; to talk about equality and have exclusive events. It speaks to the headspace that the people who follow this ideology inhabit and that headspace is entitlement and elitism. The ideology in question? Feminism…

Feminism

Feminism has lobbied for sexist laws and governmental policies and obtained them meaning it is institutionalized, the very thing they claim of the supposed patriarchy, which has no such laws. It has declared a gender superior to the other (in addition to convoluting the entire conversation). It has influenced psychology such that not only psychology but academia in general hold what are typical female behaviors as the gold standard and supposed healthy behavior, while male behavior is declared pathological or at a minimum undesirable and in need of correction…by those with supposed female behaviors, of course. More than a few of its proponents call for an end to males. Should one wish to defend such an ideology by pointing out that there are radicals in all ideologies I have two things to point out. First these positions are both commonplace in the general feminist population and well represented in supposed feminist spokespeople. And second, only an ideology that practices unity through division which is to say, one that seeks to divide people to gain power suffers from this particular foible and the reason for this is simple and, to my eyes, self-evident. If you make a system that seeks power for an elite there will always be those who state their aims directly and those aims will be vile. Stating aims is a lot less vile when the policy to be created does not seek to empower some at the expense of others. If you are in fact for equality between the sexes you are not feminist, both by definition and by the evidence of history you are egalitarian. The etymology of the word feminist itself is pro-female. The reason for the formation of the group, pro-female. The formation of policy, pro-female and often, anti-male. That feminists dismiss any dissent from both males and females, elitist. It is a power block without the slightest concern for anything but power. It is as simple as that. Ask yourself why so many people who identify as feminist are more than happy to change just about any word people find offensive except this one, feminist… so much so that they will not use the word egalitarian but insist on telling women that know that they are not feminist, that they are?

Toxic Masculinity

Incidentally, that "toxic masculinity" society has such a problem with? That is insecurity instilled from father figures, prospective mates, and society at large to be stronger, faster, smarter, richer. The feminist solution, double down on attacks, meaning, no decline in the insecurity and an increase in sociopathy from those pushed past (and not recipients of) caring. If we actually want to fix these things the solution is simple. Give people room to be who and what they are. Reduce competition, the destructive external kind, self-improvement that is self-directed is the only constructive competition. Reduce conformity though the above will already go a long way in this respect. Discard terms like toxic masculinity which is divisive and completely ignores the fact that feminism is every bit as much to blame. Insecure and greedy versus unfeeling and greedy have a common theme by the way. Fix the greedy bit. It's called sharing, we learned it when we were like 2 years old, perhaps it's time to revisit it.

The irony of feminists talking about toxic masculinity and how it makes women serve men while the feminists in question literally talk about the other gender as though it is reasonable to tell said gender how it should behave, with the obvious intent that it shape said gender to better serve them…and from a top down perspective no less. It is not coincidental that most of the feminists guilty of said dialogue are female. Meanwhile… diversity… meaning conformity, like literally now also means figuratively… apparently. It might be worth noting that men do in fact already serve women as much and sometimes more than women serve men. Indeed, we are trending toward more with the chivalry and values of yesteryear in no small part still present while the laws change and expectations on the other sex decline.

<u>Recognizing a broken system for what it is</u>

So, there was a time not so long ago when it was simply understood that children would be children and so slack must be permitted for them to grow and learn important lessons in their own time and in comprehensive ways. At some point in recent history this was forgotten and children then were protected by explicit law to said same intent and to some degree, effect. This generated a means to exploit or "game" the system as adults could utilize the young to bypass laws intended for them (the adults). The children cooperated in part due to need or ignorance and in part due to intent. Soon after this trend came the disregard of said laws intended to protect children (youthful offenders) with young offenders being punished fully and, in some senses, worse (remember they can't vote or earn a wage yet) than adult offenders. More on this later. This is a simple cause and effect chain and likely is not a substantial surprise to most. On the surface there is no fix and people simply use any system to get over, right? The underlying system present here is capitalism, however. A system whose very purpose is precisely to celebrate and excuse that very behavior with megalithic figures irrefutably proving both that it is acceptable and (less actual but no less believed) obtainable. Simply stated, the fixes are to the symptom rather than the cause and so do not, indeed, cannot fix the problem for long and often produce undesirable side effects (like perhaps embittered youths, justly so). The fix requires something deeply ingrained and false be corrected. Not surprisingly, the establishment does not wish to change the establishment else they would not be it and so it continues until disillusionment and revolution and so the cycle repeats. Break the cycle…deliberately and with forethought to what is desired. Have sincere dialogue and cease false division. Or live eternally in strife and misery… it could not be simpler… or more impossible. Which are you in favor of, the simple or the impossible? It can be either. It's up to us to choose.

 Feminism has always had and will always have a pro-female agenda. This notion that feminism is about equality is deliberately lopsided. The only question is whether said agenda (women's rights) is actually currently or not currently deficient. Given how and why feminism started though, it is completely logical that it finds itself in this place that it is now. The etymology itself, of/by/for women, should be hint enough that one needs, at a minimum to dismantle their movement when its purpose is achieved lest it go…where it has gone. The fact is, however, even feminists who (still identify as) loathe its current face are culpable for its current levels of entitlement and bigotry. Even when it was first conceived it disacknowledged that the real struggle was with respect to classes (the poor). Middle and upper-class women were fighting for the right to have "careers". Women already worked... and alongside men, at that…in back breaking working (albeit typically lighter duty back breaking work out of simple necessity). Much of the early feminist movement was comprised of entitled people and as such it is no surprise that while they were talking about how to get what they didn't have no mention was made of giving up some of what they had by way of nonuniform egalitarianism. That's right folks, men were afforded rights…and responsibilities women didn't have. Similarly women were afforded responsibilities (emphasis feminist dogma) and .. rights that men didn't have. Before I go on, briefly, the real problem here as in most things links back definitively to that wonderful (sarcasm) flawed concept known as capitalism. If money is power and all things should be linked to money then comes the pay for everything argument, which, like the rest of feminism fails to identify the root cause. Society does not hate women, or ethnicities, or any other demographic, to include men counter to what some of you may think I think at this point, it loves money, because capitalism sharpens greed rather than dulling it. It is a tenet upon which to build a civilization that is…anti-civilization. Don't believe me? Define civilization and its purpose. Now, define socialism and its purpose. Striking similarity if you were honest, isn't there? The fact is every society still standing has used socialism to remain upright, the more sparingly the more violent, as a rule. But back to feminism shall we. Feminists only concern themselves about men's rights to the extent that they look for things they believe prove men have more rights so they again can shout for women's rights. Similarly, they do not look at women's rights to see when women have more and if those are pointed out they ignore them… at best. Whether you believe feminism started from a position of oppression or not it should be clear to most that, at a minimum, women are not oppressed and worse may, intentionally or unintentionally, be oppressors. The fact is gender roles, while not entirely correct and to some extent manipulated by society are, in point of fact, more accurate than not. Put another way, gender roles are the rules, there are exceptions and there must be room for those too. Dismantling norms of nature for a land in which only the exception is supposed to exist is not only fantasy, it is dangerous. The masses will not be denied forever and their anger at being treated so is just as right as when there is no room for the exception which will itself rebel. Now to back up a moment, the present shows pretty clearly that while feminists don't like gender roles they do in fact apply as a generality. History also upholds this implication. Meaning the generality of gender roles itself is not a social construct. The imposition of that on the populace as a whole, is. The experiment has been run. The data is in. Women, as a generality, are more emotional than men…which can be positive in some environments and highly destructive in others. Let's say they aren't more emotional, in general though, or even that they are but that they are held to the same standard as men. Explain to me why there are no male quotas or incentives in female dominated fields? Ask yourself why as women climb to high places in academia they shout how women naturally should be there, suggesting they are smarter…and yet in spite of the fact that women still lag in the physical sciences it must not be said (for proof refer to Harvard president fired for a start) that women are, *perhaps* (note that the perhaps denotes that it is simply a possibility) not as capable as men in physical sciences. This learned gentleman was fired for merely speculating a possibility that is supported by evidence of numbers. It should also be noted that the physical sciences do not allow for goalpost moving… I wonder if that might have had something to do with why women have not yet been declared superior there too? Note, I say superior not equal here because many of those feminists I have spoken of say exactly that, but it's about equality, right? I suppose I should take a moment and address the term goalpost moving. So, goalpost moving is the tendency of certain parties to constantly declare a new goal. Now this is to be differentiated from continuous forward progress, primarily because it doesn't acknowledge validity from any other source. For example, a person declares a statement "all x are y", is refuted via "all x are not y", shifts the position to "most x are y", is refuted again, moves to "some x are y", but never changes their conclusion even though these are supposedly intrinsic variables. Or it is expressed in its mirror. The conclusion constantly changes, but the variables stay the same. Simply stated, their equation does not match across the equal sign. They poorly account, giving both too much and too little credit situational to who they speak of. One could simply say bias, but it is a specific kind of bias. The most toxic element of feminism is probably the insidious tendency to declare one thing, get what one wants and then simply change said declaration… that endless need and unwillingness to acknowledge wrongdoing coupled with the entitlement that allows them to do it again and again without a twinge of conscience, there is a word for that, right? I think the word is sociopath. Ironically, a label applied massively disproportionally to…men. Ironic as it is part and parcel of feminism. Let me take a moment to reiterate, feminism is not the disease, it is a symptom. Capitalism, unification through division, social hierarchy, what do these have in common? Different ways to name the same disease. Who is surprised when the bean counter and the decision maker agree to pay themselves more than everyone else doing whatever task is at hand? No one, right? There is, however, no valid reason for this behavior, merely opportunity that should be eliminated. The best attempt offered up is scarcity. Funny thing is, by and large scarcity isn't a problem unless you make it one through market manipulation. A sane person doesn't need something just because it is rare and a gifted person(rare) should be helped into a position in which they can help society at large. I'm sure this sounds utopic and infeasible to many. The thing is, the proof is all around us every day and we ignore it…in the small ways… since society has not formally recognized the truth even while seeing…and partaking constantly. Who do you ask advice from? Which household member would/do you ask to push/fix your car? We know who around us, more often than not, is talented with respect to something that we need or desire. We could make that global and create something that has the utility of hierarchy without the power play by virtue of sharing said information communally. It's something we already do, it just isn't implemented formally and/or with the broader community in mind. Why? We incentivize dishonesty and manipulation because it is about wage and power more than it is about responsibility and community and it always will be with differential rewards. They are, in and of themselves, fracturous to humans.

The fact that we live in an increasingly feminized society has resulted in what are clearly some odd conclusions. By way of example I use playgrounds. For those of you who are old enough to remember, playgrounds were far more entertaining and more dangerous places. Not only that but they allowed for a greater degree of creativity. They were less structured. The justification for the playgrounds being made safer was that many children hurt themselves on playgrounds: a fact that is absolutely true and misses the point. Young people are learning their limitations. They're learning their abilities and they're testing those. Older playgrounds allowed more flexibility with that. And they did result in injuries but it wasn't primarily due to the design of the playground. The older playgrounds allowed for children to actually test their abilities. The number of playground fatalities that were not the result of shootings or stabbings is, and was, very, very minimal. But more important is this: it was a designated place where the children could go and would go to test their limits. Meaning that if they were injured, you knew where to look for them. Children do not have full knowledges of their faculties, and I don't just mean their mental faculties. They need to learn physical agility and strength in an environment that allows them to test those things. The current one does not except at the lowest of levels and there is such a thing as too much structure. There is a reason young children heal quickly and it isn't just because they are children. They are expected, by nature, to receive injuries in the course of developing their abilities. That is a lesson in itself. Now, all of this is proven by a point that some people would actually take as proof that the current, more feminized thinking worked. I am quite sure there are less injuries on playgrounds now. The reason for that is because they, meaning playgrounds, are more quickly rejected. Our youth grow out of the current playground model more quickly and polarize to either extreme athleticism or sedentariness. The playgrounds are, by virtue of specialization, divisive. The rate of injury is probably comparable to what it's always been only it happens elsewhere so the playground does not receive the onus. And frankly, many of the injuries are happening later when our young peoples' ability to heal is impaired relative to their younger selves, and they're injured more significantly. And the reason they're injured more significantly is twofold. One: they never did develop those gradations of the recognition of the limits of their abilities, the gradations that were developed by the old playgrounds. The other reason is related to the first. Due to the fact that they did not develop a recognition of their limitations and that they're older and bigger and more repressed, the manner in which they push the envelope is more extreme. I use the term extreme for a specific reason. It is around the time of the construction of these and other feminized laws against our own wishes and best interests (bike helmets, restrictions on parks, reductions in P.E. and recess) that we see an emergence of the extreme games. You do not eliminate the desire of people, particularly the young, to test ones' bounds. But that's just perspective. You also don't eliminate the need. The more nanny state you make it, meaning protecting oneself from oneself, the more extreme the rebellion will be. One does not make laws with such in mind but education. The people must have choice in order for the supposedly valued diversity to flourish. Balance is called for, which to my eyes, the old playgrounds had. And frankly, there's something very sad about the idea of an 18-year-old male hitting the obstacle course in basic training never having seen a set of monkey bars. And if you're going to suggest the 18-year-old boy shouldn't go into the military at all, that's fine, say that rather than achieving an aim through a backdoor. The fact is, we're not dissolving the military, and the poor, meaning economically disadvantaged, boys that are the dominant group enlisting only have public parks to prepare their bodies for adulthood. On the other hand, for the feminist agenda of not only safety but making women more able to compete with men by making men more like women, this'll do a fantastic job by disallowing them to harness their natural gifts. Which is not to say it's impossible. You're just taking away a vehicle by which to do it. And incidentally, it's not that girls can't use the parks too and it's not that girls don't use the parks too. They just don't get the same results, do they? Consider well that the reduction in the physical fitness of our children is not just the availability of media but the reduction in worthy outdoor and physical activities. I addressed parks previously. What teen would get meaningful interaction from them as they exist today? What I am getting at here folks is that we *should* prevent others from actively hurting us. We *should not* prevent our society from hurting themselves, however. Making information available about safety is fine. Attempting to deny people the ability to live and choose, and worthy places to do that, is not. Indeed, not only are physical limitations learned by doing something painful, empathy is as well. Our society is trying to be a nanny state in many ways and a nanny state is fascist because a nanny state tries to protect people not from others but from themselves. This point can be debated at great length via the example read. The gist is people must be free as much as they must be protected. Autonomy is one of the vital components of a person's wellbeing.

<u>Media Attention</u>

It has grown so insane that some think a benefit to themselves is, in fact, a liability. There are those who think positive attention they don't want is a bigger problem than the counterpoint, negative or no attention.

Feminism has been presented so heavily in the media that clearly feminist broadcasting is "the norm" making the speaking point that substantially sexist feminist productions are labelled as "not feminist enough".

10 years ago, most males on television were either clowns or jerks. Moving forward to today the situation is so much worse. The valid male figures have diminished further, the macho male figures are replaced by "macho" females even while macho males are disparaged. The level of buffoonery has magnified. All the while the female characters are the ones that keep things together and are intelligent and articulate not to mention clearly being in charge whether in an official capacity or not. If it was sexist

before, and I say it was, relatively passively due to acknowledging social averages, which created a feedback loop on gender roles and averages, it is not less so now. In fact, today it is more sexist than ever. It doesn't even acknowledge averages but rather is full in your face constructed and insulting to… about half the populace. The result of the current narrative? You didn't get rid of gender roles you just took several male ones and gave them to females and made the buffoon an overwhelmingly male role. It is in fact, more sexist than ever. You didn't dissolve the gender roles at all. You merely made them more offensive. Male more or less equals bad and you can get away with that because males will just increasingly not identify with other males. Competition and division increase. Superficially it may seem like women, being in predominantly positive roles is a good thing, but in my experience, women are competitive with one another. This too will increase division. That said we don't have to delve deeply to see how offensive the trend is. Five minutes of honest observation of television, movies, or even commercials is enough to make a person who has removed the calluses turn off the television as it is insulting to ones' intellect, damaging to ones' image, and frankly, for me and many others, not very entertaining.

Even if no one else in our society held these views academia and the media preach them. You can choose not to go to church and dramatically cut down on their rhetoric in your life. Not so for the education system and the media. These views, easily demonstrated to, at a bare minimum, be questionable, if not outright ridiculous, as I hold them to be, are for all practical purposes, omnipresent, immersive, and divisive. Imagine a born-again Christian, should you happen to not be Christian, entering your home every time you turn on the television and every school being a Christian one. Christian or not the implication is clear. This is indoctrination.

<u>Pay Gap</u>

The pay gap is still spoken of by acclaimed speakers in regular parlance in spite of the fact that it has been examined and soundly rebuked time and again. First, it is not true from the perspective of work hours and experience. In other words, those who work less hours and have less experience get paid less but that is not, under our system, discrimination. Second, it doesn't even touch the fact that in the lower tiers of income, women are given physically easier jobs, of necessity, in fairness, for what is often the same or more pay. The pay gap tries to compare actors and athletes which is that much more absurd, under capitalism, as these people draw, in most cases, less audience and so less money, or its inverse, and are paid accordingly and regardless are not wage employees but contracted professionals… with agents. More comical still, on the subject of sports, we made women's sports, with their supposed lower pay, so that women could be in professional sports in the first place. Imagine how many female athletes you would see if there was one coed league without quotas. Next to none, right? Because the best female competitors cannot compete with the best male competitors, as unpopular as that simple reality may be. That said there is a pay gap worth talking about but you have to change the lens a bit. You see, there is a fantastical pay gap out there with hardly a soul speaking about it. That pay gap requires viewing every-one as worthy contributors. We will get to that later though. It is interesting how much people pander to this though. Do they think women so weak and emotional as to need a debunked stat foisted at every op-portunity? Or do they merely think them pliable enough to be easily manipulated with it? It says the same thing about their views on women, only differing on their own agenda a bit.

The Point

I am all for equality, but rhetoric on pay gap isn't equality. Nor is droves and droves of pro-woman poli-tics and agenda remotely just. To suggest it is to correct for errors of the past is not only openly dishon-est or ignorant based upon an honest examination of history (comparing top men to bottom women or examining what men have and ignoring what they lack while doing the inverse for women is not hon-est), it is also vengeance at best and vengeance does nothing if not beget vengeance. One cannot make justice from injustice. You can, however, perpetuate a cycle this way and that is precisely what femi-nism, the most prolific and institutional sexism, though not by any means the gravest inequity the world has yet seen, does.

I would love to see gender roles eliminated. Feminism makes more. If you make quotas for roles you reinforce roles. I would love to see people paid equally. That doesn't mean a certain percentage of rich women need to be added. Indeed, how is that not the very definition of injustice? You wish to correct for people being disadvantaged by disadvantaging more people? I agree wealth is a source, *the* source in fact, of injustice. Feminism says so too. And then they say we need more rich and powerful women? Not less rich and powerful people? The very source of the imbalance they wish to remain, so long as they get a greater share of it. People who, by their nature, seek advantage, will not stop seeking it. As such one does not fix the problem by dribs and drabs as those seeking advantage will shift faster than the masses.

The correction cannot be special interest but must be united. Any other way empowers those you oppose, or you are them.

Men and women are not competitors but complements of one another. That the system we have tries to make them adversaries is truly repulsive. For this reason alone, we should think carefully about fostering the competition that we do, but of course this is only the beginning. Our survival as a species has always relied, at its core, on cooperation and that becomes truer with every scientific advance, every increase in population, every natural disaster, and every day that goes by. So, should we be rivals or should we look out for one another?

If at times in this writing it seems as though I am angry it is probably so. These things should have never become so lopsided. To me they seem quite obvious and the injustice of them is, well, it is appalling. We can do better and we must. The policies above are not just unjust, to be clear. They are destructive to the psyche of those affected. It seems to me the two most likely results would be a rise in sociopathy to defend the ego from such a pervasive assault or any number of neuroses for those who continue to care as they are assaulted for innate traits with baseless attacks. That, of course, describes those attacked by the dominant views. Those affiliated, often without their consent, with the attackers suffer for this division as well.

The consequence of declaring one side the side of interest or in need of protection for any reason other than overt action, which gender and sexuality are not, declares the other side the aggressor. The only category in which it is not discriminatory is the one that is obtained through action, wealth. You cannot justly treat all men as assailants or even potential assailants and all women as victims or even potential victims and claim justice with any degree of honesty. It is the very essence of bias. Worse, it is extraordinarily exploitable and further is fantastically naïve to believe that which genitals a person possesses dictates the extent of their morality or immorality. If you think such is possible you almost certainly hold a number of views of morality that have nothing whatsoever to do with it, whichever side you assign to either sex. In other words, maybe you have constructed one sex's normal behaviors as abnormal and the other's as normal, hmm? Do not confuse this with justification of all. It is not.

Our oppression does not come from the fact that we are male nor does it come from the fact that we are female. But oppressed we are. Our oppression does not come from the fact that we are straight nor does it come from our not being straight. But again, oppressed we are. There is a more honest reason and this is no more than a symptom and a tool of the true cause. Read on.

As with the case of sexism so too goes the case of racism. I understand that there is in fact racism in our country, culture, and systems. Again, I would argue that it exists primarily because of systemic inequity allowing for differential exercise of power. That power is not that of color however, but by virtue of its predecessors. Those being wealth and numbers. As to the numbers issue it is a passive force as the majority does not identify as such except by passive measures, barring the issue of wealth which people do indeed identify closely with and which, through differential access to resources, the necessary by-product of wealth, allows something that is nothing more than preference, and occasionally ignorance, from any side, to become something far more serious and negative. Racism comes from both sides and any justification of it only perpetuates it.

Success in America

A thing that is actually starkly different often looks the same and so it goes for the supposed meritocracy of America. America is not a meritocracy; it is a mediocrity. The suggestion is that if you work hard and are capable, you will succeed in America and nothing could be further from the truth. There are few slots at the top and the futility of achieving them is obvious to any sane person… any bright person. Thus, the people who continue to hammer away obliviously are the not-so-bright people. This is the pool from which success (financial) is drawn in America. Note, even from this pool not everyone succeeds. But those most likely to achieve success are those who disregard the facts before them because they are incapable or unwilling to acknowledge them. Hence, we are rewarding dogmatic and irrational people or at a minimum those willing to act thus on the off chance that they will be selected. This can be verified by either of two very simple methods. First, examine the people who have withdrawn themselves from the race. You will not find all of them to be the brightest society has to offer but you will find a substantial quantity of them—disproportionate. Second, examine the people who have achieved success and their myopic views regarding such topics as human rights, safety, dignity, fair play or any other virtue that you would assign to a person considered sane, moral and/or wise.

Are poor white people poor because they're stupid and lazy or because of policies that affect them as much as, and in some cases more than, they do black people? If they're poor because they're stupid and lazy, please refer to the rhetoric about why black people are poor. Do you sound like them? If they're poor and it isn't because they're stupid and lazy, then it is because of government and socioeconomic policy, at least as much so as for black people, in which case we move onto question number 2. If they are also affected by government policy, do they then deserve reparation? Yes or no? If no, then hypocrisy ensues and they will be angry with the black community and the racial tension continues. If yes, then where do the reparations end? Answer: the reparations end when you fix the wealth gap for everyone. Any alternative will result in continued injustice and hostility. Please note the alternative is to do nothing, which is a solution that operates under the delusion that it's fair because everyone has to struggle to raise themselves. This solution is delusional because it is literally impossible for many people to raise themselves up and because many do not have to while still benefitting. Many people rightly disagree with this being a feasible or even plausible solution. But they haven't considered the other side. You cannot be part of a community if you haven't considered your contemporaries. Understand that the fostered notion, that of fellow man being competition, is why we are where we are. And I don't mean that in a good way.

If white people cannot possibly understand the black experience, then black people cannot possibly understand the white experience. If that's the case, those that are complaining about a demographic not their own are necessarily complaining about someone they don't know anything about at least by the argument that these people express. In which case, they can't complain because they're just at odds and there's nothing that can be done which is fatalistic and supportive of status quo. Or one could acknowledge the fact that white people are as capable of understanding the problems of black people as black people are of understanding the problems of white people. At which point, we can stop saying it's a black thing or a white thing and can address the individuals and the other groups at play. And maybe, if we do this, we can reach a resolution if not only one group or another does this but rather if everybody does this. As long as people play the "you wouldn't understand" card, there's no speaking, made more lamentable by the fact that, presumably, in such a circumstance, the other side has at least tried to speak and perhaps understand. There's no moving forward with this mentality. This behavior makes a bigot of those who would claim others are. People like this don't want resolution, they want to complain. Resolution is necessarily predicated on the assumption that it is possible for the other party to understand. If it is not, there is nothing to talk about. Therefore, if we speak we have tacitly acknowledged it is possible and having spoken, should we decide to claim others cannot possibly understand, the motivation is manipulation (overt dishonesty).

This slogan disacknowledges that the speaking points apply to anyone else. It makes minorities of those who are affected who are not black. It then suggests that said minorities handle that problem on their own. In short it does precisely what they are speaking against. Worst of all it makes a poverty problem into a race problem. It is the poor who are affected by these problems. Oprah Winfrey has about the same chance of this happening to her as does Bill Gates, little to none. On the other hand, it is correctly a very real concern for all poor and working poor people due to proximity. The police patrol these neighborhoods, bad cops do bad things. Bad policies produce opportunity to exhibit bad behavior and the number one policy problem is that we have said poverty institutionally present in this country and, largely, people wish to systematically ignore it in favor of the symptom issues, like the above. 50 percent or so of prisoners are black it is said. 30 percent of the population is black and so it is said that blacks represent an excess of arrests. What is ignored is that about 60 percent of the country is poor and with very few exceptions only the poor really have to worry about prison. We could go on to then say too many blacks are poor…but you would have learned nothing from the above…Too many people are poor and they need not be but they cannot be otherwise under our current policies. When will people learn the difference between uniformity and equality and seek equality…

Put simply, 'black lives matter" would be better said as we must put a stop to state/police violence and oppression. If you suggest falsely that it only happens to blacks and thereby separate blacks, who then are we telling that black lives matter and why should said group care? If you are telling the police it is because they show, according to the rhetoric, that they do not believe they do and so the words are meaningless. If we are telling whites, why have we distanced them from black people by both alienating and accusing in the slogan? I am sure it would sound ridiculous to the ear of a black person to hear "white lives matter" and yet there would be much validity in a similar appeal. Whites are killed as well, albeit in smaller percentages, not, and this is important, in smaller numbers. The simple truth is police officers patrol heavily in poor urban areas. Areas higher in the sorts of crime our system punishes with greatest vigor. It is also true that the greater number of whites killed by absolute numbers, are in no way protected by being white nor are they targeted for being white. The statistic that tries to analyze this by race completely ignores the real variable, class… yet again. Incidentally, the crime in question that is more prevalent is nothing more than capitalism, practiced by the poor. Not a pretty picture, is it? It is no better when practiced by the wealthy but for the fact that it is often on someone else's shores and is vilified far less with only the most egregious of behavior receiving punishment and lesser punishment at that as somehow, white collar crime, which is to say largely invisible in execution but quite grand in effect crime, is somehow seen as lesser. And clearly that too is not because of class, right? But back to racism and, in specific, BlackLivesMatter. Which group being killed by police officers and our system in general should we care about? If you can pick one I say you are immoral. Does it mean that the group you did not pick should be silent to their troubles because some other is presumed under some metric to have it worse? Or perhaps the problem is that the makers of said slogan feel that the white folks somehow deserve to be maltreated and ignored, which is at best, vengeance, and sorely misplaced as it will apply, unsurprisingly to the poorest and the most powerless. None of this even touches on things like affirmative action for whom the white male is the only group not protected and so therefor the only group that it is LEGAL to discriminate against. How is that for institutionalized racism? Oh right, it has been amended to be about the power group…And which group does a poor white male have more in common with, a rich white man or a poor black one? The answer is clearly a poor black one meaning money not color is the true issue. From here it is not hard to understand that the slogan divides from support that is required…by ALL poor people, black or white, weakening both. And the makers and speakers of such a slogan deliberately separate the very support they require and, supposedly, desire. This is division politics in a nutshell.

Do you know which kid it is in the family that gets away with punching the other kid, then crying and getting their way? It's not the hated kid. Incidentally, in case you're confused still about which kid is which, the kid that gets congratulated for Cs while the other kid is reprimanded for B's? It's the one with the Cs that isn't hated. That's affirmative action.

When one suggests that black people are oppressed, who is it that one is suggesting is oppressing them? Because if it's black people that one says are oppressed, it's a given that one has chosen a skin color that's oppressing them, else it is not racism but, for example, classism. Now here's the problem with that, in case it wasn't obvious. When one teaches that white people oppress black people, one is not teaching that some people oppress black people. One is teaching that white=bad. This is exactly as much of a problem as when the circumstances are reversed and white people are saying black people are bad. It should also be addressed that the people actually responsible for this behavior are being held in common by skin color when the issue is an ideology that they do not share. Saying generically that "white people" oppress black people is the same as saying that black people are shiftless and lazy. It's a generalization that has consequences both for those who fit the stereotype and, more importantly, for those that do not. I know it's popular to say that one can't be racist if one is supposedly not of the power group. This is false. Power is situational. Anybody who guides the development of children has power. Anybody who's capable of picking up a brick has power. Anybody who's capable of poisoning a group of people against another group of people has power. And do you know who that is? Anyone. It's tempting to think of this as resistance to those who don't want to acknowledge their culpability. The problem is, this resistance that some hold up as virtuous is being applied to people who didn't do what they are accused of doing and in large amounts is being applied to people who are, frankly, more power-less, by virtue of a complete absence of social acknowledgement coupled with the fact that they never had, and at the rate we are going, never will have, any voice on the matter. Let's be frank here, anyone who argues that a homeless straight white male is privileged, indeed supposedly more privileged, than a wealthy homosexual black female is either completely oblivious or completely disingenuous. So, are we to condone treating people badly because they look like people that treated someone among us badly? What is the certain outcome of that? That, folks, is exactly what racism is. And that's how it keeps roll-ing. There are specific individuals (not groups) responsible for this situation. And the trait they share most strongly in common is not the color of their skin. It's the weight of their wallet and their lack of humanity.

Pro-Black

 Much of the argument against this has already been said with reference to Black Lives Matter because it's essentially the same issue. However, a simple economic acknowledgement might be in order. If you create a social movement or more importantly a social program that is racially oriented (not that race exists), what you have effectively done is charge the people at large (via taxes) to improve the lot of a specific group. The problem with this can be made rather clear. Were you to say we should eliminate wealth disparity across all ethnicities, all genders; in other words, stop people from being poor- not black people, not women- people, everybody would pay the taxes and everybody would receive the ben-efits- everybody would be deserving of them. When you switch it to a particular demographic, however, everybody pays the penalty, only some people receive the benefit. Now that, in and of itself, is very ob-vious and only the greatest of fools can't have seen it. So let's move onto the point that is going to be ignored by most. Let's say that the people that we are trying to give a hand up to are black people.

Surely there are poor white people. Surely there are poor yellow people and red people. It is difficult to adequately address in words the tremendous insult heaped upon a person when they are asked to pay for another person's privilege when they have none themselves. And when you make your social justice excessively targeted as in this case, the natural backlash is to push back with questions of merit. You suggest that this demographic deserves these acknowledgements because their situation is presumably worse. So now it's time to find out whether it is in fact worse and for everybody else to shout about how they have those problems too. This isn't inappropriate behavior. It's normal and in fact you invited it. You invited it by saying that these people deserve it more than those people. You invited it because you're making people pay for it that need the same care. Most importantly, it doesn't resolve the problem. It only changes the victim or worse (and likely more accurately) worsens their status as in the case above, in which they are already victims. This all is presuming, of course, that you're not one of those lovely people that thinks that all poor white people are poor because they deserve to be. Because that is the necessary conclusion if they have all of this privilege and they're still poor. They must be inferior. Right? The point could be made, quite validly, that poor white people in this country have it worse. The fact is we have myriad social programs that are not for them. People don't want to hear it. They aren't even supposed to speak on the matter. The they in question is specifically the poor white people. Those effected are disempowered from speaking, institutionally. This holds true across all manner of quota-based social justice programs. The group one tier above before the corrective actions ends up one tier below, at least. All it is is a transference. It is worth noting that urban centers are poverty-generating centers. This is not to say that there aren't plenty of poor people in rural areas. The point here is that urban centers generate poverty fantastically. They are a centralization of jobs. However, in centralizing those jobs, the wages for most of those jobs gets driven to rock bottom under the system of capitalism. This is consistent. The rural centers develop poverty as a secondary effect of this as towns cease to be large enough to be self-sustaining, having lost their population to urban centers, coupled with the inflation that occurs from the urban centers.

There is per capita a higher concentration of poor black people in this country than white people. This is not an accident. In fact, it makes quite a bit of sense. It is a fact that a chunk of white people where elevated to middle class for a time when the middle class was created *by the wealthy*. And they created the middle class around the time that they freed the slaves. Any way you slice it, the white people in America had some wealth advantage in general over black people. This is not to say that there were no rich black folks. This was at that time a color line and intentional. But it would have happened even unintentionally based on the circumstances, being a large influx of immigrants and, ultimately, wage-earners, not to exonerate the wealthy as they were the cause of the importation of both and indeed, that was their intent, this being the vehicle to greater wealth and power for them, a fact made possible only by setting castes of people. The fact that the divide wasn't deeper is due only to the fact that the wealth of the supposed middle class that they just created was also carefully restricted with top down economics. Since that time, the line has very much blended between black and white. And in the past decade or so, the line has also very, very much blended between middle class and poor. The only thing that persisted about middle class thus far is the mentality. A mentality that was fostered of superiority. This is, of course, a general statement. Not everyone from the set adopted the mentality, but it was clearly present. It's clearly fostered today. The funny thing is it's fostered among black people in the set as much as it is among white people in the set. The people that go to prison are poor. That 50% of prisoners are black isn't nearly as remarkable as that 50% of them are white. The prison population is overwhelmingly made up of poor people. It should not be startling to anyone that a large percentage of poor people are black, considering our system entrenches poverty. And placed at the beginning, the vast majority of people of that socio-economic status with that skin color were poor. Only a fool would deny that there are white people amongst the poor and black people amongst the middle class. And only a fool would deny that the vast majority of people in the prisons are of the poor. What this says about our society is that it isn't skin color that determines wealth. If this were the case, white people would not become poor and black people would not become rich or even middle class, but it's entirely possible, even obviously more likely, that one become middle class than rich. That is the ladder that doesn't get climbed too often by design. So what's the variable? It's ideology. Money doesn't want anybody to obtain money that doesn't support their views, chief amongst them being control and "Capitalism". At the end of the day, they don't want competition, period. But if the competition allows them a larger share of the global market and is in line with their thought processes, they can suffer it. It's simply an ideological war that can be summed up with the word "elitist". Note elitist and elite are not the same thing, just as arrogant and confident aren't. Being elite and/or confident is to be capable and sure that one is capable. Being elitist/arrogant is measurable by insecurity and toxicity. Being elite does not preclude sharing. Being elitist does. Being capable doesn't mean that others aren't. Being arrogant does. So, back to the point. They aren't locking up black people. They're locking up poor people. Black people are often poor. Should that be rectified? Yes, absolutely. But not separate from everybody else who needs it rectified. All at the same time. The redistribution doesn't need to come piecemeal. In fact, doing it piecemeal will only make the problem worse as everybody clamors for their piece, rightly so. And wouldn't that be fun? The only people that need to clamor are the 10% at the top, done correctly. To clarify, they wouldn't need to clamor, but they would because they would seek to maintain their largesse, most of them. And this would be no surprise. It's human nature to try to keep what one has obtained, however one has obtained it, and whether or not it is fair, just as it is human nature to ascertain whether or not it is fair. Ask yourself why so many studies ask about race, which doesn't exist, ask about gender divides which are shockingly consistently misrepresented, ask about sexual orientation, which is completely irrelevant, ask about anything under the sun except the one thing that everybody's chasing and most people are never going to have enough of. Ask yourself why these above questions are being asked if they aren't to divide and distract. Is there another reason? And after you have that answer, ask who wanted you asking the other question. Did it take money to push this into the media? This distraction? Did it take money to push this into the school system, to indoctrinate with this, which can only divide? Who has money, especially that kind of money? And then ask yourself why you listen to anything they have to say.

Race doesn't really exist at any rate. Nationality exists. Race is akin to species. There is only one species of human. I don't understand how people don't get this yet. People point out that supposedly black people from other regions came from Africa. And yet they still think there's a racial divide based upon color. Meaning necessarily white people did not come from Africa. That would be their implication, right? The science that provided us with the premise that blacks elsewhere came from Africa is the same science that told us, just as explicitly, that whites came from Africa or said slightly differently, that Africa is the supposed origin of our species in entirety. One choosing to point out one and ignore the other is a result of racial pride, which is extraordinarily misplaced as race does not exist. People then attempt to boil it to ethnic pride, converting it from the race that doesn't exist... equally misplaced, as the Africa that one would be ascribing it to is no more theirs than it is everyone else's.

The ancient Africa of which we are speaking could not be properly called Africa at all anyway, first, because the Africa of today likely bears almost nothing in common with the Africa of yesteryear of which we speak and secondly because it wouldn't have been known as Africa and wouldn't be "your" Africa or "their's". Indeed, the people living in the area that were proposed progenitors of the human race likely were neither black nor white but of a medium tone, increasing the likelihood of successful adaptation into the various climes in which humans found themselves assuming it is in fact our origin point. This is all predicated upon the notion that humans originated in one location and migrated to various locales, implying that we have shared common ancestry, and localized adaptions, which is, incidentally, reinforced by our fertility (I would say interfertility, but that gives too much credence to race) and the amalgamation of our traits that results. To identify these supposed progenitor people as non-white is to be racist just as it would be racist to suggest these people are non-black, unless the only thing of relevance you have to discuss is their degree of pigmentation and the things directly linked to that. What is directly linked? Relative risks of skin cancer and sickle cell anemia and the obvious aesthetic differentiation. That's about it. Because they're just as non-black as non-white. And conversely, rather than observing their absences, observe their presences. Why would one wish to claim credit for being more closely related to the progenitor people? Presumably one assumes that being closer to the progenitor people makes one somehow superior. The obvious counter-argument, just as valid, is that it makes one inferior, more primitive. Neither of these is ideal. Both of these are elitist. These progenitor people have what is necessary to produce both a white person and a black person. Does this make them superior as people? No. Nor does it make them inferior, and frankly, few if any of us have any claim to them other than as distant ancestors. It simply makes them capable of adapting to a greater degree of environments and to be less fully adapted to any that are not medium but are antagonistic. Put simply, specialization has pros and cons. You are special. And so is everyone else, and that's not tongue in cheek.

You can consider everyone better than you, worse than you, the same as you, and/or different from you. All of these are wrong (and half right). The best way is just to consider everyone. Be respectful without toadying. Cooperate without surrendering yourself. Social justice has gone too far. But it exists for a reason. The issue that is truly problematic in social justice at this point, the thing that people do not wish to speak to except under the guise of race or gender or some other nonsensical issue is that of wealth. It is not possible to reward people at massively divergent rates and have a healthy, productive society. Each is contributing to the welfare of the society and in the simplest terms possible nobody makes millions without many, many people working for them. Which means, very simply, that they were overpaid and their workers were underpaid. Even if there were ethnic and gender issues regarding equality (btw equality and uniformity are not the same thing), they could never be resolved while wealth is massively disparate, because wealth is power.

So long as we use currency to eat and to have a place to stay, being able to manipulate what amount of income a person has grants control over their life-- control you shouldn't have-- if you're wealthy. The problem is this is an inescapable consequence of wealth disparity and one need not intentionally seek to exploit this for it to have the above effect. It's not a mystery what happens when that situation festers. Crime and discontent are the inevitable consequence. For what is crime other than the decision to no longer abide by the social contract which, it should be noted, in most cases was already breached to the detriment of the soon-to-be criminal. This is simply slavery by another name. It should be noted that for all practical purposes, the middle class are slaves of a moderately higher station, much like the house slave vs. the field slave paradigm. And it isn't blacks or whites who are enslaved. It isn't men or women who are enslaved. It's the poor. And the poor are comprised of all of these. If you jump up and start screaming and shouting about who has it worse, you alienate your allies and you start squabbling over who does in fact have it worse rather than trying to determine how to fix it. Now who does that benefit?

Black Lives Matter suffers from exactly the same problem as the feminist movement. It is a movement that presumes that a particular group is, was, and always will be the disenfranchised. Ergo it can never work for and disacknowledges the existence of the supposed exception. The problem is the exception is no exception at all. Regarding the feminist movement, there are a ton of disenfranchised males. In fact, there are more of them. I won't try to make the case that there are more disenfranchised whites. I probably could but it wouldn't be quite as clear. I will instead say that focusing on color when it comes to poverty makes poverty racist. You don't need to look at a person's skin color to acknowledge that poverty is a problem and poverty needs to be fixed. You shouldn't look at a person's skin color for this purpose. It is a secondary and irrelevant trait. Before you balk at that statement, let's say the only people that were poor were black and you didn't focus on black at all. You focused on poor. Would the black people's lives improve? The answer, obviously, is yes. Let the focus lie where the focus should. You comment on media propaganda and then perpetuate it. When you speak of poor people, you don't discriminate against a particular color. You don't discriminate against a particular gender. The only people excluded are the ones who aren't poor. It's easy and it's obvious. It was, is and always will be the case that there are those who will try to take from others to give to themselves. They do not care about your skin color. They do not care about your genitals. They do not care about your ideology. They care about being more powerful than you, and that is it. They will use any means to achieve it. The easiest is misinformation.

<u>Correlation/Causation</u>

Are you aware that drowning and ice-cream sales have a corollary value (which is to say when ice--cream sales go up, so do drownings)? There is a difference between correlation and causation. Correlation is when a thing occurs at the same time as another thing, but we do not know that it is necessarily the cause. Indeed, the cause may be another variable entirely that increases both simultaneously. This refers to the lurking variable, only lurking because it is not yet understood that it is the relevant factor. Causation is when the variable is known to be responsible. Many people presume that because a thing changes when another thing changes, that it is the cause. This is often premature and either over- or under-generalizing. It seems clear to me, as demonstrated by a number of points above, that what is being attributed to race and/or ethnicity is correlation, not causation. That there are more wealthy white people has nothing whatsoever to do with whether or not white people are the cause. Wealth is the cause. Wealthy white people on the whole do not feel the slightest solidarity with white people. Some of them may find it useful to foment the division, but if you really care deeply for an ethnicity, as a wealthy member of an ethnicity, you wouldn't have such a divergent wealth imbalance between yourself and those you cared so deeply for. And there is and has been for the entirety of the duration of capitalism and before, in its predecessor, feudalism. Frankly, there is not much solidarity between wealthy black people and poor black people, either. If there were, again the gap would narrow, not grow. And this core imbalance has significant staying power. Poor white families tend to stay poor and white. Poor black families tend to stay poor and black. Poor tends to stay poor. The divisions persist, both due to the behavior of the system and the individuals in it. Ask yourself a few simple questions and see what conclusion they lead you to.

Q1: Do you know ice-cream sales increase in the summer?

Q2: Do you know that drownings increase in the summer?

Q3: Do you believe that ice-cream sales cause drownings?

Q4: Do you know that wealth tends to perpetuate wealth?

Q5: Do you know the majority of the people in this country are white?

Q6: White people are rich and poor. Which do you think is more prone to privileged behavior?

Q7: Is it possible you conflate white privilege with wealthy privilege and make racism out of an admittedly unjust capitalism?

Two things can exist alongside one another and have nothing to do with one another. Wealth perpetuates wealth and you need to look no further to figure out why there's a wealth divide. Overwhelmingly, the people that came from money have money. And overwhelmingly the people that didn't don't. And that is not because of some supposed merit to their bloodline. It is because of the nature of wealth. Particularly wealth that relies upon the nature of concepts such as compound interest. But even without interest of any kind, the simple fact that you have more means that you have more, meaning you have more power, you have more authority, you have more access, you have more privilege. If there is any difference between white people and black people on this issue, it is because of the perception that, wait: white people have more money. It's based on a generalization that does in fact exist. They're playing the numbers to make money. But that does not somehow equate to privilege, as the basis for those perceptions is exactly the same with regard to poverty. The term trailer trash comes to mind readily. The term poor white trash comes to mind readily. The "they are not like us" thing that various socio-economic groups pull (and it is socio economic groups, not racial groups) each layer of the stratification does the same nonsense. And the nonsense is they are not like us. Any justification they can provide will be used. If you want proof of that, even look at the stratification between old money and new money. You're talking about people in a tiny percentage of the populous that still divide and separate themselves from the rest. Old money is, of course, more entitled to be wealthy than new money or so they would say, in general. After all, what is the point in pointing out that these newcomers are new money if not to suggest that the old money is somehow superior? Now consider the fact that old money is primarily the string puller (obviously) since they have had money for generations so have had influence for generations. And yet many of them even look down their nose at the new rich. It goes without saying that they probably look down their nose at the middle class (new or old) and the poor (new or old). It goes without saying that they would think that they're better than them. Those are the generations-long string pullers (as in they have been pulling strings for generations). And yet some don't think the problem with wealth disparity is wealth. There is a point where obliviousness becomes willful ignorance. Most of us know there is such a thing as old money. We know that they have influence and power and have had for some time. We know what that can afford or entitle them. And yet people are still in denial that the problem is wealth, that the imbalance, that the injustice, is wealth. People still need to be reminded of this obvious fact, for some reason. I would say that this is because of an unwillingness to think for oneself coupled with an abundance of propaganda supporting the narrative that wealth, and the people who have it, are generally good, which is particularly egregious when you consider the narrative for the opposite, that poverty, and the people who possess that, are generally bad. This reality alone should make you very seriously consider what, and how much, propaganda you consume. The question then is why would people choose to believe something that is so obviously biased? It's wish fulfillment. It is comforting for them to think that maybe someday they will be in the advantaged position, so long as it's still allowed. They dream that someday they will be the lords and masters. They are okay with there being lords and masters so long as they might one day be one. It's the "I put in my time attitude", so now it's my turn to treat others poorly, which is to say it's infantile and destructive and works about as well in society as it does in the workplace, incidentally, which is to say not at all well.

White Fragility

Incredibly condescending, disingenuous, and communication destroying. Imagine starting every conversation about what is and is not wrong with our system by identifying that people of a particular skin color are weak and neurotic. Do you suppose that is, in any way, a genuine discussion? Imagine doing it to manipulate and gaslight people into agreeing with you even when you might be wrong. Does that sound like a person to respect or revile? Imagine that slapping a sex or ethnicity label onto any discussion is racist or sexist right from the start with an eye toward division. Does that sound plausible? Imagine reversing the various currently allowed race and sex labels and how those would be received. Would that be considered hate? Because hate is hate be it from a majority or minority, folks. Here's what it would look like. White pride. Black fragility. White lives matter. Womansplaining. I am not defending these. I do not want to see them. What I want is simple recognition of the fact that their counterpoints are every bit as hateful and ignorant.

Differential Crime Statistics

The variable is centralized poverty. The poor are patrolled. Cities are easier to patrol for quantity of people per area. Most poor black people in America live in cities. Poor white people in America live in both the city and the country but, relative to black people, disproportionately in the country.

Differential Reporting

Ask yourself why when they have large numbers of blacks and whites they could show on television they display mostly blacks. If you said because they hate blacks and they want everyone else to as well you missed a very important point. They also want blacks to resent whites and to believe, completely falsely, that whites are not being treated similarly. This is what it looks like to divide people, intentionally and falsely.

Affirmative Action

Not only a division but a handicap. You cannot complain that the perception is that you are not as good and leave a system in place that has as its express purpose the acceptance of candidates that may well in fact be, not as good. Reject it if you do not need it and in fact resent it. You should resent it, you do not need it, and you think the fallout from it is unfair. The simple and obvious solution is to get rid of it. Furthermore, it is blatant racism, only racism for a group that claims to be oppressed, which makes it no less racism and is directly in conflict with antidiscrimination laws. Racism for is every bit as destructive as racism against.

Reverse Racism

There is no such thing as reverse racism. That is true. The reason that is true has nothing to do with the commonly accepted narrative. There is no such thing as a supposedly oppressed person being a reverse racist because the word reverse is a qualifier, an allowance, an excuse, and there is no acceptable excuse. Racism is racism regardless of which ethnicity perpetuates it. You will never end racism by excusing it from any group for any reason. You will perpetuate it producing future generations due to such qualifiers. You want to end it? So do I. Stop doing it. Everyone.

Race

This is a false narrative in the first place. Race doesn't even exist as it is utilized. It most nearly means species or sub species as it is used. It was divisive and ignorant and superior when the term was created.

Why are we still using something that has been generally proven to be both scientifically false and socially destructive? Because it is a very easy way for the haves to keep the have nots divided of course. And if you think white people are the haves, first, return to the top, second, you are wrong for several reasons to include Asians and Jewish people identifying as non-white (these days) and holding an appreciable amount of wealth as a (illusory) demographic.

Ethnic Pride

The inevitable consequence of having pride in a trait that has nothing whatsoever to do with you is that you will have hate for another because pride in inconsequential traits is elitism regardless of the trait and regardless of the group. Would you be proud that your eyes were blue or brown? Why? You had nothing to do with it. Would you be proud that your skin was light or dark? Why? Short of tanning or bleaching you had nothing to do with it. If you did tan or bleach what about that is worthy of pride? Nothing. A choice based upon a preference does not make a worthy location for pride. Would you have pride if someone with the same skin color as you invented something wonderful? Why? What did their skin color have to do with it? More importantly what did you have to do with it? This behavior is nothing but the allusion that some completely contrived group is superior to some other completely contrived group which, of course, will naturally be opposed and the inevitable conflict between the two self-superior groups will lead not only to conflict but hate because emotionality and pride have been attached to non-accomplishments. Even worthy accomplishments should not be sources of pride, ethnic or otherwise. Worthy accomplishments are made possible by what has come before, what gifts one is born with, and the resources society has made available. There is no group short of all of us that can be given fair credit for said accomplishments. Indeed, even negative contributors contributed via a greater understanding of what not to do, as important a lesson as what to do ever was.

Cultural Appropriation

Fun fact, claiming a thing is cultural appropriation is racist. You are claiming that group x can use or do a thing and group y cannot, based upon "race". That is literally textbook racism. How ironic that the group most responsible is the same group that sees racism everywhere, no? It seems to me that fits the profile of projecting rather succinctly, does it not? Culture is not owned and it does not form in a vacuum. If this confuses you refer to the problems on intellectual property rights for some additional framework in the following chapter. I also speak to culture later. Neither is strictly necessary to understand the above, however.

<u>The Real Problem</u>

I have a solution for you. It is slow and you might find it less satisfying but, that being said, not only is it more effective it is, contrary to apparent popular opinion, more accurate. Imagine what would happen if you and others acknowledged that the color divide in this country is. first and foremost. a class divide.

 Do not take that to mean that those of darker skin are more or less qualified because that is not what I am saying. There is, however, proportion of poverty among this group. This is incidental though and I will tell you why. America's social and economic structure requires it and so it comes down to which group shall it be shuffled off to. Do not take this to mean that this is fair or just or even that it ought to be group A or group B. On the contrary, this is incredibly unjust and should be fixed. It will not be fixed by focusing on greater respect or economic opportunity for blacks or any other group. It can only be fixed by making that the goal for all. Anything less merely shuffles this injustice off to some other group, protected or otherwise.

None of this is to say that those of darker skin do not often have great cause to be angry and depressed. The simple fact is they do. Equally simple is that this is true for nearly every person in this country and on this planet. This is not intended to be dismissive. It is simple truth from the perspective of one who also is but is somehow not entitled to be. In any event if you address the wealth gap on its own merit the logical progression would place emphasis on poverty, removing the emphasis on skin color associated with poverty.

Should we be fortunate enough to see progress made regarding poverty, skin color would fade into the background still further as wealth gaps shrink both due to greater economic power and due to lesser emphasis on the arbitrary identifiers of who it is carrying said wealth. If at the point that wealth gap is relatively reasonable you and others saw an excess of injustice surrounding skin color you might then address it but as it stands it is simply not the issue but a symptom of a much larger problem. The elephant in the room is real and so very few want to see it. As an aside you might also stop alienating those who would be allies. Or we could justify the source oppression and let people continue to quibble over who should be the ones getting more and less, which will never be ok for anyone.

The source of oppression is not that we are white or that we are not. This also does not prevent us from being oppressed. And again, the cause is elsewhere with this nothing more than a symptom and a tool.

If I make a point in this section that does not at first seem to be about class ask yourself if it is about economics and haves and have nots. These things are the root of our classes and classism that follows. That we have multiple economic classes is not a necessity and is the underlying premise behind many of these observations and thoughts whether they speak very directly about class or address the ramifications of such. Indeed, the point I try to make is that class is literally and inherently classist, which is to say prejudiced, and fully socially constructed, and curiously, the one issue both the left and the right do not, in any meaningful way, speak on, but please read on and decide for yourselves if my points ring true.

Most of us want generally the same thing. To be comfortable and relatively autonomous first and second to be part of something greater. Where the disagreement occurs is in how to arrive at this. I intend to make points demonstrating that there is really only one option forward, at least in a general sense, here.

That being said, there is more than just classism to found in this section because many of the causes and effects of classism are also covered here. To omit them would be to leave large and unnecessary holes in the point and its conclusion.

<u>Capitalism and Driving-</u>

Driving is a perfect representation of capitalism, particularly driving at rush hour. Everybody's chasing the dollar (or in this case getting home or to work; same difference). The effect of that is everybody goes when they feel like going how they feel like going. The conflict is continuous and toxic. Most of the slowdowns aren't from accidents. They're from a basic lack of cooperation, both on the part of the person in the advantaged position (in the lane) and the person trying to merge. One is usually too aggressive, the other is usually too passive. Interestingly enough, if everybody drove at a similar speed, adjusting as the situation warranted for things like oncoming cars, changed lanes when it was appropriate, didn't hog lanes and adamantly refuse to adjust speed (for those who wish to go faster), rush hour wouldn't exist. The highway is more than capable of handling that number of cars. It's the people who aren't. Interestingly enough, the ideal situation that is described most closely resembles socialism.

Capitalism is supposed to improve things through competition. But as in the case of traffic, we see the same in the economy. Nothing is improved. Everything is degraded. In the realm of consumerism, specific examples: one high and one low. Walmart strongly practices the tenants of capitalism. The result: less choice, less variety, lower quality. Contrary to the tenants of what capitalism is supposed to bring. On the other side of the coin, pick a luxury car, let's say a Jaguar or a Lamborghini. Take your pick and substitute one that is what we would consider an affordable American car. Is this an example of building a better mouse trap? Undeniably. The luxury car is clearly a superior product. Is it within the reach of the people? No. How many more years will go by before all of the cars are the luxury car? I wouldn't hold my breath… if we can't make a better we will continue to make a worse in our system. Entrenchment. So… when capitalism is producing a better product, the people cannot have it. When capitalism is producing an affordable product, the people would not choose it except that it's their only choice. Please explain to me how that's better than the worst examples of socialism ever. And then consider that the worst examples of socialism ever were more in line with fascism and nothing like what socialism is supposed to be. Frankly, it looks just like feudalism. It's rather sad that social policy hasn't improved in centuries if not millennia. And it's completely unacceptable when you consider that our social policy hasn't changed whilst our scientific knowledge, our ability to destroy ourselves, our ability to control and exploit our fellow man which IS destroying ourselves has increased exponentially in that same period of time. It isn't for lack of ability. We allow people to hold the reigns that have no interest in the one and a great deal of interest in the other. And let me stress this: ALLOW. They could not do it if we collectively said "no". Note: COLLECTIVELY. And that's the threat of socialism. And that's why we don't want it. And that's all.

<u>Is it Complicated?</u>

Let us make a scenario that while theoretical also no doubt happens. Let us take a rich person and a poor person each with $20 in their pocket. Let us further presume that each of these individuals is deeply uncomfortable with this prospect due to reasons of scarcity. They do not like having so little available to them in case of unforeseen events. Many will think that said poor person should be used to it, routinely having little or nothing and that for a rich person that would be disconcerting indeed. On some level such people would be correct. However, the poor persons constant scarcity does not ameliorate the problems of constant scarcity. In other words, the poor person in spite of exposure has every reason to feel this way and constant exposure should not ameliorate but magnify it. Will such an event become toxic? Of course it will. That does not make it disordered though, just as a person with a runny nose will dehydrate...the toxicity is elsewhere. We do not as a society treat it thusly because we actively ignore one particular toxicity in the.hope that it works to our betterment. Incidentally, the rich person in this scenario gets sympathy for dealing with scarcity... How ludicrous is that? The poor person gets derision for the same systemically.

So, is it really complicated? I don't think so. It's just not the preferred answer.

Libertarian Dreams

So, Libertarians want lower taxes, no subsidies on poverty, and a strong military and police force, right? This means a shrinking poor class one way or the other. It then means higher wages for all jobs due to reduced competition (assuming all goes as it should according to them). These two facts both inclusively mean the cost of raising an army rises sharply as there are fewer interested and capable candidates and they have better opportunity outside the military meaning much better compensation must be arranged (presuming it is even possible to raise them in sufficient numbers at all considering the plenty they are being asked to leave). Let me make the above clear, the military, the greatest expense (or near the top) that the US already pays...would INCREASE sharply and is payed for with taxes...so taxes at a bare minimum would not go down and would likely go UP. This is not the only tax that would increase and yes, the poverty ones would be eliminated regardless...but not really if there were still poor and during transition, poor have cost whether you do or do not subsidize them. Be aggressive enough to them and they aren't going to be beggars they are going to be vandals and cutthroats. Everyone can and will fight to survive. It isn't that hard, really. The parties position is fundamentally dishonest and actually structured on the plausible deniability of responsibility for services they want, need, and use.

Conservatives

Conservatives- people who believe in a divine being, formerly thought to reside in the sky, that extended them the right to take what they want and do what they want in his name, who believe that they should have the right to defend themselves either directly or tangentially through strong police and military, who believe that their fellow man are to be trusted to run their business in a reasonable, ethical, safe manner. Now in case you didn't get the irony, they want the right to defend themselves… from people. But business owners are implicitly trustworthy, and so do not need regulation. Obviously, it doesn't make any sense that they believe people are implicitly trustworthy. Otherwise, why do they feel the need to defend themselves? So it is reasonable to infer that they do not believe people are inherently trustworthy, but simply do not want regulations upon their own actions, presumably because they do not plan to be trustworthy themselves and/or they plan on taking matters into their own hands should some-one else prove to be untrustworthy. This is a position I can fully get behind should you attempt regula-tion and regulation fail. This sounds to me, though, like they don't trust anybody to regulate them, but they're perfectly fine with regulating others. After all, how is businesses being able to do whatever they want not influencing the lives of the people around them? It's simply regulation from a private citizen. For instance, if someone goes out and buys up all the produce, they regulate the food supply. They are now the FDA. The fact that it's not a gov't institution just means there's no institution to turn to. Vigi-lanteism is the only option. Simply stated, conservatives believe in might makes right. They do not have a problem with regulation. They have a problem with regulation of them. They do not trust peo-ple. They trust them. So, tying that back into the whole Christian (no it isn't just Christians but we will come to that) thing. Christianity is attractive because of divine right. They're entitled to go out and take what they want. They're perfectly fine with having a community so long as their community is very much like them. This is, of course, infantile logic. This is entitlement at its finest. These are people that believe in might makes right in terms of take what you want, but socialism in terms of "I need peo-ple to protect and defend me while I take what I want". Where is the socialism evidenced? Police force that all people pay for that they expect to benefit and serve them. Military- same issue. Taxes are theft to these people, but profit isn't. No matter how much profit, no matter how it's obtained, no matter how modest the taxes, no matter how much benefit the people paying them receive from them. These poli-cies are selfish. They are immature and they are, above all, arrogant.

<u>On 1 Percent</u>

Everyone has heard about the 1 percent having 50 percent of the wealth. Most understand, at least in general, why this is a problem. Yet, a person will declare themselves in agreement with you based upon only disagreeing with 1 percent of your point. This is a problem...a big problem and I can show you why. Let us say we agree on everything...literally everything except one point. That point is that I think wealth is the cause and the thing that needs correcting to implement a just society and you think it is ethnicity primarily or gender. You will, presuming you speak on and otherwise act on your point push ethnicity or gender to the fore. I will push economics. The result? You divide people that are fundamentally the same. You entrench wealth (more rich ethnics for instance not less rich people) while I oppose wealth entrenchment (which incidentally automatically benefits the groups you claim are oppressed and others you do not acknowledge). I pull people who have intentionally removed themselves from the whole (along with vast resources). You separate ever more people into smaller boxes beholden to some absurd other box, essentially infinitely. I speak for justice, you for injustice but yeah, it's only 1 percent, right? They are literally opposite. On a large enough subject or over a long enough time very small differences produce very large (even opposite) differentiations. We need to debate to define this, to let the most just solution show itself...most however only want to argue or dismiss, either being emotional appeal.

<u>The Wealthy are the Oppressed?</u>

This is just one example of thousands spoken by those who are pro wealthy… various John Galt sorts suggest the wealthy are treated as "Second class citizens"? The 1% are treated as second-class citizens… So, the people that live in mansions, drive luxury cars, make their own hours, eat the finest food, drink the finest wine, travel the world because they want to and can afford to (both in terms of money and time), implement policy either with direct bribe or via lobby as individuals… these are the people that you defined as second-class citizens. These people who, incidentally, received this largesse off of the fruits of the labors of MANY, not themselves. No person is capable of making this kind of money off of their own efforts. When you credit the fact that they established something as them being entirely responsible for it in all capacities such that they deserve the overwhelming majority of the compensation, this is obviously dishonest. No idea, no matter how good, can be implemented so easily. It absolutely requires the support of those masses these individuals look so down upon. That some then feel no compulsion to compensate them is why it is done via taxes.

Charity

Charitable giving on the part of the wealthy is a sham. First, the wealthy collect bankable goodwill by the appearance of charitability. In other words, it can and often does literally pay for itself and so is not even charity on the first order but a transaction. Second, is the tax deduction element. They have already collected goodwill and then they collect tax deductions. In other words, they have been paid twice as they shed their liability. Who do they shed their liability too though? Why, the same people who they collected goodwill from. Many businesses these days ask for donations from customers during transactions. This is the third order of magnitude. They literally take your money to get your goodwill and use your money for their deduction so that you can pay their share of the road maintenance…which incidentally also serves them prodigiously more than you… and people thank them for this… The fact is wealthy people are wealthy because they charge more than they pay or, simpler and clearer, they take more than they give. They have enough money to give to charity without receiving anything in return, that is in fact what charity is supposed to be. This stack above though, several order of magnitude deep, is a scam that has poor people thanking rich people for helping the poor stay poor. The wealth gap grows and corporations and franchises are asking minimum wage workers for a dollar while sneering at a homeless man on a street corner… It is repulsive, but hey, maybe I'm the one confused.

Welfare and the Entitled

There is this oft pushed position by primarily republicans but generally ill-informed people that the poor, be they welfare recipients or otherwise, somehow defraud the system of millions or even billions of dollars. It seems necessary to point out that with almost no exception the poor, when they receive benefits, whether they be legitimate or otherwise, receive very few. It is a meager living. Now if you examine the other side, and you look at the ways that the wealthy get over by avoiding paying taxes, by dissolving corporations and reincorporating to avoid liability, by just plain not paying litigation costs that they have been found guilty of (and incidentally none of the behaviors are atypical for the extreme wealthy), it's not hard to see who is in fact defrauding the system of millions or billions of dollars, and at least as important, who doesn't deserve it. Steal millions, live like a king, and you're not considered entitled. Be provided your daily bread in exchange for respecting all of the laws of the country you live in and you're entitled. This whole argument has been had a thousand times, a billion times throughout history. And it boils down to shut up, be a good slave, get your ass back in the field so I don't have to do any work. A palatial estate and a plantation, well, they look a lot alike. They've got a lot of land. They've got a very nice house. They've got lots of people working there. The similarities don't stop with appearances though. All the people you see working there, (or don't see because they're not technically in the field) they (the poor) pay for that (estate). They (the working class and poor) pay for that by being paid badly. That redistribution, the original redistribution, from the poor to the rich is the source of much of the wealth of the wealthy. Last but not least, the wealthy industrialize. They automate. They don't just ship jobs overseas. They literally replace human jobs with robot jobs, which justifies a reduced workforce and the designation that the people that they do still have are low-skill and low labor. They just have to hit a couple buttons from time to time. This is in an environment in which there was already an insufficiency of decent paying jobs and an insufficiency of jobs in general. The expectation that everyone must work for their daily bread in an environment where people with too many resources in the quest to generate still more resources remove themselves from the community that is supporting them by not supporting said community back. They want people to buy their products but they do not want to pay them. It doesn't take a rocket scientist to figure out that that is unsustainable. That that makes the rich richer and the poor poorer and further deteriorates the options of the poor to find a decent job. People still argue the fact that they deserve these benefits for having worked X amount. While that's not untrue, you do deserve something for having worked, the truth is if we're going to allow automation to continue (and btw most people don't want automation- the consumers are not given a choice), if the trend of automation continues, it is an obvious and inescapable conclusion that people have to be entitled to their daily bread without working. In fact, what is the benefit of automation if not that? That's what automation is for. It's to free people from menial tasks. You can't free them to the point that they can't have food else it is an act of war. The class warfare that anybody who speaks for the poor is accused of fomenting, it's already happening. Why do you think the wealth gap increases? It's been happening; it's just one-sided. Unions are a terrible solution. Incidentally, a quick and effective fix to unions is for them to remain unions, which is to say the union rep or boss needs to be omitted. It defeats the point of a union to place a person at its head that is a singular point for bribery and manipulation. The point of a union is the strength and diffusion of the numbers. The problem is, so long as you have people in positions of power who see nothing wrong with increasing profits at the expense of their labor, they're the only solution. If people in such positions saw that they have an obligation to their workers (not just their shareholders, customers, selves), none of this would be a problem. But when a worker equals a cog in a machine and you can get the cogs a penny a pound or at least that's the attitude because people have to work and everything after that is also allowed: market manipulation, automation, then that's where you're at. All that's involved is following a simple chain of logic to its logical conclusion. Every society who has ever disregarded these rules has Bastille Day in one form or another. You can do this to the poor for a long time precisely because they are *not* entitled. But if you do it long enough, if you do it hard enough, they will buckle. And the tanks and the prisons won't stop them. And what difference if they would? Because then you'd lose your giant free workforce (and consumer base).

You cannot nail down exact values for social phenomenon as those numbers change not only while you measure them but more often than not literally BECAUSE you measure them. So there is nothing to be done, right? Wrong. This is precisely the purpose and value of generalization. Measure of that which cannot be nailed down is what generalizing is for. It is in point of fact what truly is being used to separate, for instance, humans from say monkeys as far as definition goes.

<u>Pizza Party Analogy</u>

So, we get ten people together and have a pizza party. One person had the idea to do this. One person grew the grain and pounded it into flour. One person raised cows and milked them. One person grew tomatoes. One person made said tomatoes into sauce with some basil from their own garden. One person took the others milk and made cheese with yeast they had. One person took the flour and made dough, also with yeast. One person gathered clay and made bricks. One person made those bricks into an oven. One person used said oven and all those ingredients and made pizza. The pizza was cut into 10 identical slices… and the person who came up with the idea took 7 of them, leaving the remaining 9 people to share the other 3 slices… Oh, the first person also watched these other 9 work. This is capitalism. Do you understand what is wrong with capitalism now?

<u>On Gentrification</u>

Gentrification: the process in which the wealthy come to a low cost of living area with the intent of benefitting from such low cost of living while simultaneously raising the cost of living for all native inhabitants without raising the wage, in order to remove gems. Rochester is a very attractive area to live, in spite of its awful laws and its economic depression, because of its natural beauty and at the end of the day the awful wage isn't as terrible as it might be because the cost of living isn't as awful as it might be. Gentrification makes the cost of living more awful but does not improve the wage. Said simply, the wealthy come and absorb the value of the area. The natural beauty of Rochester might well not last, but even if it does, the people who live in Rochester will not be able to continue to live in Rochester should the gentrification continue. Because while in the most superficial of senses, gentrification appears (and is claimed) to add value to an area, it does nothing of the kind. It takes it away. It takes from those who had it: it takes from the poor and it gives to the rich. And it's worth noting that part of the reason it had the value it had is because the poor didn't seek to exploit it. It's no mystery that the bulk of the desirable vacation spots in the world at a given time are those places that are or were until recently "underdeveloped". I've heard it said by the wealthy, politicians, conservatives that the poor are the parasites. That the poor are the leeches. This is one of those situations where there's an obvious truth and people simply say the reverse of it. The groups that bleed the value from an area are the groups that "develop" it. They bleed it of its potential and their supposed "vision" is no vision at all. The only vision they had was the vision of dollar signs. You can't eat dollars. You can't drink dollars. And when you seek to go to vacation, you can't go to vacation on dollars. Yes, you can spend dollars on those things until there are no more to be had. It is not the poor that are the destroyers of the world, and they are not the parasite, and they are not the leeches. They are not killing their host. That is, was, and will always be the wealthy. The poor do not make places bad, that they can move there means that they have gone bad already and are consequently affordable. It is misappropriation akin to the belief in Europe ages ago that tomatoes were poisonous when, in fact, their plate was.

Thousands of Reasons Raising the Minimum Wage Doesn't Work

"Thousands" is an absurd overstatement. There is literally only one reason. The word is greed, not economics. Economics teaches you the basics of supply and demand. That is not the emphasis of what is being taught in economics classes today. What is being taught is the concept of maximizing profit and the acceptability of shorting your resources to do it. That means slash and burn. That means cutting the wages of your employees who are the very vehicle by which you generate your wealth. Not only that but they are also your customers in many cases, probably most cases. You are impoverishing both the partners in your business (that's what employees are) and your customers. And this is considered to be fair business practices, so much so that it's taught in school. Let's return to the top. The word is greed. If your business cannot sustain itself without paying a living wage, it should not exist. But the truth is most businesses could, they simply wish to maximize their profits and consider this an acceptable means to do this. If you want an example. please refer to the Walmart of yesteryear and today. It was sustainable enough yesterday (back when it didn't do these things or at least did them less severely) to be what it is today.

<u>Prices</u>

Greed plus market. A reasonable person will charge a reasonable markup to afford staying in business and being moderately comfortable. In other words they will pay themselves and do so reasonably. Unreasonable but within tolerance or relying on desperation…or manipulation, is rewarded better monetarily though… and soon becomes mandatory because their ilk do this to all markets. This simple phenomenon alone could drive inflation but another is at play as well. Compound interest which may well have been done to control for the above ultimately just gets used by the greedy and the gulf widens. There are so many systems in place to try to ameliorate the one fundamental flaw of our system. Our system not only allows but celebrates greed ideologically. Even in our system most are not fundamentally greedy, controlling and exploitative. Most simply want a modest and comfortable life. Yet poor neighborhoods are either divested of their best resources or costed out of living there via gentrification. Either way the money takes what it wants and there is nothing, within the law, that the poor can do about it, at least not individually, a problem a person with wealth does not have. Pretty much every family unit teaches sharing within group. Perhaps it is time to recognize the larger group. The problem, of course, is that even if a wealthy parent did attempt to impart such values to their children, lifestyle of the wealthy, all by itself, says otherwise quite loudly. Your children do not learn by word alone but by deed and putting business before people, profit above all, and maintaining a lifestyle separate both geographically and economically from others, well, it says a lot about how elitism is ok and that you do, in fact, believe you are better than others. Even if wealth and poverty weren't intrinsically linked due to finite resources this narrative as played out time and again can only teach one of two lessons. The system is fine and we are superior or we are not better or worse and the system is deeply flawed. Many of us are better than others at many things, from all classes, and worse at other things, but none of us are better than anyone else. We all have essentially the same needs and while they are currently not consistently recognized for all, we also have the same rights in no small part based upon said needs. Thus, the system is in fact flawed. We can, should, and must do better.

<u>Median Income</u>

First, and most obvious, $50,000 is the median income where? Because if that median value was in Rochester, it wouldn't be too bad. In fact, it'd be quite decent. For Rochester. However, I'm confident it isn't. Second, it seems likely the median value would be considerably lower if you count all the people who literally have NO INCOME. And they exist. I am also confident that the income of prisoners is not in that equation. You know, the ones that make like a dollar a day. Third, somewhat related to the first, what are the opportunity costs of making that income? Over and above the simple unavoidable costs like costs of living, what are the opportunity costs? For that wage, do they have to maintain a licensure, take courses, have a student loan? Fourth, $50,000 is the median but I bet you if you went by tens upward (you know, from the 50% mark to the 60% mark or vice versa down to the 40th percentile) you'd see a great deal of similarity in the wage and with an incredible spike in the earnings in the last 10% and a precipitous dip in the last 10%. Fifth, what happens when basically no one makes the median because all you have is highs and lows since the middle class is vanishing and all, right? That curve has been argued to resemble nature. This argument tends to forget some things. Like what happens in nature if one animal collects a big ole heaping pile of stuff for itself with the help of the other animals in a group and then refuses to share it. It isn't pretty. Put another way, while the number of people in the various ranges may be consistent with nature the magnitude of the compared product, wealth, is not by any means in keeping with nature. How is it that this above point was missed and omitted? Additionally, the problem is the social conventions imposed living in a society are not natural to most people anyway. They're anything but. So you have principles that argue essentially that might makes right and social Darwinism coupled with laws that demands that people not act like wild animals with the barest hint of recognition of natural rights. This does not equate. I could go on but it's clear that the number does not mean what it's supposed to mean. It is supposed to indicate prosperity and the reality is contrary. Values such as this are not compared with enough to make them relevant in most cases. What does a median income tell us if there is no standardization of cost of living or goods? What does it tell us when said average has people at all ranges along it and selectively omits populations? What does it tell us other than an approximation of how much to charge to ensure that most people stay in poverty? And speaking of the various prices and wages in various areas now seems like a good time to move to economies of scale.

Economy of scales/High inflation areas and low

Economy of scales as I am using it here refers to the notion that some areas have high wages and/or cost of living and others have low ones. The relevance of this is that this environment creates endless opportunity if there is a portion of the populace that is wealthy but also that even a person of moderate means should they come from a high scale area can do better in a low scale area for no other reason than the scale they come from. Put another way, say $100,000 is an average wage for job x in region y but in region z the same job, job x, pays $50,000. In region z the cost of living is half of what it is in region y so this is fair so far right? Except that they each saved ten percent of their wage for retirement and both moved to region a. Now, just like that, two people who did exactly the same amount of work and the same kind of work at the same quality of work and live in the same region have wildly different retirements. The same holds for all sorts of issues. One can pay half as much in wages in an economically emerging area (or less) and have the people readily accept said low pay because it isn't low pay there. Put another way $5/hr. is $20/hr. in a place where the cost of living is a quarter of elsewhere, sort of, as mentioned above. Inevitably such a business wants to sell the products in the market that isn't emerging however for its higher typical costs and so greater mark up. Businesses and individuals think this manipulation to be clever. It isn't. It is rudimentary math coupled with an exploitative nature and a deeply flawed system that produces poverty and crime, both in the developed and undeveloped areas. For example, who is buying your product in the locale you just removed wages from and how? That is someone else's problem no doubt even though said business directly put it into play and anyone who doesn't follow suit is supposed to just eat the cost and so it goes. Capitalism makes for great conformity mistaken for freedom but more on that later. The solution is simple and difficult at the same time. These economies of scales need to be balanced. Tribalism, nationalism, and various other unities through division actively oppose this process however. The mechanics of correcting it are simple. The support… less so and it must be done with support or it won't last and it will be pointed to in perpetuity as the excuse for why it shouldn't be tried. I say excuse because few succeed at anything they try only once and most fail several more times… on relatively simple things.

Poverty is just one more economy of scales. Gentrification is a simple example of how such is exploited… the poor are not elevated they are kicked out of another neighborhood. Nothing more nothing less… because prices are set to poor but poor can't outbid wealthy…prices rise poor aren't benefitted but rather must move. This is, of course, yet another unaffordable expense.

Conformity is not Freedom

Capitalism is not freedom enhancing, it is conformity enhancing both due to need to follow business practices such as exploiting economies of scale and conformity needed to secure allies essential to capitalism. I'm sure many of us have also heard the turn of phrase "love it or leave it" as well. Curious kind of freedom, that. The fundamental denial of truth from the other camp is no better. We can only agree to disagree if we first agree that there is no truth. The problem is this first agreement is self-refuting and disagreeable. Put another way this is the same echo chamber conformity nonsense. For those who wish to be clever, no, truth is not conformity. It exists outside of us and is recreatable. Contrary to popular thought these days not everything is a social construct nor is everything not a social construct. Some things are and some are not but more on that under relativism.

Insurance

I find it funny that most people who have a problem with socialism have no problem with insurance. Insurance is just all the worst elements of socialism. Everybody puts their money in the pot, and if someone gets hurt, it gets divvied out to them. Only most of the money gets kept by the company.

While we are here it is worth pointing out that the policy from a recent supposed leftist president for mandatory insurance primarily subsidized insurance companies that already give, in many cases, inadequate care for too much money, at the primary expense of the poor of the US in order to claim that we have something approximating universal health care. That it took and continues to take money primarily from poor Americans and gave care as determined by said insurance companies and those doctors who would even accept it in the first place (the cheapest policies are both inadequate in coverage and often not accepted) is not remotely what universal health care is. This is the antithesis of said health care. The poorest pay more and get less. It's only commonality is its mandatory nature. I suspect it is also common for the cheapest plans (those the poor must default to or simply pay tax penalties at the end of the year) to have the highest copay, meaning that even should the poor get said insurance they can't afford to use it, meaning that it is strictly for appearances and grand claims to be able to say all Americans are insured (if it were even true). Meanwhile the wealthier people routinely have coverage anyway usually on top of an absurd pay differential and in some cases, due to more insured, even have been effectively subsidized. The simple truth is that said policy was yet another tax on the poor and tax relief for the wealthy. If you doubt me just take a look at tax rebates for low earners a decade ago to those since this program. If they opt to pay the penalty their return is lower (it likely is relatively lower even without this but made obviously worse). If they opt to pay the (unused) insurance their take home is lower.

<u>Economics and Roles</u>

What is the purpose of business? Most today would tell you that the purpose is to make money- to make a profit. If you asked 50 years ago, most people would say the purpose of business is to fill a need in society. Something that the people want or need. This isn't a flaw in the understanding of people. This isn't a mystery. This is simply what happens. This is the difference between late-stage and early-stage capitalism. This is a flaw of capitalism. Whichever position you hold as the proper place of business: that of providing goods and services or that of making a profit- either way, any sane person would recognize the fact that business requires regulation. People who want to provide goods and services might not necessarily consider the big picture. People who want to generate maximum profits absolutely will NOT consider the big picture.

So that brings us to what is the purpose of government. The purpose of government is to regulate and redistribute. That is its purpose. The commonality of those two things is to protect the people. Because the people (collective) have little power, individually, except of course the wealthy, yet again. They keep cropping up outside of the rules, don't they? Consolidated power is found in most any business. The people's purpose is to provide the labor and to consume the product. You can always count on the people to do their job. They always do and they always will. Many, many people have made mythical claims to the contrary which have literally never in the history of the world been true. They're fearmongering. Where the problem lies inevitably is with business or government. And frankly I have to say it is almost always with government. Now before you think me a conservative and show yourself to have very superficial thinking, understand that while the problem is with government, it isn't because they do too much regulating and redistributing. It is because they do too little. Every time the gov't fails to perform its duties, it is in the same direction. It is because they have been bought by business. This is without fail.

The Wealthy vs Government Argument

If rich folks and government are both doing what they should there is little difference in how they conduct themselves as it pertains to the working class and the poor assuming, of course, that the wealthy are not predatory by nature as one might infer but which is a necessary postulate of the conservative set as if predatory is acceptable or even desirable we must release all those predatory inmates as they played by the same essential rules only, generally speaking, from a disadvantaged position. So, the difference is in when they go wrong and the correction of such. If a wealthy person does something wrong and begins abusing the trust afforded by their wealth there are two recourses. There is the predatory, as above, which need not be specified but is justified if outside the civil contract. Then there is government correction. That being the only entity with sufficient power to correct people of that stature without departing from the social contract and if said government is just then it is again the people who have gained justice as the government should be comprised of and for them. To be clear it is supposed to be of and for them due to voting. Clearly the buying power knows no bounds as one piece at a time the very people who government is supposed to limit the power of have bought additional power directly from the regulators or, on another note, sold off the power of the people (sold something they did not own) to seek redress. Thus while clearly government is something that takes diligence and perhaps the occasional cleaning of house (charging government officials with treason for selling the power of the people should probably be strongly considered)it is the only means to remain within the civil contract, that structure by which we acknowledge to play by certainly rules and receive certain benefits as members of a society without which, it should be noted, there would be no infrastructure…which wealthy folks rely on heavily and which ultimately is primarily funded by the non-wealthy. Just one of the many examples of socialism in any country…most of which, to be clear, benefits the wealthy…EVERYTHING benefits the haves more than the have nots by necessity…else they would not BE the haves.

The people, to their fault, will often prefer to assign the status of scapegoat to an individual or subgroup rather than acknowledge that things have gone off the rails and society is disordered and unjust (but correctable). "It isn't capitalism that's the problem, it's …rich people/black people/white people/poor people/men/women". Anything but that it is the necessary eventual outcome of a plainly broken system. Acknowledging the actual problem would mean it is correctable and if it is correctable they should be DOING something about it. Thus, they resort to any category that relieves them of said obligation, "that's just life". It is clear that they have an inkling that they do this however. If you address the issue the question becomes what are YOU doing about it which of course disregards that the act of considering and sharing said information is in fact the most important thing one CAN do about it assuming people are unaware, as they present themselves to be. YOU fix it while I try to profit from it is how that boils down which of course makes fixing it impossible particularly since the solution is a global one requiring all or at least most to participate.

Privatization

There are those who argue privatization is fiscally responsible, which is to say that we save money by taking services out of the hands of the people collectively and giving said to a sub-collection of individuals to convert said services into a business in order to reduce costs and even perhaps generate profit. What is wrong with this argument? Several things. First, is how said business accomplishes this. They cut wages and decrease services. The cuts in wages create pockets of poverty or grow them if they are already there. This in turn damages the economy of the area in general over a longer period of time. Poverty is directly linked with the kind of crime our society most focuses on trying to stamp out, which in the case of the prison industrial complex literally manufactures more, more crime, more prisoners, more profit. It is, of course, just a wealth transference, as usual, from the bottom to the top. Worse, as the process of privatization cuts services, reducing the very thing they are intended to be providing, the wealth transfer becomes their only purpose. A 90% savings on a service that is not rendered still leaves the cost 100% too expensive as you are paying for nothing or worse, a detriment. If all this weren't enough, the fact still remains that the tax payers payed for the infrastructure of these "businesses" which operate like businesses in terms of profit but government in terms of monopoly because what private business can compete with the one that payed zero for infrastructure? It is worth noting this is a product of capitalism, a mere eventuality of leverage when profit (theft) is the primary goal.

<u>The nature of Poverty in capitalism vs Christmas</u>

Let us assume that we have national holidays to unify people into some sort of collective that we refer to as a nation. As such, Christmas is intended to be unifying. It is a forgone conclusion however that we also excuse various practices in this country under the heading of capitalism. Capitalism of this sort unsurprisingly commercialized Christmas among other…all other, national holidays. Now we must consider the poor as they essentially comprise a rather static 50% of the nation. I know some peoples measures on and what constitutes poverty vary in this respect. Suffice it to say those people have not lived in the category of the poor or the so called "working class" which is simply poor with employment for any length of time or they were blind to the realities around them while they were. In any event a sizable portion of the country is as little as a month away from being homeless if any of a number of very realistic possibilities were to occur and many of these at the whim of people with a great deal of excess resources. Now that the poor are adequately defined for this purpose let us move on to how that interacts with National Holidays. The poor can either subscribe to this expensive capitalized holiday and further entrench their poverty or they can reject it. While they do this those who have will speak loudly about how the poor are poor because they are lazy or foolish and so should work harder or behavior more prudently with their money. We will examine the farce that is working harder shortly, but first the notion of being more fiscally prudent. The poor under this heading should reject this commercial Christmas entirely and save their money. It cannot be overlooked however that if this happens in any meaningful quantity prices will climb for the most basic items to compensate and maintain the status quo as those wishing to maintain such do indeed have tremendous pull with pricing of basics like housing and food. In small numbers a few can make some meager progress by this method or similar ones like college but if it becomes a strong push the same response inevitably happens under this system. In short, prudence only works if the representation from the poor is small. If it is large it actually impoverishes them MORE under this system. Let us not overlook the fact that while under these very specific circumstances when it does work it never works particularly well. The gains on meager resources are necessarily meager excepting the very most absurdly rare cases. Cases such as these almost always involve something that would generally be considered either immoral or unethical or both should those words still retain any real meaning. Of further relevance to this issue is the fact that should a sizable portion of poor reject holiday commercialism and other money pits they will be the ones blamed with the "dissolution" of America and destruction of our "National Identity" for choosing to do one of the two contrasting things deemed mandatory by their supposed betters, I might add. Those same betters that literally created this circumstance in the first place.

The other issue is the farcical notion of the poor working harder to escape poverty while simultaneously maintaining our (Commercialized) National Identity. This is nonsense of the highest order even before the addition of National Identity argument but let us look anyway, shall we? First, the poor, by long tradition, do most of the most physically demanding, hazardous, and distasteful jobs out there. As such they are already literally working harder and yet they are poor. The argument is already defeated but let us persist. So, they should work more hours then, yes? Never mind that doing work such as this has an absolute threshold for every body and yes, those bodies are different in this regard but each has an absolute threshold nonetheless. It is also true that the poor work as much as or more than the most industrious of the wealthy. Perhaps they should simply approach National Holidays in a thrifty manner then, yes? Never mind that that already stirs the dissolution pot and answer anyway. So crafty skills are presumed to be possessed by the poor and they are presumed also to have the time and resources not to mention the drive to pursue them, yes? As to the presumption of skill, that argues that they are talented…if so they are underpaid. As to the possession of resources this is precisely what they lack, hence poor. As to the presumption of time, as they lack the resources they must work more to gain the resources and then still more to make them into crafts…the same people that work on average as much as the most industrious wealthy… As to the drive, a substantial amount of drive is consumed simply living in the circumstances of poverty, should they have surplus again you argue their superiority. The mere fact that you are poor in a land of plenty is disheartening enough but it is only the very tip of the iceberg in terms of the emotional and mental health effects of institutional poverty. What is worse is that the more moral, truly moral not lip service and false attribution, the more fair-minded to be clearer, the worse, the heavier the burden of said lifestyle.

<u>Human society mimicking insects</u>

Human societies that are hierarchical in nature tend to choose roles for the members of society. It may come as a shock but the system by which this is done is essentially that of the insect world, not the mammalian. This is why they invariably collapse and prior to that the fit is ill. But let me be more specific. Every hierarchy chooses drones by some method. And leaders. Breeders, etc… varying roles. Let's focus on the drones, though. Whether your hierarchy chooses their drones based upon heredity, testing, qualifications… none of that matters. There are going to be people who are not appropriately labeled whatever method you use, every generation. And the discontent will necessarily grow. The people who are benefitting either because they're labeled correctly or because they're getting over based upon their labeling will naturally be content with the status quo and seek to preserve it further cementing the certainty of dissolution or collapse. The problem is not that humans have to necessarily function this way, with the rise and fall of civilizations. The problem is that civilization, when utilizing hierarchy, is nothing but an insect hive so is innately poorly suited to human life. Even the basest of us are not born to be "drones" and even the most gifted are not born to be "queens". We are not insects and excess specialization denies us an important part of our nature. Maybe the problem is that we aren't hierarchical but more on that later.

<u>On Hierarchy</u>

Consider well the implications of this next statement. A person, granted the title of leader, who falls behind in a race, call it a footrace, can simply reverse their direction and declare themselves ahead. Such is the folly of following a leader. Thus what is objectively better or even best becomes conventionally invalid and relativism rules the day as behind suddenly becomes ahead and worse becomes better.

That ones' talents lie with planning or organizing does not entitle one to rulership by authority as found in hierarchy nor impoverishment as found in industry. It requires more talent and effort to motivate people neither starved of resources nor autonomy but that is as it should be. The presumption that it should be otherwise is the very essence of elitism… and mediocrity. Few decisions truly require immediate and unilateral action. Emergencies only in fact and only those that are unforeseen by everyone, since if everyone has a voice there are few (emergencies), perhaps none, that escape the eyes of all. We know all too well what happens when emergencies are manufactured. Rights soon depart.

Think you the wealthy are our shepherds? Consider well the ramifications of the farmer and their cows when it comes to humans interacting with humans as their shepherd. The farmer cares for the cows and depends upon them, but not to the standards of the cow or for its sake. The cow is only wanted healthy because the farmer wants to eat it… or sell it. And the only rights a cow has are the ones the shepherd gives them. And shepherds are the positive side of hierarchy folks, it only goes downhill from there. Do not mistake this for meaning that we do not need positive role models and modelling. These two things are absolutely essential. You are not a shepherd though when you do not have authority over others. We need positive role models but we also need autonomy. We will not, even should everyone see value in what I say, arrive there tomorrow. Many of us, most even, will need to try and fail many times to get close to following even half of what I suggest. Worse, enforcement must come from the people themselves with no more authority than anyone else which means the people must be all of the best virtues of a police officer with none of the flaws commonly found with central authority. They must look to themselves and to their neighbor. What makes this different from most systems is that one's neighbors talk to one's neighbors for support rather than calling said centralized authority. Authority such as that, sooner or later, will be abused, either by the callers as a means to gain competitive advantage over fellow man ala red scare, or the system itself, having grown corrupt and abusing the authority vested in it by the people. Simply stated you cannot transfer responsibilities such as this to another and expect them to not be abused. What I advocate here is people again being complete and responsible people. People who think before they act and speak and look on themselves and others but not out of hate but love. Is this utopian? Of course it is. Is it attainable? Absolutely. Is it a long and bumpy road from today to the goal? Beyond a shadow of a doubt. Is there an easier way? Only if you want quantifiably inferior results which, generally speaking, put us right where we are today. We must get and be better for our society to improve, each and every one of us. Do look to your neighbor, but do not forget to look to yourself.

It seems to me a great deal of effort on the part of the supposed shepherds is spent in the process of trying to create sheep of the people. If such effort is required it strongly suggests one can stop making sheep and consequently stop needing shepherds. Said simply, the narrative of a need for shepherds is self-refuting. We do not have perfect knowledge but that is true of all of us and the narrative that none of us was promised the world holds true for the top more than the bottom, as they are the ones claiming it as their own.

<u>Wealth as Energy</u>

Half of the problem of wealth is the way most people perceive it and those who have it. Wealth is not kinetic energy it is potential energy. But people treat it as kinetic energy much like how many people perceive someone full of bluster or swagger as strong when generally that would indicate weakness or insecurity in the animal world. Because people perceive wealth the way that they do the wealthy often do not have to actually use their wealth to affect change on the world. Consequently, it does not get depleted nor does it return to the economy. Indeed, it often grows because said exertions often have that very purpose and obviously minimizing expense is a good start to making more money especially when one does not have to go without the things that said expense represented. Basically, having wealth is considered ennobling by many in our society and the reason is obvious. We celebrate money… and consumerism. It is the most prolific religion in the US and possibly the world… and also the most divisive. Sit in a factory break room and hear about how some billionaire athlete or actor got robbed because they only got 10 million dollars for their last project and tell me I am wrong. Meaning sit someplace where many of the workers are temps making minimum wage and most of the rest are making between 30k and 50k annually. This mindset is sad and it's taught. If the issue itself isn't problem enough consider that said mentality is only possible by creating heroes of very fallible wealthy people. You need not wonder where the young get their values from when this is how things are done and so wealth is also social energy, again without need of spending for it. While it seems like perpetual energy it is merely leeching more from it's surroundings while spending very little.

Diversity

The difference between preference and prejudice is primarily one of wealth imbalance. Preferences are normal, natural, and healthy. Prejudices are damaging and unhealthy but what turns a preference into a prejudice? The power to impair access of others to survival and the ability to flourish, differentially from the whole. And what gives preference this power that it becomes prejudice? Wealth imbalance. Wealth imbalance has the ability to turn a simple harmless preference into an indictment against anything or anyone, with the teeth to make that preference destructive to that subgroup or individual. It makes the preferences of people who are wealthy elitism and manipulation/control of the populace rather than mere likes and dislikes. It makes the preferences of the poor express as cultural unrest and group think. If the people had equal access to wealth this would not be the result. It would simply be preferences with the power to secure said preferences without the power to deny others their own preferences. In short, preference is essential for increased diversity and preference is made possible by equal access to resources. Without such. preferences become prejudices, both imposed and self-adopted that narrow the band of what is and is not acceptable to express, meaning less diversity and, of course, less equality. Both preference and equality are essential to diversity. Equality is not a largely static representation of unequally rewarded people as we find in class under the current social justice model.

Gun Violence

Gun violence in America doesn't come from guns being legal for ownership or sale. They are not being used legally when violent crime ensues and them being illegal wouldn't change that one bit. It doesn't come from mental illness. Plenty of mentally ill people don't commit said crimes and plenty of people who would only qualify as mentally unwell from the fact that they committed an act of gun violence with no other indicators of poor mental health, in other words they are declared mentally ill because they did x, cause and effect confusion also known as confirmation bias. Some will want to argue this last, think on it this way, if every person capable of violence is insane then everyone is insane or on a narrow band every ruler of every nation in history has been insane, clearly that position has problems any way you try to argue for it. They do do it because America fosters an environment of competition and division. On the competition front rules are made to be broken, because they are made by your competitors or you made them to apply to your competition. It isn't hard to see under such circumstances why people would be inclined to do such a thing. On the other side of the equation we have division. When people see themselves as belonging they are not inclined to act against those who they belong with. The fostering of division removes that restraint. So, our society gives reason to seek gains at the expense of others and also makes everyone else an 'other'. Why would gun violence be a surprise in such a scenario? You cannot make the guns disappear, they exist and would be available by illicit means or self-manufacture regardless. Furthermore, the notion of preventing violence by making anything dangerous unobtainable is a nonstarter. There is little that has no potential for danger, every human being on the planet is capable of acting as a predator. No, you fix this problem by fostering cooperation and inclusion. You give people reason to both not have to compete and to see their fellow man as family. Understand that both of these variables affect the outcome. Foster cooperation but also division and you will still have these issues, albeit in a diminished rate and/or intensity. Look around and look honestly and tell me I am wrong.

Let us not forget guns were made as an equalizer. The majority of the self-professed "elite" have, throughout history wanted the masses unarmed except when they send them to war. These same elite when they have this in hand tend to step on the necks of said same masses. The armored knight of feudalism was quite unhappy with the invention of firearms. They attempted to regulate them with perception (unchivalrous) and law not so different from now, yet again failing to recognize why they(guns) and their like are invented and why they are used. Hierarchy is undeserved even when not abused but is almost always abused and if we compete, we escalate. Simple as that.

Law Enforcement

If capitalism was really about working hard to secure success, or even to do so cleverly, we wouldn't see the poor being barred from the pursuit and exercise of wealth via the passing and selective enforcement of laws, etc. If you have any doubt that this is the case, consider the criminal pursuits of a poor person that is prosecuted to the legal activities of large businesses that are not. The lesser evil is punished, the greater is rewarded. Indeed, who are the laws not only enforced for and against, who are they made for in the first place. Law are made regularly to entrench both wealth and poverty in their respective places.

The Rules and Class/Caste

Class places people both above and below the rules of society. The wealthy make the rules but said rules rarely if ever apply to them negatively. They benefit from them but in instances where they would be detrimental to them they rarely apply. The poor are, unsurprisingly, the inverse of this. The rules apply when detrimental to them but rarely to their benefit and of course they have little influence in making said rules in the first place. In theory the lobbying power of the poor is tremendous but they are kept occupied with basic subsistence, divided, and on the whole have accepted the implication that there is nothing they can do about it. The correct position, naturally, would be for the rules to be made by and apply to all for good and ill or for there to be no rules for those who think, incorrectly, that society is and should be a survival of the fittest competition.

Class is Caste

The primary difference is one shines a light on the fact that some few slip through and celebrate these exceptions so as to suggest they are virtuous while the other hides these exceptions claiming that they do not occur and that everyone remains in their "ordained" place. The caste not at the top, slaves.

Homelessness

This was a reply of mine to a person suggesting homeless people are parasites and that the gentleman (Arnold Abott, a WWII veteran) who was feeding them deserved to be punished. I could make a section for it not in this format but what I said fairly captures my sentiment and sometimes anger is required. What follows was my comment. "If you don't want to be inconvenienced by the existence of homeless people then make sure there aren't any. That means you can either lift them up or you can kill them off. Both of these will be hard. Which do you want to do about it? Wanna ask me what I am doing about it? Red Herring to disregard that you made a complaint and it has been addressed. So, which would you prefer? Start knocking them off small scale and go to prison? Start knocking them off wholesale and prove you're a sociopath? Lift them up small scale and be seen as a saint? Or do the fucking right thing and fix the systemic sickness to the best of your ability that produces this and other ills and be an honest to goodness citizen and human being."

There is no excuse for people to be without basic needs with the resources available in this world. There is even less reason for people with enough to look at people without enough with loathing. It is simply unacceptable. Whatever reason a person has become homeless, and there are many, it is clear they lack something important.

Poverty and Slavery

You do understand that poverty and slavery are synonymous in general but particularly in a society in which it is functionally impossible for most anyone, particularly a poor person to be self-sufficient (living off the land, neither burdened nor a burden to society), right? The slave received room and board and had some small measure of superficial choice, at the pleasure of the master of course. What has changed? Table scraps and a couple simple pleasures, then and now. And to use psychological controls rather than physical ones, because it increases morale and reduces the cost of guards and general maintenance. I have a later section on this that does a back and forth on slavery but I did not want to excessively break the flow here.

Slavery and wage

Subsistence wages is slave rental rather than purchase. A net gain for the wealthy. They only need spend on a slave while they have use of them and need not worry about the resale. Clearly we aren't partners or our wage would not be mere subsistence. And make no mistake, the wage, subsistence wage, does not go to the slave even though it touches their hands. Room and board, neither of which they own with very few exceptions.

Social Contract

Disregard social contract at your peril. Those not granted the protections of social contract (food, shelter, safety, opportunity) are under no obligation to abide by it. Literally, the laws do not apply to them, not to be confused with whether they will be held accountable to it. Unsurprisingly, this is backward in America currently. The wealthiest are the ones not bound and also best protected. Our obligation to obey the rules of society is not a one-sided relationship. Society also owes us something for the degree to which we are part of something more than ourselves. If it does not honor its own end the breach of contract was not ours should we cease to abide the rules. Duty has a wage.

Living Wage

If you think unskilled workers do not deserve a living wage then you are content not to receive the work of unskilled workers, because they could not live without a living wage were there not subsidies to allow it. I would like everyone to make a long, comprehensive list of all the "unskilled labor" that we benefit from in our day-to-day and them tell me that we can and would be happy to live without it. And if the answer is no you cannot or you do not want to be without it, then it has value. Living wage and min wage do not go far enough, merely enabling rather than eliminating poverty…

Value of your Life

Your wage is, in a very real sense the value of your life. And yet again I believe this speaks directly to the lack of fairness of capitalism. Not the nebulous, less clear, gender-based wage gap but the very real fantastically disproportional value of life that is represented by massively different wages which literally represent peoples' lives as they spend most of said life (waking hours) doing it. Your wage is in a very real sense the value of your life even to the extent of how much a company or individual must compensate you should they disfigure you or otherwise do you harm. And not even based upon true potential either, could you have been a model someday but for the wound to your face? Could you have been a surgeon but for a wound to your brain or hands? Your potential is declared from the moment of injury and your value fixed. In an egalitarian society your harm is a tragedy and one you wouldn't need pay for since you are already being taken care of and will remain so. In capitalism the harm to you is merely a transaction… that didn't involve your consent and your value, determined. How can that be different for anyone in a just society?

Literally working half your life is not even enough for a one-bedroom apartment for most people in the country by the way unless you work two jobs so basically all your life, barring subsidized housing, unless you want to count sleep as recreation. No surprise about how people shack up, is it? But that's just another dissolution, right?

Productivity

The source of productivity is a moderate amount of comfort. Usually meaning and acceptance are included in said comfort as requirements. There will be similarities and also differences between one person and another on this. For this reason, equality and diversity are crucial to a society even if you do not care, on an intellectual or moral level, for either. Not only do you lose productivity of individuals when you shirk these things, those individuals affect the comfort, meaning and acceptance, of those around them, either affecting those who care most about them or those who care least, in a more active role. The more discontent there is the more there will be, compounding, and it is foolish and short sighted to suggest that those people pushed to the fringes just get over it or conform, many will snap. Our diversity is our adaptability. It is ironic indeed that we are, in our time and place, asking people to adapt to us rather than our environment. That is not adaption at all, which comes from the external sources, but conformity, called adaption by those arguing social Darwinism. We are literally trying to remove our adaptive population when we demand conformity. If this seems confusing read on generalizations, mirrors, and/or cycles. Social adaption is not adaption at all but an attempt at homogenization. And again, this is hierarchy, with environment there is no confusion over who should adapt but people aren't environment. Any of us could as easily say you should adapt to us. The reality, we all should, without surrendering ourselves. To be clear, we are not our money.

<u>Hard Work?</u>

There is a narrative you hear often from on high, with no shortage of repetition from the lower tiers. That narrative is that you must work hard, and smarter, and better if you wish to climb the ladder socio-economically in the US. And then they tell you precisely how they want you to do whatever task they want you to do and if you go off course the odds are quite good you will be fired, or worse, receive negative credit for the problems that arise but no positive credit for whatever good elements arose. This applies to both the smarter and better elements as well. But then maybe they meant you shouldn't work for them… in which case they know working for them is less rewarding than it should be. As to the harder element, when one works harder one draws the ire of one's peers, presumably due to fear of not being promoted themselves or worse, not being retained (fired). The thing is, the harder working people are the ones more likely to be fired due to complaints from peers (in a competitive environment this is assured/opposite in noncompetitive) that management just doesn't want to deal with or results in bad public relations elsewhere (the same element, popularity) or because management themselves sees them as a threat to their own position. If they aren't fired they are unlikely to be promoted. They want the hard worker working… at what they know they are good at. Meanwhile they do promote the backstabber… both because they won't promote the worker and again because the backstabber has demonstrated a trait that is useful to upper management, disloyalty to labor and politicking. The hard work narrative being the recipe for success is great for getting more work out of the work force while simultaneously having them tear each other down. Which is to say, it is a terrible structure for a fair society or for achieving success in an unjust one. Not that there is anything wrong with hard work, just hard work and poverty.

Meanwhile the wealthy do not work harder or smarter really, unless you count taking the path of least resistance smarter. I do not for various reasons, some of which I will make clear shortly.

Let us say that our pyramid scheme of a society (capitalism is essentially this) is a mountain. Let us say the path of least resistance is a stream bed. Let us say labor is the water being directed via the path of least resistance (the stream bed) by the wealthy. The steep slope of our mountain (capitalism) demonstrates the sheerness of the divide between the classes (the climb is severe). With such a slope, labor (the water) is hurtling down the mountain (capitalism) at a great rate (high productivity) carving the streambed ever deeper (path of least resistance) creating a chasm. This chasm that is forming means both entrenchment of the path and a substantial obstacle for those not on the path. Additionally, the bottom of the chasm, formerly the path of least resistance, has become rough going with rock and the like everywhere. Any number of other paths would be superior at this point but for the fact that this is the lowest point (high wealth gap), made so by entrenchment. Divergence is no longer feasible without substantial change. It seems to me that in nature and society a mountain is not so hospitable a place to live. A nice level field with a slow-moving stream and many tributaries is fertile ground in both nature and society as well. The thing is that society is shaped, so our metaphorical mountain is man-made which is good because the change to the rivers course in nature after the formation of a chasm is usually catastrophic. Perhaps it is time we made a field instead.

We aren't working 60-hour weeks because there are people on welfare, unemployment, or disability who can't work. We are working 60 hours weeks because we can't afford to pay rent working less hours. Other poor people are not the cause of this problem. Wealthy people or the system itself are the cause/s. Hating your neighbor for becoming broken in such a system, mentally or physically is foolish and is either what those who created the problem want or proof that they cannot handle the responsibility of wealth. Either way wealth imbalance is the problem.

<u>A Funny Thing about Businesses</u>

Business expects service from employees and in turn pays them. Business thinks itself in charge in this relationship.

Customer expects service from business and in turn pays them. Business thinks itself in charge in this relationship.

You see the disconnect right?

Smaller population group. Consolidated power. And now they have human rights? Which they have basically stripped of you. Don't think so? You don't have freedom of speech on social media, right? Even though most of interaction is happening there. I could go on and on.

Business divorces itself from feelings. It uses logic but logic absent morality because logic that pretends feelings don't exist is a denial of the existence of morality, the problem being amorality in humans IS immoral as they (feelings) are a vital component of our nature. It is all a given that business is immoral though because businesses primary purpose is profit. Profit is theft that pretends it is not. Theft is, from this camp, declaring a firm belief in the concept of private property and then summarily declaring that said belief does not apply to oneself the way it does to others. One cannot take from others AND believe in private property but as an excuse to prevent others from taking from them. Business justifies profit as a supposed need for business but objects to tax, the redistribution intended, sometimes unsuccessfully, to redistribute back to the whole what was siphoned by profit, which was no less illegitimately gained. This is what currency has given us. Why not move past it while acknowledging that every person deserves a share of the resources that we must all share. A universal credit and a true free market can emerge with this. We need only keep accurate accounting of available resources for such to work and what better use for all the automation that we produce which, in our economy does nothing but put people out of work and consequently out of resources without merit? Furthermore, this allows the capitalists a truer free market than they have yet had and the socialists a community of one and all with maximum possible diversity. Everyone can be an individual and this is desired in some form by each side.

The expression "it's just business" essentially declares business sociopathic and people expendable… openly. Think about that.

<u>Capital and Time</u>

Name one world shaping capitalist icon with an idea or product that won't see a return for 120 years? What's my point? Capitalism is about short term gains and losses. Period. Meaning? Long term consequences are not considered by the most powerful and influential people in your society if your society is capitalist…by design. Worse, the consequences are not considered on the part of these supposed innovators from the perspective of anyone but them and theirs. That doesn't even touch on the whole profit is the point mentality. Can you think of a graver citation than this for this system of socio-economics? Civilization was built upon notions of far distant futures. What do you suppose happens when that is removed from the equation? I suspect it means we fail to see the ever more prolific and significant (due to our technology) hazards before we arrive at them, largely unprepared. Profit is wholly unsuited to such a reality both morally and in terms of vision.

<u>Loans</u>

So you think loans are an opportunity for you, huh? You do understand that the reason they would approve those loans, best case scenario, is because the world actually needs/has room for what you are trying to accomplish with that loan. Meaning they want you to have it, for them. Not sure? Did you take out a loan to get a degree… maybe in nursing, or physical therapy, or to become a therapist, or a doctor, or a computer programmer? The world wants those things…and not just the world, the wealthy. But if they can get you on the hook and get what they want so much the better, right? I haven't even gotten to the fact that most loan takers are just starting out in life and earning less than they should while simultaneously being, via loan, on the hook for most of the rest of their lives. Certainly, the entirety of their youth. This doesn't sound like slavery to you? How about if I also touch on the fact that the interest you pay… that you can't afford, goes to the wealthy making them wealthier? No, literally. You see you pay high interest and collect low when you have nothing, you know, when you need a break. On the other hand, you pay low interest and collect high when you have more wealth. Meaning the system makes much of its money, probably most, from the poorest people and gives the bulk of the benefits to the richest people. Remember a little while back I said it's a caste system. Does this help? And somehow that doesn't sound predatory and upside down, right? Think about it like this, that money the bank gave you for your loan came from a rich person's account, the most neutral reason being it isn't likely to be withdrawn by them because they don't need it, to pay your way through school BECAUSE they want more of what you are studying. Sounds to me like they bought you and made a profit. Is this the only way? Of course not. We could make rich people actually pay for what they want. They are the greatest beneficiaries of an educated populace in the system we live in. Better yet, we could count all education a social service or if you prefer, a right. If we don't want to call it a right, fine, call it a privilege, just so long as it is for all with the ability. Naturally student loans aren't the only loans out there. Home and business loans aren't measurably different however. Folks do not want homes lying empty and loans also allow home prices to remain high, along with rent rates. Why? Because sellers don't have to come down to what cash is available or what the local economy now looks like, again under this system. Business loans, well who doesn't like going to a new restaurant to try the fare? Who cares if it folds in two years though? The bank got most of theirs and we got to eat someplace new, right?

Let me put this another way with some simple numbers. Banks are directly responsible for inflation. A seller wants 50k for a house. No one in the community has it so the seller can either not sell it or settle for less. If settling they can take 40k via installments over 30 years like a bank…or maybe you CAN come up with 20k cash and the seller might consider it… a choice they don't have to make because of banks… so the prices creep up. Indeed, the people that do have the cash are wealthy and or out of area economy of scales beneficiaries so they aren't buying a cheap home to live in they are buying an investment property to rent out. The cheap homes are bought and rented for more than the mortgage, meaning rent is too high but there are no homes to buy in the appropriate price range of those living in the area because they can easily outbid. This touches back to gentrification, economy of scales, loans, interest, inflation, the wealthy and capitalism. One can see how it starts to stack up.

Interest and penalties

All interest is usury. That will have more than a few people outraged but wait there is more. Penalties, the next step in the usury chain, are much more dramatic. The purpose of penalties is to award money to the lender to, ostensibly, cover their loses from your late payment. Penalties, of course, more than do this and are usury +1. Let's do a simple logic chain on a very close parallel though, to demonstrate this and more shall we? So, you pay your bill 15 days late every month for years. Few would be foolish enough to argue against the observation that this can easily net you thousands of dollars of penalty fees. Now, pay your bills 15 days early for the same period, what does this net you? Interestingly enough it again nets you nothing but loses… Hmm, how's that then? Well, you didn't receive a credit commensurate with the penalty and you removed money from an account that could have been interest bearing itself. Icing on the cake? Say you are a more typical payer with some early and some late payments. Say you pay 2 months' worth of bills every 45 days making you 15 days late for the 1 and 15 days early for the other… this is literally a wash…but you still pay a penalty, don't you? Enough said? So, penalties are really just a way to charge more interest than an already too generous system allows. That doesn't change the fact that the interest itself is a problem. There is the fact that interest is payed more to people with more money and less to people with less and I do not just mean sum but percentage itself. This strongly reinforces wealth gap growth and caste. Then there is the fact that on outgoing interest this is reversed with lower payed rates for people with more money. So, the people with more money pay… less money? Why? To make the loan more attractive to people who need no enticement to chase money, at the direct expense of those with less money. It is, after all a zero-sum game. The bank plays with the money it has access to and if that wasn't sufficient proof there is also the percentile element of the equation. This also doesn't touch on whose debts are forgiven and whose are not. Too big to fail indeed. Buttress an institution fine, buttress one above us, much less fine. Entrenchment of wealth 101.

Taxes in Capitalism

My tax burden as a single person who made 22k for 2016 was approximately 1500 federally. My tax burden for that same year for making 45k was 1800 under same conditions. Without doing the math it is painfully obvious that the POORER people are paying a greater percentage of their lesser income to taxes. This makes sense to who and how? But the poor are the parasites, right?

To make it simple, 100 percent increase in wage/20 percent increase in tax on an income that already has more disposable income than the lesser one. That is without complicating it with tax breaks and the like that become more commonplace with people who have more assets.

Planned Obsolescence

I suppose I should first define what I mean by the term. Planned obsolescence is the practice of building things to fail and/or be replaced. Most industries do this at least passively, choosing to build something cheaper rather than more durably. Many do it more intentionally with a clear desire to render previous products unserviceable with little to no benefit from the new product. Either is a problem. The digital age is no exception here, with a simple example found in the recurring release of near identical products for the price of brand new cutting-edge products. It is a cash grab. Planned obsolescence is also a corner-stone of capitalism. What does the elimination of planned obsolescence bring. however? For a start it brings substantial resolution to landfill issues, global warming issues, and waste in general. To be clear, I am saying planned obsolescence, aside from being a shameless cash grab is strongly culpable for the depletion of our natural resources and destruction of our habitat. I am saying the face of said policy is landfills, garbage islands in the ocean, strip mines and deforestation. It also eliminates jobs and manu-facturing. one might find this a fault, especially under capitalism. What if it wasn't eliminated under cap-italism, however, but something else? Eliminating the need to manufacture as people have serviceable items that last generations does not just eliminate jobs. it eliminates the need for said jobs... so long as people are entitled to live somewhere and have access to food. These things are acknowledged under various forms of socialism… and as the availability of land does not increase and population does... it is a given that people have some entitlement in this regard. Gone is a time when everyone could literally provide for themselves. That makes farmland a public resource or one to be raided, like it or not. Inci-dentally, with less manufacturing and service necessary farmland actually can increase as land that is being used for these other functions no longer need be used for such. Poorly made, derivative products are not needed and are bad for, at a minimum, our environment. Shouldn't we do something about the thought process that produces what amounts to garbage for a quick buck?

<u>An Anecdote that Isn't</u>

There are two supermarket chains in the area that I live. One is found in the city regions and the other the suburban regions. There was overlap but it was largely eliminated. The one in the city regions which, not surprisingly, are also lower income regions has higher prices and both lower quality and selection on average. The suburban one has better and more consistent price breaks with greater variety and general quality. This trend is not exclusive to supermarkets, in fact it follows for most every business but food is, of course, a necessity. How is this not predatory? The poorest people pay the highest prices and get the least selection in like items. Now, it is true that the poorer people can theoretically go to the other supermarkets and benefit and no doubt some do. That said the poorest people also are more likely to not have a vehicle, yet another thing many of them cannot afford. One might make the argument that businesses don't want to deal with the poor because the poor have less money and while a problematic narrative we can see where it would come from but then why higher prices on people who have less money? This is how caste is made and bias confirmed. You can see how easily the problems in a system can stack up.

Invention under Capitalism

If your motivation for invention is money then whatever you made what you were actually trying to invent was a bigger bank account. The problem with this is that it is inherently inferior to even a markedly smaller amount of invention motivated by genuine interest. Furthermore, invention not precipitated by money has a greater chance of considering ramifications outside of the product and money...like, for instance… human rights, global ecosystem… or even something as simple as durable goods.

Intellectual Property Rights/Copyright

The only reason we need these things is because of capitalism. We need these things under capitalism so that we can potentially benefit from our ideas gaining the resources we need to survive and thrive for our mental energies, right? Except the winner, meaning the wealthy, take even these spoils in a number of ways such as, by way of example, owning the patents of their employees, among other methods. Why should we care? Well, contrary to the stated purpose of encouraging innovation I believe these things stifle innovation, if one presumes we are all entitled to our share of the worlds resources. Numerous innovations are shelved because it is more profitable for the innovator or their owners to not use them than to use them. If you ran a drug company and accidentally found a cure for cancer, and I say accidentally because that too is an issue, that is not the research they fund in the first place as it might put them out of business, would you release the cure knowing that your long-term profits would be negatively affected? So, we have suppression and we have narrowed scope but there is more. How many excellent ideas are simply not heard or credited under such a system or are not offered for fear of predatory institutions claiming them. Call it opportunity cost if you like. The fact is profit is anathema to sharing, and insight and knowledge are to be shared. This is in no way to implicate the drug companies. This is not unique to them. It is endemic to capitalism. Profit trumps morality. Profit trumps life, so long as that life is not their own. But returning to the point, the need for intellectual property rights is only because of capitalism in the first place and secondly, it does not encourage innovation, lest you count derivative innovation like that of the latest model of cell phone, almost identical in every way but for the steadily increasing cost. Not only is this not innovation and incredibly wasteful it is filling landfills to appeal to, primarily, elitism. If that were not enough there is another layer to this. You cannot own an idea. I do not mean the law cannot grant you claim to an idea. No, clearly that is possible. We live that reality here and now. No, what I am saying is that at any point in time a thousand people might well have had the same idea you have. Not only in our own time but throughout time the awareness of various realities reasserts itself making itself apparent to myriad people. Not only that, said ideas are predicated upon two things. The ideas of others and I do not here refer to copying though there is nothing new under the sun so that too applies though how does one copy one that has never been heard by oneself, though I have an answer for this too. I refer to the fact that one does not come to ideas from within a vacuum. One comes to ideas from observation of reality and the ideas of those around oneself whether in agreement or disagreement. Stated another way, nature (of reality) and nurture (of peers). The other point has already been hinted at. Reality itself is the source of these ideas, be it correctly or incorrectly understood. How does one lay claim on reality for simply having witnessed it. What colossal arrogance is that? Most amusing and disheartening to me is that under the economic system we have we need, but don't really have intellectual property rights for various reasons. Under the system we do not have, we would not need it. Meaning, like every system that is part of a system of inequality, it is really only there for the haves if not by design then by the processes wealth affords one.

<u>Trade is not what money is for.</u>

What is the purpose of trade? The purpose of trade is to facilitate (the natural phenomenon) of transitioning high concentration gradient and low such that they are relatively equal without conflict or at least without violence. (to prevent war)

What is the purpose of profit? The purpose of profit is to gain more for something than what was given or to increase high to low concentration distribution. Profit is war.

There are those who conflate profit and trade. These same people make absurdities of logic like "the thing is greater than the sum of its parts". If the sum is greater it is because you took value from something else or failed to appreciate the value of what was there. It is that simple. In such a world is it any surprise labor is underpaid?

Deception

The world we live in today and most of what is wrong with it is the consequence of rewarding deception. Everyone cannot "profit" except if there is no profit but sharing. Everyone is not the same. The truth is not a relative construct lacking objective reality...nor an objective thing lacking all relativity. Every truth requires both to be true. Rewarding the lie ultimately makes everyone discontent in spite of the short-term gains. The "reality" created by stacking one lie on the other only produces a reality that for whatever comfort it brings, increases misery more. Further, every lie brings us another step further away from real correction if and when we wish to fix it. It is made tenable by not living within it, an attractive mosaic comprised of unattractive pieces, or so the wealthy think. But the mosaic can only grow or be dismantled, it cannot remain the same. So, they too find themselves in, rather than gazing on the mosaic. How so? Global problems created or at a minimum deepened by those shaping the mosaic become their problem too, however they insulate themselves. They might well have the last sip of fresh water but scant consolation that, once it too is gone, no? Lies, like cancer, are destructive, hungry and inconstant. They show holes which must then add another layer of lie or walk back to the truth.

A Simple Truth

Business, and by extension, currency, necessarily leads to widespread or at a bare minimum, upper echelon sociopathy. Profit is anathema to concern for one's fellow man. Indeed, profit comes directly at their expense, be they customers you overcharge, employees you underpay, or products you cut corners manufacturing. Do not confuse this for trade. Trade does not predicate profit, currency and especially business do. Profit being more for less or, more clearly, something from nothing...which is nothing more than a lie.

Capitalism, far too many claim, usually in maximally dismissive and condescending tones, more often than not failing to even bother to reason or debate, is the best and only reasonable system and ensures improvement. Those who hold this view always point to countries with myriad socialist policies as proof that capitalism works. Said social policies are literally the only thing keeping the people from naked revolt or naked enslavement, the continuous and inevitable result of anything even vaguely resembling a pure capitalist economy. Somehow, they think that every single person will compete and none will form a power block, unchecked by government, to better compete. They are wrong on both counts. Or perhaps they think that the other inevitable power blocks will keep them in check...except of course that all this actually predicts is a cycle of endless war...on the very land you live on no less, with one faction or another temporarily winning out until one does win...at which point... you have government again. You want to go backward and call that progress rather than forward. The path forward has a fork. That fork is to choose, as the people, to be...the people...or you can wait until the choice is made by necessity and inevitability. This latter "choice" has not worked out well at pretty much any time in the past. The government that is less perfect than you would like, the mandation of birth rate in Chinese citizens that could have been done with early recognition and education and autonomy...

An ounce of prevention beats a pound of cure...but it requires an ounce of forethought...which requires thinking about something other than money...and it will be unpaid thought...unless you count the whole better environment for everyone thing...Bah, that's crazy talk. Or so far too many say, but then that's actually a pretty good indication it might have some merit isn't it?

The Ambitious

The ambitious think those who are cooperative and/or content to be stupid and/or lazy. In so doing they pick a fight with people who had no quarrel with them. There is no quarrel until the ambitious mandate ambition via policy or hoarding of formerly plentiful resources. You wish to strive and excel? Do so. It is its own reward. If it is not you reveal the real reason for your behavior. You have declared a resource or conformity war. If this is not your intent reexamine your justification for differential reward. If you compete to better yourself kudos. If the peace of some is a declaration of war to you then you are a tyrant, grasping and guilty and needing to make others so to feel better about yourself. That is not competition nor betterment...that is cowardice and a need for control...uniformity, seen both on the left and right.

Do you believe such ambition is not mandated? Can most live without spending over half of their waking hours serving someone who will become wealthy from their services while they will not? Work ethic is not slaving for 40-100 hours a week. Work ethic is doing a job thoughtfully and well. This misappropriation of language goes far to demonstrate my point.

Think on this, would it be a bad thing if we did not have millions of voices with nothing to say clamoring to be heard? Do not confuse this with the fact that they should have the right to say it. They do not clamor because it is their right. They clamor for the spotlight. A thing most would not naturally even desire but for it being attached to one's bread.

Any trait can be positive or negative. Perseverance can be particularly problematic in our system though primarily when coupled with greed or simply, short-sighted thinking. Indeed, I would argue that the slew of stacking disadvantages to the poor and stacking advantages for the wealthy come from precisely this phenomenon yet the notion that perseverance wins out in the end is supposed to be a positive notion. If a person or people methodically seek to institute advantage at every turn and opportunity for themselves with, at best, no regard for others and worse, active maliciousness for same, how can we expect this to produce anything remotely resembling a just or even desirable community? Most would acknowledge that a hypercompetitive environment is what we have at the moment. It would seem that not enough recognize that such an environment is hostile and tends to destroy that which it seeks to save or champion. We do not get better this way. We get worse. Any appearance to the contrary is nothing more than the concentration of resources that has occurred. It is essentially the work harder so that I can get more cocaine so that I can work harder argument and few who do not turn to a drug or other cheat in such an environment can compete, but then the competition was destructive long before that. When we want people to be a particular trait we call it by its positive name and when we don't we call it by the negative. This is a manipulation. Or have you not noticed people that are determined on a course we want persevere while on one we do not want are said to be dogged? Eccentric is what we call someone odd that we value, usually someone wealthy or famous rather than calling them odd, strange, or even disturbing.

On Achievement

We live in a world where many, not all, are scrabbling for achievement. Other than money and recognition, name one reason for this behavior? The world doesn't want, need, or even have room for much of it. If it did the fight to do so wouldn't be nearly so intense...but for that whole money thing again… as if we needed another proof of the problem inherent in money and particularly, wages. So, people face constant rejection and hostility in the competition to receive things that there are, in all honesty, more than enough of. Why? To feed some monolithic insecurities? Most people do most of what they do most of the time to belong, because we are a cooperative species. The problem is a thing can go so far to one side that it circles around, which I will get into more later. This means that a person's need for acceptance can actually be expressed as pathological levels of competition which is both ironic and extraordinarily inconvenient for nearly all concerned. You see this commonly when people go to extremes to differentiate themselves or when a parent is very withholding on affection, often due to absenteeism, often because they themselves are busy obtaining achievements, and so it goes.

People driven by their insecurity, seek accomplishment to feel less inadequate. Attaining accomplishment, they then tell themselves they are superior because of their accomplishment as they cannot merely measure up, being insecure in the first place. So, the accomplishment, a testament to a weakness real and one perceived (insecurity and whatever metric triggered it) becomes proof of superiority rather than inferiority or even equality and so the lie begins, though in fairness it started with the insecurity itself which started with the need to be the same when no one is. Thus, ultimately the right is every bit as conformist as the left, only differing in the particulars of how they express it. The right claims superiority, the left often strives for uniformity from the same root.

Most people, I believe, want acceptance and belonging. They aren't going to get that by being rich or being poor. Poor get ordered about and derided. Rich get toadied too and also derided. You aren't going to get it by going to a religion. Whichever one you choose has its faults and at its core considers itself better than all the others else it would not need to exist. Thus, you are an elitist and will treat and be treated accordingly. Unity is not formed through division and acceptance and belonging are unity, without the sacrifice of autonomy or diversity.

<u>Tragedy</u>

The grande tragedy of our world is that the middling of intellect routinely think the intelligent naive. The intelligent show profound patience as they must, since most understand less. Some from the intelligent camp at some point have a break of patience and some are raised from the beginning to view such patience as weakness. Enter the sociopath, typically from the wealthy and opportunistic, though these, when they occur, tend to be groomed, but back to the point. Said patience is seen by the middling as naive and so great intelligence is seen magically as lesser intelligence. These middles should know better having interacted with intelligences below their own, the low intelligence, that they themselves must be patient with. Yet how can we be surprised that the middle fails to note something the high do not miss? We cannot. It is not, I suspect only a failure to note, however. I believe the middle does to some extent recognize the great intellect fully and merely uses the offered patience to undermine it out of basic jealousy. Whichever is the dominant reason this is why the strife is endless. There are those who note jealousy to be the culprit and even those who note that it is jealousy of intelligence. Far too many of them believe themselves entitled to more for their supposed intelligence, however. How does an intelligent person miss the interdependencies and varieties upon which we all depend? It seems to me such a failing of vision can only come from those in the middle, smart enough to outwit many, half to be clearer, base enough to miss the endless destruction that follows this path. Still I am sure some intelligent people walk that line having lost patience or been groomed, in many cases since birth, with the notion that they are superior and therefore deserving of more. Were I born to a wealthy family I might well have the same thought, living in an environment where everything I have and learn says I am better. These points too originate in competition rather than cooperation. One is loath to see one's competition rewarded and clearly one should not reward inferiors the same, right? Never mind that one needs to remain blind to conclude that any of us is inferior or superior based upon class and every human being has as much right to the resources of the planet as any other. Reward all equally and you will see a great deal of this reverse itself in short order as intelligence then becomes a responsibility rather than a reward. This too speaks well of cooperation and poorly of competition. Most readily accept their relative possession of any other virtue but this one. I suspect more than anything else it is because they do not want to find themselves unentitled to speak. A valid fear in a competitive environment and a baseless one in cooperation in which anyone might, but usually doesn't, produce the best ideas. In fairness it isn't just with respect to intelligence. The issue is that the mean, due to being the mean, which is to say middle of the road, often mistakes a numbers advantage for superiority, which becomes self-fulfilling prophecy should that notion be believed and acted on, again due to numbers without acknowledging the value of either side of outliers and certainly not both, commonly not even recognizing there is a "both" for said same reason. This is not a necessary eventuality though, but for competition encouraging the dismissal of those one can outcompete, however that is accomplished. The mean is needed, as are we all, but they know what it looks like when someone outdoes them being middle of the road and so they know they have those under them who surpass them. Honesty, hard as it may be, is required. The same goes for those pandering to the numbers knowing they are lying.

Another Absurd Irony

If I oppose you I am capable of all manner of insight (people see genius and malice in their detractors) while if I cooperate I am an idiot (people see sharing and cooperation as naive and weak) or so goes the narrative for those who favor competition, yes? If this is so then they themselves should know that their position is folly. I realize the thought is that competition is a must, however they have tacitly agreed that one is brilliant for opposing them and an idiot for agreeing with them thereby acknowledging they are an idiot and one, in opposing their narrative of competition and advocating cooperation is brilliant. Think on the irony, absurdity, and most importantly, truth of the above.

The Not Really LURKING Variable

The presence of social injustice for minorities and women and the like is its own thing. It isn't money. That's why it is measured in terms of money, right? That's why it is to be corrected in terms of money, right? No, clearly its money. We just can't have poor white males included in the group that needs help. As a bonus, maybe some not so poor women and minorities will do even better by it. And has this happened? Of course it has. People arguing against injustice creating it. And worse, smoke screening the real problem actively and by stealing needed support while they are at it. There is one group of oppressed people in this country. That group is poor and it is comprised of all demographics barring the financial one. Every demographic should be on board for fixing it, which starts with calling it what it is. Generations of blaming poor people for the tribulations of middle America however makes that unlikely. Now who pulled that particular hat trick do you suppose? Oh, the wealthy, right? And "identity politics", quotes due to the absurdity of both the term and the reality that it has almost nothing to do with your identity, soared around the time Occupy Wallstreet rattled some cages, didn't it? Must be some great coincidence, right? Simple question, what does having more mean? Does it mean someone else HAS to have less? I know words are coming to mean little with the word games being played but this one should still be pretty clear shouldn't it?

<u>Another Analogy</u>

You have bologna and salami. They are, with respect to meat and fat content, quite similar. Consistency and appearance only differ due to a narrow view of distribution. The salami is coarsely ground while the bologna is fine ground. Each distribution is roughly even in quantity and each is evenly spread with meat next to fat and fat next to meat. That said the salami has more distinct flavor and a generally firmer consistency. The fat and meat of salami are not differentially treated when you eat them though and both are vital. It is simply apparent that they are distinct and complementary. Bologna on the other hand has had all distinction blurred. The meat is still meat and the fat is still fat but your eye and your tongue both have difficulty distinguishing them in spite of their nature remaining the same. They have simple been ground too fine for it to be apparent. Do you prefer salami or bologna? Steak or meat paste? Distinction is critical. So too is valuation of all the elements. We need more salami and less bologna but, in the process, we need to remember that the fat is just as important to the salami as the meat is and so worth as much. Socialism...not homogeneity. If salami can do it you can too.

Note the salami has half of what the right says...and half of the left on the positive side. Bologna the same, only inverted. Homogeneity...and capitalism. Or perhaps you think three differentiations of people, the classes, largely mandated to homogeneity, are more diverse than a situation where everyone is an individual, and having equal access to resources, we no longer have one group getting the best of all and another getting the worst of all but rather myriad differentiations according to taste as no one could hoard the best or be relegated only the worst with equal access to wealth or better stated resources?

<u>On Culture</u>

Culture doesn't exist, per se. Culture is taking habits and familiarities that were determined by region and time and making them a source of division, or weaponizing them. Literally everyone has habits and shared habits due to shared environment is no great mystery. Pride in a physical feature (or shame) or the region you were born, things you had no say on and that do not reflect on who you are can only be divisive. Harmony is not born from people being the same. It is born from differences and similarities being nothing more than traits. Add badges of honor and shame and its war...or culture.

<u>Culture and Values</u>

Many of the differing views on society that we attribute to culture are really little more than environmental and the ensuing interaction with people from different environmental circumstances. Living in desert instills frugality. Winters instill industriousness. Long mild summers instill a relaxed air. People then take these dispositions and upon meeting others conflict ensues and competition results. The fact is that in the world we have now, one in which we can travel the globe at ease, in which scarcity of vital resources is a social construct rather than the result of nature, we can and must take a more conscious look at our values and beliefs. In so doing we can, to my eyes at any rate, either cooperate as a species or we can, sooner or later, and likely with little warning, destroy ourselves with one form of war or another. We can do it competing on tech that gets out of hand, deforestation, global warming, the production of sterile food stocks, or just good old-fashioned war, to name a few. As many means as we have today, and we already have more than enough, we will have more tomorrow you can be sure. Our physical sciences badly outstrip our social sciences. Surely no one thinks these medieval ideas with a fresh coat of paint are where we should be at in a world such as we have at this point? What we do in our own backyard is no longer only relevant to our own backyard…if it ever was. The scale has changed. We share a neighborhood. It just happens to be called Earth. Too grandiose you think? Take a look at the oceans or the landfills then. We are well past due for this folks, and it is showing. We are just trying really hard to not notice.

<u>Group Think</u>

You think socialism fosters thought policing and capitalism fosters free thought? Think again. Socialism is better for real scientific innovation first of all. Real scientific innovation absolutely requires free thought. There is only one thought not permitted under socialism. Which one? How can I make this about me and screw everyone else? Everything else is fair game. Now let's look at capitalism, shall we? Capitalism is about competition. Competition requires allies but not too many allies or very poorly compensated allies because you want more, right? The idea of allies is about group think. You want to be my friend in this dog eat dog you have to say you are just like me. You have to act just like me too don't you or they won't buy it? That's where all these groups come from. Do you honestly believe that the people who identify as in any of these groups agrees with one another on even half of what they claim to believe? Of course they don't, but since they are already fighting some superficial group that they clearly do not belong to it's make nice time. If you are honest, this is the source of thought police and yes both the left and the right do it and they do it for the same reasons. They want more than whatever outgroup they created in their heads and it can be literally anything… You want the freedom to think for yourself? Drop the power blocks which means drop the competition. The first thing a power block wants is for you to think like them. Here is a simple proof of concept. What is a Christian supposed to think like? What is a Conservative supposed to think like? What is a Liberal supposed to think like? And now the winner, what is a human supposed to think like?

How many people, do you suppose, have a deep and fundamental problem with the system that we live in and only pretend otherwise out of need or social expectation? I believe most of us are truly not ok with our system and go along because many believe they are in the minority or that they cannot make a difference in how our society is structured. This is incorrect. How many people have stopped trying? How many people have stopped feeling? How many people have even stopped living out of revulsion of how we have structured this supposedly cooperative venture we call a society? The time for change is now. The way I see it, as the poor masses, we have only three options to be heard on these issues. One is revolt and none of us from any class want that do we? One is to petition our government in vast numbers, which could work but we will miss work, many of us to do so. The last is to strike, also in vast numbers It seems to me that two and three are natural synergies as we would miss the work in either case and by putting them together we have more potential to affect change. I know for the poor this is very difficult as we live paycheck to paycheck but that's the game isn't it? How else can we get their attention while maintaining our dignity? Does anyone else have a better idea on how to get heard? Because one thing is certain, without many dollars we will need many voices. But I want you to think it through yourself. These pages are my proof I have done mine and rejected both the left as they do not serve the people.

Unity Through Division

What I refer to as Unity through division is the process by which people attach themselves to groups, which are really subgroups, presumably to obtain allies (unity) when in reality it nothing more than a power block to compete against others (division) for various resources (competition over cooperation). We see all manner of such behavior and few seems to realize that each of these codified groups that forms is just one more source of strife and competition, ultimately making whatever ease they hoped to achieve still further removed from them, for most, most of the time. Religion is a fantastic example of this. What purpose is served by hundreds of pockets of people saying emphatically what they think of some, to all evidence, imaginary being, that, even if it existed would likely consider us beneath it or be just as unaware of us as we are of something ten steps below whatever the lowest particle we are presently aware of and if it did know of us, how narcissistic would you have to be to believe it would favor one group of paramecia over the other? It is a fight… over nothing… except ego. It is simply a declaration to all the world that one is either with them or against them and on their terms. It is division and hierarchy personified. The same goes for nationalism. A country is only as good as its policies and all of them have at least several flawed policies. The fact that we have so many countries is simply a testament to our inability to share at the same times as we, ultimately do, that those countries exist in the first place. We can and must be diverse. Being diverse does means assigning a billion labels. You will never make enough boxes to encapsulate human diversity fairly… except by only using one. Unity through division is predicated upon the notion that the only reason you want cooperation is so you can better compete. You do not want cooperation to cooperate. In short, it is a lie.

<u>Religion</u>

Whether religion started from a place of innocence and adopted flawed concepts of morality to make its appeals or religion started as a dishonest means of population control that incorporated kernels of truth to make it palatable to the masses one thing is clear. Religion has both truisms of morality and falsehoods of morality. The problem with religion in this respect is that it is not particularly more likely to discard fiction than truth based upon either the structure of religion or the passage of time. There is a reason for this but first another element needs to be addressed. Religion is not the sole determiner of morality. Indeed, it isn't even the best determiner. Logic and emotion (feelings) together will tell you what is moral and what is not. I would specify that honesty is also required but such would be redundant because if you are using logic to determine truth a lie is not logical. The feelings are required because we are feeling beings and so that component cannot be ignored. By simple demonstration, imagine that we maximized productivity and that said level caused physical and mental pain in everyone who participated. It would not be an honest maximum, would it? Because it ignored feelings, be they physical or mental. But back to the point. Religion is not a reliable and certainly not the only, or even a primary source of morality. Religion is a wonderful source of dogma and conformity however. Religion is a power block in a world that competes. It represents itself as unity but is in fact divisive. Every member of any religion is necessarily not a member of another religion and more importantly is likely not examining their beliefs but rather being indoctrinated into them and expected to conform. Religion is unity through division and I can prove it with a simple question. What is the difference between the expression "God's chosen people" and the expression "master race"? Pretty much every religion out there has a "God's chosen people" doesn't it?

Media rating and Capitalism

Outrage sells. Divisions pays in more ways than one…but only for the immoral and the top. Everyone else is harmed. If everyone were in fact immoral, they aren't, it would only pay for the intelligent and connected, true now but truer then. The intelligence narrative is a common misappropriation of fiscal success. The intelligent do better at whatever tier…but intelligence is not the dominant indicator of tier change. Morality, or rather its lack, has a stronger connection. How easy is it too fabricate cause for offense endlessly? And what's the harm, right? As I said, immorality. It is not possible to be amoral and human. We have feeling and among them a conscience. Intelligence is capable of recognizing consequences other than the most proximal. Put another way they should know better and failing that, be held more accountable but then they aren't the only ones, are they? The only real question is whether they knowingly foment the division that enables so much oppression or whether they do so in ignorance of the damage that they do? If the former they are malicious, if the later they are unqualified to have such access to the people. This of course also presumes they are not simply tools bought and paid for themselves, doesn't it? But then the only thing that changes is the tier not the observation isn't it?

On Defenses of Capitalism

To the meritocracy crowd, where is the merit in being born or raised a lion? How did you earn it? You did not.

There is no such thing as a meritocracy. Declarer of best picks self. Two people of differing abilities both literally work themselves to death, which deserves more reward? They may not have equal ability but they paid equal price. Or would you like to suggest a eugenics program right now?

To the Social Darwinism crowd, how do the rules of mankind equate to the rules of nature? One is inviolate, the other is predicated upon the circumstances of who holds the reigns. You argue that the best will be rewarded most and then declare what the best is, ignoring all the rest that you fundamentally depend upon. In other words, you claim Darwinism while literally preventing it with rules that artificially dictate both might and right. Darwinism doesn't declare one trait superior to another. Socially constructed rules and enforcements do. It's basic confirmation bias. Self-fulfilling prophecy. And it is usually coming from those claiming to be science minded. You are not a lion in fact. You are a human and human rights do not depend on how gifted you are. You argue for the dissolution of rules while depending upon and demanding them.

Both of these are rationalizations on why capitalism is not unjust. Both are easily and obviously refuted.

Understand if we are competing you don't get to make my rules, only your own. Which means I have no obligation to follow your rules unless one of two things is going on. Either we are cooperating or we are servants, which is to say complicit cooperation aka duress. We aren't cooperating of course because cooperation has us as equals. Massive wealth disparity proves that one false. Which leaves that we are considered servants also known as slaves. The rules apply to us, indeed more than they do to those who make them and we do not get even stake for following them, we get much much less. This analysis is clear, honest and accurate.

The everybody is better off today argument, poverty is better than it used to be, is disingenuous. First, you cannot make a convincing case for the fact that a person isn't poor because they can afford a cell phone even though many people own a home and some own a jet. Relative scale cannot be dismissed so casually. Both relative and objective measures should apply and relative measures to present standards are at least as relevant if not more relevant than relative measures to past. A simple demonstration of that fact would be done by taking…pretty much anything from a person in the present. The kind of people that make the argument that I here counter would object strenuously if we took anything from them in the present but dismiss the present from their relative scale of poverty instead comparing the poor to the past poor. It is dishonest, intentionally or accidentally, on every level, ignoring the argument that poverty shouldn't exist entirely and ignoring present relative comparison which they would find signifi-cant, should it affect them, in favor of past comparison. In other words, they prove present is more important to them by complaining if you take something from them, in the present. Otherwise, the fact that they used to have it (whatever you took from them), a past condition, would be irrelevant. Yes, every group has done better courtesy of cooperation, enforced or otherwise. That is not in debate…much. The point is that some have claimed more than their due and this argument simply tries to walk around that. It is a strawman of epic proportions. Second, is the fact that every group at a lower technological level throughout history gets steamrolled by the one with the greater technology whether accidentally by virtue of them simply being beneath the concern or observation of the technological group or through active exploitation and malicious intent. The poor operate, if it even needs saying, at a lower technological level than the wealthy.

<u>Supply and Demand</u>

Supply and demand are pointed to as the reason for both prices and wages. This would imply that they are the fundament, the bottom line, on a causal relationship. If supply and demand are the reason then they, being the base, should be unalterable by less relevant, higher tier factors. Yet both supply and demand can be and routinely are altered both deliberately and accidentally. What this means in simple, irrefutable terms is that supply and demand are not the cause of prices or wages in our system. That which alters them is. What is it which alters them? The extent to which a given, human, business, or system is greedy and so willing to manipulate the factors of supply and demand is. We already know that said factors ARE manipulatable. The diamond industry is a classic example with rather blatant artificial scarcity, considering carbon is one of the most common elements on the planet and what diamonds are comprised of, plus heat and pressure, but again, natural or man-made, diamonds are not scarce. The demand? Manipulated perceptions of status and affection. Are diamonds unique in this regard? Of course not. The manipulation of supply and demand happens in most, if not all, industries under capitalism. But if you can alter the supply and the demand then it is disingenuous to point the finger there for why low wage workers are low wage, isn't it? It is disingenuous to rationalize high price goods and services for the same reasons, particularly when these things are needs like renting or owning a home, yes? If we compete, greed not supply and demand controls the price. If we cooperate and only if we cooperate is it truly supply and demand. Businesses that operate based upon greed do not really provide whatever goods or services they purport to anyway. Their purpose is to bleed wealth. What they provide is simply the vehicle to do so and they provide this other service, whatever it may be. grudgingly and at the minimum threshold they can get away with to continue with their true purpose.

Capitalism does not now, nor did it ever, own supply and demand, what capitalism owns is the manipulation of supply and demand. It is, in essence, the system that disregards supply and demand to the greatest extent possible. It respects class, like any number of thrown down systems before it that did the same.

The Post Scarcity Argument

I have heard it said that the only way socialism could work is in a post-scarcity world. This is a poor extrapolation. Cooperation is required in scarcity not in plenty. It is its very purpose. Anarchy would function fine in a post scarcity world. Anyone could do and take what they want and the conflict would be minimal as there is...no scarcity. Plenty for all.

Socialism, by contrast, is about managing finite resources for the benefit of all. It is only needed and indeed, only useful in a world that has scarcity.

Capitalism more closely resembles anarchy than socialism… at least early stage capitalism. Late stage capitalism always resembles a very particular form of socialism because someone has amassed fortunes and now dictates the rules...only this person never does so for the good of the many, due in no small part to how they arrived here. It is much like how the current left sounds very much like the current right, each with their bigotries toward demographics they attribute to the other. Crony capitalism, as it's called, is not socialism it is feudalism, capitalisms' predecessor come back around. It isn't socialist unless it is for the good of the many, whatever someone wants to call it. Clearly the left aren't the only ones guilty of ignoring definitions and morphing words to suit them.

Pyramid Scheme

There will, under capitalism, never be enough seats at the table. Working hard is never going to be enough. The people at the top will surely appreciate all the hard work though, as you try to outwork the next guy neither of you getting your due. The same goes for intelligence. Indeed, how many patents today are owned by our "employers"? And guess who dictates what you devote your brain power to in the first place? It is also worth noting that since capitalism is about this funneling of wealth and many workers know it well, the work ethic suffers across the board. You get averaged work from capitalism, not socialism, because capitalism is prolific for stealing the energies of laborers. The rebuttal? Unpleasant work environment from on high. The rebuttal from labor? Various forms of theft. Downward spiral anyone?

Capitalism Requires Socialism

Socialism does not necessarily require capitalism, but capitalism requires socialism. Your options for capitalism are to give the poor what they need using tax dollars for that source and eliminating the poor at which point you're almost as much socialist as capitalist. Or you can spend that money and probably more ensuring that the poor who do not have what they need harm one another rather than entering your own neighborhood and harming you. That such an outcome is a necessary eventuality of predatory policy and specifically capitalism is beyond question. And if you don't notice that that's what going on, you're not paying attention. The police attempt to keep the poor in the poor neighborhoods and that with some rudimentary socialist comforts already in place. Regarding this latter form of capitalism with its social controls only to keep the poor separate from the wealthy, what we have is essentially feudalism which is essentially might makes right. Which is to say, no government at all, as a government that doesn't serve the people is not a government but a private interest seeing to its own. To make this point, here we have many billionaires in the US who could, can, and do influence people's actions on epic scale to serve their own interests. Are each of them a government? As to the other form of socialism and its approach to poverty, it doesn't have an issue with poverty because it would effectively eliminate poverty. What it would have as a concern is a population problem, which would necessitate education and compliance on the part of the people as it pertains to population. Population control is a requirement in a situation of plenty, as otherwise the population could only grow and in doing so would necessarily pose a risk to itself.

It seems to me that capitalism is natural bedfellows with fascism. Socialism is natural bedfellows with democracy. Limited voices equate to wealth imbalance and fascism. Equal voice can only come from equal resources. Now plenty of countries call themselves socialist that aren't, to be clear, and yes most of these are fascist. Spin is stock in trade of fascism….and capitalism, is it not? You can call the moon a cow but it will be giving you neither milk nor beef, will it?

Competition/Cooperation

I use capitalism and socialism frequently here. I know that these terms mean different things to different people and that some of these perceptions are rooted in fact and some are not. Let me clarify what it is I am advocating. I wish to see competition with our fellow man be minimized. I wish to see it minimized by encouraging and allowing cooperation which means among other things, reducing artificial scarcity and baseless fear. It means having a system in which our efforts serve humanity as a whole rather than some wealthy self-interested person or puppeteering manipulator. I believe, by logic and the evidence of my own eyes, that unity and diversity are compatible and desirable but not without autonomy and wealth equality (upon which autonomy in no small part resides).   I do not care what you call your system if it does these things. That said, capitalism, whichever form you practice, does of necessity of its mechanics allow and even encourage division. In its ideal it is intended that all people benefit but profit comes from somewhere and someone. It can only work if everyone competes and everyone competes freely and everyone is born equally capable and no one colludes, collusion functionally being neither self nor community but special interest, in order to obtain advantage. In other words, it is by its very nature only capable of division, masked as unity.

The very first thing most people teach their children is to share. The very second thing most Americans teach their child is NOT to share…with "them" whoever them may be.

Selfish Intelligence?

Being self-serving doesn't require great degrees of intellect. You have only to consider what is best for one and grant some small measure to those you require in order to thrive. No, considering the needs of many or indeed all is far more difficult a task with far more variables. Celebrating one's intellect on the ability to fool others and gain for oneself is hardly a measure of intelligence even in the short term, to say nothing of the long term in which case it is significantly worse. The long term doesn't exist for such people except in the most myopic of ways with themselves as the only people on earth or at least the only ones who matter remain or so they clearly believe. Far more impressive to not only consider the many but the future and yet the previous would have you believe the latter are simple, stupid or naïve. The same for appealing to base nature versus our better elements. Sure, we are comprised of both. What happens when you encourage the base? Lowered bar, right? How did those oh so clever miss that, do you suppose? They didn't. The would rather rule a weakened and foolish populace than be one part of a stronger, smarter and ultimately more prosperous one. Or they did miss it… in which case they aren't as smart as they thought, right?

<u>Capitalism and Manufacture via Car</u>

So, capitalism makes things better, does it? Why then do the cheapest cars of today not only cost more than yesteryear, they are more poorly designed. They handle worse. They are fundamentally flawed of design. The knowledge has not been lost, has it? No. It seems to me that it is quite typical that things at the bottom price bracket are literally made intentionally badly. We are not merely talking about cheap materials here folks. That would be no surprise for the cheapest products under capitalism, would it? We are talking about fundamentals of car design and steering that we have had locked down for decades that are pointedly NOT incorporated into the automobile producing a vehicle that handles worse than it has any right to considering the knowledge has long since been developed. Its equivalent in produce would be for us to genetically modify a potato to be less nutritious and then sell that one to poorer people. This is the exact inverse of what capitalism purports to offer. The poor don't get the old best someday, no we design a special new bad just for them. Why? To encourage people to buy the more expensive things of course. Except no one chooses to be poor so... back to class warfare, right? If you can't raise the bar or don't want to you can maintain class division and wealth inequity by simply lowering the bar of the other group. It sounds absurd, and it should, but that makes the fact that it happens all the more sad. Supply and demand meet greed and elitism.

<u>Automation</u>

How many businesses are offering dramatically different pricing to customers to encourage the removal of a need for staff? How many phone systems literally make you listen to everything the company has to say before extending you the option to talk to a human? How much of what you listen to is pertinent to you and how often? How is that worthy of your dollar regardless? They are not serving you at all... often in a situation where what you are paying for is literally service in the first place. When they eliminate the jobs who buys the products? Will the rich folks suddenly see the need to see to the poor once they have entirely replaced their dependency on them by having them build the infrastructure intended to re-place them (the poor)?

Capitalism is division. Classes are just the start of it. The extended family becomes the nuclear family becomes the broken home (single parent or separated). The sexes cannot tolerate one another. The ages cannot tolerate one another. The ethnicities cannot tolerate one another. Every piece of this intolerance and outrage is profitable to the top. The divisions do not merely disempower the bottom. They literally enrich the top. How many more houses or apartments does divided living require? Double at a minimum right? But more, because there was a time there was no shame in living with family. There is now, is there not? Think not? Clearly you are not a male of dating age. Superficially we can thank feminism for the fact that women lowered the wage by doubling the workforce and also expecting males to be some form of material provider but feminism is a symptom not the cause. Or perhaps it would be fairer to call it an intentionally delivered pathogen. But not one intentionally delivered by women. It is a tool of the wealthy, nothing more and nothing less. We are at a place as a society in which products are intention-ally made badly to INCREASE revenue. Soda companies use additives that while ostensibly for other purposes, like emulsions and preservatives, counter the desired effects of the product. Put another way, the up you desire from the caffeine and sugar in a product is then countered by an inserted low. Why? To make it habit forming and so that you have to consume more for the desired effect without ever real-izing the crash you are feeling is not a sugar crash at all. Let's not pick on the soda industry too much. This sort of business practice of maneuvering to make people pay more for less is standard in our soci-ety. Inexcusable and unnecessary but standard. Do you honestly think that this predictable verifiable pat-tern that just so happens to coincide with the rich getting richer and the poor getting poorer, as evi-denced by among other things a fast grown and growing wealth gap and vanishing middle, the place everyone should be, or maybe, just maybe, this is intentional? How much proof do we need and for how long should we gather said proof to know that, first, capitalism is about haves and have nots, and second, haves and have nots is not a just society. We can do better and we must.

On employment

We seek to weed out and otherwise disqualify. We do not want to qualify because there are too many applicants (to feel a need to) and more importantly because of competition. If everyone in our society held a Master's degree and McDonalds was not automated yet what level of education would you require to work at McDonalds? The answer is a Master's Degree. You think what I am saying is absurd perhaps? How many jobs now require college and frequently as much as a Bachelor's degree that required no college previously. Do you think the job became more difficult and that the college requirement is justified? It did not and it is not. The truth is the vast majority of jobs in our society could be done by…a computer or a trained monkey and they are working on doing just that. Not only that, if you did have specialized knowledge there is an excellent chance you would be asked not to use it as they will tell you exactly how they want you to do your job even while degrees become ever more required and ever more exacting in terms of what degree qualifies for what job. Why not, if they can just send people back to the loan mill and pretend that is opportunity rather than obligation?

The true injustice

There is a strange phenomenon in our society. Many people are perfectly content to suggest that a person is bad because of their skin color or gender or even their age. Most of these same people feel, however, that it is unfair to generalize the wealthy as bad. The preceding traits are all ones for which the person is utterly blameless and yet those, to them are valid reasons to hold a person as contemptible. There is, in fact, only one trait up there that is within the power of the people possessing it. Wealth is active. It is not passive. Wealth is not only the root of the injustice it is completely mutable. One need not remain wealthy. And having wealth while others are in poverty necessarily means having more than you need with the full knowledge that others do not have what they need and yet keeping it, is this not so? One need not continue the pursuit of wealth once one is comfortable. How many philanthropists become middle class or below? How many philanthropists spend their money trying to change the nature of the wealth imbalance itself? It seems to me a wealthy person that gives and remains wealthy or even more common, becomes wealthier still is not a philanthropist at all. They have merely bought good will…and a sizable tax write off. Being able to avoid your tax obligation thus at the highest levels of income is just more burden for the rest of us. They have enough to donate to a cause they believe worthy without shedding tax liability, do they not? Were we to eliminate such a loophole we also eliminate much of the need to check on the legitimacy of their contributions in terms of graft and nepotism too do we not? Ultimately, I do not blame the wealthy for this either. Few indeed could have such power and privilege and willingly surrender it, especially when the system is such that someone else can merely take up the mantle. That our system not only enables but encourages exactly this paradigm is what I believe we must change. One simple means is to turn wealth gap into wealth cap such that people having amassed as much as they are allowed no longer have reason to seek and hoard more. This is a mere stopgap to my eyes as it reduces but does not eliminate the myriad issues of wealth inequality but it shows gradation in just how wanton our practice really is. The truth is there are many solutions superior to what we use now. The shortage is in pursuing them.

Intelligence/Academia/Meritocracy

I posit that we have an interplay problem with education, meritocracy and intelligence in our capitalist system. The bar in education is set such that a person of relatively average intelligence can, with effort, fairly consistently obtain top grades, A's if you will. A person of slightly below average in this regard can expect to pull C's consistently, a passing if not exceptional mark, with the occasional A. The reason, one would presume is to hold up the notion of meritocracy thereby justifying differential reward. The insinuation being that it is obtainable to all. There are problems with this mentality from every angle however. First and foremost, the gifted vanish into obscurity. How so? Well, the most gifted on such a scale can obtain the A without effort and while that is handy in terms of having some free time the fact is the supposed merit measure is rendered irrelevant. There is no indication that your straight A's where obtained effortlessly or through effort. Superficially this is fine but since the bar is entirely arbitrary in the first place it should actually identify the various tiers and it does not. Additionally, we do not need everyone to have and/or qualify for a degree. There are myriad jobs that should not require them. This whole scenario is only necessary because of differential rewards and a need to create the illusion of full potential for upward mobility. This fails because in a pyramid there are never going to be enough seats at the top. It is immediately obvious... or should be. The education is diminished, and presumption that it is an actual qualifier for positions is discarded. With uniformity of reward regardless of what one's strengths are we can restore the true purpose of various institutions, education being key among them as it becomes the qualifier it is meant to be rather than the keystone to upward mobility it should never have been…but which is irresistibly profitable in capitalism.

Equality means having to state your case to your peers for ideas that impact others. It doesn't mean having to produce a cover story to control the spin should information that we don't intend to get out gets out anyway. That's several tiers deep of hierarchy, obfuscation, and entitlement. The world does not belong to whoever has the most money or whoever can lie the best. Some likely think that the above is indictment of one group or another, be it big business or government. It is both, they operate far too similarly, both forgetting they are servants of not only themselves but the rest of the community that they belong to instead choosing to see themselves as part of an ever shrinking and more elitist society who is not beholden to the rules they, more than anyone else, make in the first place.

Equality means accountability is more or less uniform, not sparse for those in positions of authority and not only present but excessive for those at the bottom. Indeed, if these should be set unequally they should be inverted not because people at the top deserve more punishment but because if anyone is to be held to a higher standard it must be those with the most ability to do harm, a condition authority grants.

Equality means holding lying as a serious issue. Deception has, at a minimum, the purpose of obfuscating the truth. This is the baseline for keeping people ignorant of what is and is not going on, who does and does not have power, who should and should not be held accountable, who is and is not guilty of wrongdoing, who is and is not reaping more or less than they sow, and my personal objection, it brings people piece by piece to the notion that truth does not exist, a position that makes people incapable of separating fact from fiction going forward and one in which anything becomes possible but only from on high because the bottom is not to state what is true but merely to believe it. It is authoritarian of the highest, or perhaps I should say lowest, order.

The jealousy that is ripping our society apart expresses in the differences but it is not its source. People are trying to make sense of the fact that we are differentially rewarded and it is something that makes no sense. We do not choose our gifts or opportunities. But they are told, we are told, that these, not the system, are the cause and so all differences become cause of hate and discontent. This is a wholly untenable position. There are infinite differences among us…and more importantly they are not the source of this division.

If these observations have been made by others, great. Perhaps if we get enough people on board we can finally make this eventuality happen, ideally sooner than later. That said what I have shared here are my insights and observations having lived in the world that we share. The evidence is all around us. The system we live under currently does nothing that it promises and much that it would not like to own. Moreover, it is intrinsic to the nature of the system and of our own. We cannot have a gentleman's agreement on how to conduct our competition and then declare the majority of the populace not gentlemen. The flaw is immediately apparent. The system in question declares most people unworthy out of the gate, makes its own rules only answerable to their supposed equals and the rest of us are supposed to accept being seen as nothing more than chattel to these elites. Think me too dramatic here? Affluenza kid ran over how many people with what amounts to no consequence with a defense of "He was too rich and sheltered to know better" fairly paraphrased. They may as well have said "let them eat cake". This system has never worked throughout history and always leads to revolt. There is no valid reason for people to be above one another. And if history has shown anything it is that people are incapable of handling being above one another. War and revolution are the inevitable consequence of such, not only based upon history based upon simple logic. Every strength is also a weakness in the right circumstances. We cannot afford to allow this trend of attempted dominance followed by war or revolt going forward. Our technology is simply too great to do so responsibly and I use the word responsibly more than a little ironically here as war is never responsible.

The social justice movement gives short shrift to the discussion of classism, the most significant, indeed the source injustice, vastly more significant than either sexism or racism which are spoken of both frequently and at length. Worse than merely shortchanging this conversation, it is not hard to demonstrate that said movement in its current form is actually entrenching classism for a variety of reasons most simple and significant being the distribution concerns about the above sexism and racism. If one seeks to ensure that there are equitable distributions of wealthy women and non-white ethnicities then one is not trying to defeat tear down the walls of class, are they? In fact, one might well be increasing said division would they not? They are not unique in this regard nor in the misdirection other than the specific flavor that it takes but that does not excuse it. It merely demonstrates that not everyone who says they want justice does in fact want justice or even know what it is. I offer many arguments from many directions all pointing to the same conclusion. Hopefully my own argument rings truer than those I have disputed but it is not over just yet. Please read on.

Yet again the social justice movement addresses a concern without addressing it fully or honestly. In the case of age and ageism it speaks often about what we do and do not do too and for our seniors and as usual there are kernels of truth and gaping gulfs as well as outright misrepresentation. Let us not forget that youth is an age block and one that has been largely omitted from the narrative about social justice, perhaps because many of those holding credentials are, both by circumstance and design, not young. The fact is our society is regularly trying to bar youth voice and agency in any number of arenas. Here are a few points to that effect as well as points to other shortcoming on this topic I have noted.

<u>Own the World?</u>

You do not own the world just because you were here first. Learn to share. The notion of ownership really is a root problem in a number of categories. Age is no exception here. There is a perception that being here first entitles one to a greater degree of say. There is room for such an argument in a world without scarcity as the newcomers can simply get their own pile of stuff and land. This is not a valid argument in a world in which we need to either compete (in which we take what we want) or cooperate (in which we share). In either scenario you being first or last is irrelevant. Incidentally, if age does confer wisdom then older folks should know this should they not? Also, worth noting is the fact that the wisest old person was also the wisest young person with very few exceptions. In other words, being older does not necessarily equate to knowing better than others, only better than your past self.

This condition too appears to be a root cause of injustice but is again primarily a symptom. Control for wealth and the problem disappears because then being here first has no direct bearing how resources are distributed. It is also worth pointing out that those who precede, whether they admit it or not, want and/or need the newcomers should they wish to survive long both as individuals and as a species. Also, worth noting is that creating another human to be little more than one's servant lest they be deemed worthy of more is not the great gift some pretend it to be. It is only truly a gift if they have fair stake in the present and future and a place worthy of inhabiting. To make the matter clear imagine you are born a slave, who is your life a gift to? You or your owner? Now imagine many are not so far removed from slavery, if at all, and tell me that entitlement from being first and resenting the young for their youth isn't a problem.

Make Room

Should we insist on capitalism there comes a time when the old should step aside to make room for others to advance. Not fool oneself into thinking you are the only capable ones and the eternal youth delusion. 70 is not the new 60 which is not the new 50 which is not the new 40 etc. That is spin. We may be living longer but the toll is there nonetheless and it is both physical and mental. Of course, under capitalism you do not have too and will not want to. This should come as a surprise to no one.

Under socialism you need not step aside. There is room for everyone and the compensation remains the same. But also, you can if you wish with no harm to you. You need no retirement fund. You continue to receive your wage.

Wisdom?

Age is said to confer wisdom and yet previous generations are frequently snarky and condescending to present and future generations. Shouldn't you know better by now? Speak with care and compassion but do not speak too much. There are two ways to learn and they need both of them.

Tomorrow for Today

Should you decide not to step aside I would ask that you stop selling our tomorrow for your today. You may well deserve today but so do we. And if you deserve today we deserve tomorrow. Someone saw to your future other than yourselves. And if they didn't and it was all you what do you suppose it looks like in the current environment if we look to our own in spite of you?

Bankrupted Youth

The youth of our nation start our lives with the lowest pay in the country and in recent history. Our youth start our lives with the most expensive renting… indeed renting is notably more expensive than buying in many areas… no credit to buy with because of how banking works… most expensive insurance, most expensive…well let's be direct, everything. Student loan debt for a decade followed by housing debt for 3 decades followed by… People can be productive without being indentured servants. This is slavery plain and simple. The cage and shackles may not be obvious to most but they are very much there. Social security many of us will likely never see if things continue… in no small part due to things like wages above around $100,000 being exempt from SSI. Those wages climb that high by being siphoned off the wages of the bottom… that's why SSI goes broke more than any other reason. Billions of dollars of wages go untaxed by it every year. From the top, not the "illegals" though frankly… guess who they work for more often than not?

Pay Your Dues

The resources of the world aren't yours and you do not know better. So, who should we pay our dues to and why? Hierarchy is destructive, unjust, and myopic. If you do not agree, tell me, who are our betters and why? Are those the only ones in charge? If you said anything other than the wealthy you couldn't answer both of these compatibly. If you did say the wealthy and believe them better then I apologize for failing to make clear how wrong that was in the previous chapter. That the paying of dues may have happened to you or I is remarkably poor justification to do it to others, particularly if you did not like or agree with it either. How many of our policies are little more than Stockholm syndrome from one group to the next do you suppose? More importantly, you asked us here (birth) so what makes you think we owe you more than you owe us? We can share or we can compete. If we compete we don't owe you anything. If we share we owe each other. Which have you been teaching the youth of the nation, not just your own?

<u>Adolescence? Rights and their Erosion</u>

How many people do you know that are mentally identical or near identical to who and what they were in adolescence? Many right? Maybe most? Nearly all for many of us no doubt. I am not saying we learn nothing. We all do, every day. But most people change very little in who they are and what is important to them except when a situation is forced upon them or social pressures steer the views of said person. Mature and immature people come in all ages. So do smart and not so smart people. So what is adolescence if mentally and emotionally people basically are the same from this age range to death? It seems to me it is a convenient age to declare people not people in the sense that they are not entitled to act as though they have autonomy and rights. There are those in our society that believe the age in which people are considered adolescents should be increased yet again, by the way. Why? The stated excuse is that said group is supposedly not mature enough. Never mind that their maturity can be enhanced or stunted by their environment and their teachers (not specific to academics). So, if they are stunted in terms of maturity guess who gets the credit? Their supposedly wiser teaching set, who failed right? Or it's a control game. Why do I think it's a control game? This country didn't want age restricted drinking, they wanted no drinking and they tried to make it so. It failed, the people pushed back and so a compromise was struck. 18 years of age to drink, the same age as all other "adult" rights, like voting, smoking, and in many places, sex but we will get to those shortly. They pushed the drinking age up to 21 later. Why and how? Not enough people were affected to make it a deal breaker and us/them thinking was and is encouraged so it was easy, right? Divide and conquer. Remember there are people testing the waters right now about raising the age that one should be considered an adolescent. It is important to all of this. The situation with drinking applies mostly to smoking as well. Now let me pause for a moment. The government should stop companies from marketing to children, most if not all of us agree with that. The power of business being what it is means the people would have insufficient redress otherwise at least within the law. The caveat here is that that applies to business not the people, whom you educate but do not control on matter of personal choice that only might harm oneself. That is one's natural right. No law can take it though many try. This means the people can choose these things and the businesses are kept honest. So where does that leave us? Alcohol, tobacco, marijuana, and sex should all be legal at the inception, not termination, of adolescence. Remember adolescence is the essential mental age of most people, without insult or exaggeration. So, the mental maturity being insufficient argument holds no water. Additionally, maturity is learned, and largely by action and consequence. If you think adolescence needs to be extended perhaps it is in no small part because of the curious blend of sheltering and overexposure they are presently subject to, no? The sex argument requires another bit be addressed however. Mental maturity was covered, sexual maturity was not. The fact is, the only reasonable standard for sex, other than consent, is sexual maturity. If a person is sexually mature and you tell them they cannot have sex…the list of things wrong with that is long and disturbing, ranging from overregulation and sheltering to targeting and eugenics. Statutory rape has no place in the books. It is rape or it is not. Obviously there is a cut off and it was stated, sexual maturity. Educate to consequences… really educate… there is no reason children should not know where children come from, how much they cost, but not fear based, such will backfire.

If we make mental ability a function of it we have absolutely walked toward eugenics by, for simple example, declaring people of limited mental ability unfit to both engage in sex and/or procreate. And if you think that's ok, just wait till a trait you possess or lack is on the chopping block. If you think yourself last in line remember how alcohols age was manipulated by dribs and drabs. Remember also how many people have been incarcerated for using their nature given right to, for instance smoke marijuana, a plant, harming no one, except possibly themselves, in spite of, in this case, many if not most people agreeing its illegality makes no sense, and its classification (less known) is absurdly overstated (it must have no medicinal use to be classified as highly as it is, it does and yet it is and that's just one problem). From marijuana and legality why don't we stop by the "tried as an adult bit" shall we? So, you are to young and dumb to make smart decisions about weed, alcohol, tobacco, and sex and you have not had a say (vote) in any of the laws whatsoever but you are old enough and mature enough to be held accountable for them and such a lost cause that we can and should throw you out of a society you have yet to even really be a part of for your entire life, yeah? How is that not immediately incomprehensibly unacceptable? Don't get me wrong, I think they are smart enough, I know it in fact. But you can't have it both ways and even begin to pretend what you serve is justice. You can't deny people autonomy and be surprised by a lack of maturity. You can't create a special status and expect it not to be exploited. The solution is the same for both problems by the way. Adolescents are adults and if that seems shocking to you, in most of the world, they are. Incidentally duty is not responsibility either, it is top down, directed not autonomous, and so no solution. We must use education more than governance.

Youth is on total lockdown on one front and completely free on the other. It's a carnival ride slow for safety but completely rudderless, as in the rudder was removed but not by them. These two together isn't safety its totalitarianism.

If youth we are to accept the generalization that youth is idealistic and naïve then we must also accept the generalization that age is bitter and tired, fraught with futility. What this means is that age is not a superior position for policy making either. The fatalism of age leads to a steady downward spiral of high minded ideals. Thus, in general it would seem that what society requires is a rather equitable distribution of each, ideally not in hierarchical form as that is itself a source of rather serious flaw.

<u>Where We Are At</u>

That people aren't always right doesn't mean that there is no truth. It also does not mean that people are incapable of determining truth. It also does not mean that truth is personal. There is another word for that. One should use it unless one seeks to intentionally obfuscate truth. If one prefers one of the above to the true answer it simply means one overgeneralizes. The accurate reflection of the above scenario is that not everyone is right all the time. Some people are wrong by accident, missing variables or not understanding the equation. Others are wrong intentionally. Put another way, they lie and they do so knowingly, pretty much always for personal gain or its inverse, to prevent personal loss. It is understandable that there is such confusion these days. Words are being contorted and misused at a phenomenal rate in this age where it is permissible to sell people both products and ideas with little if any application of reason. Consumerism and emotion, what could possibly go wrong? Meanwhile our elders, who spun up this ad machine are the ones who mock their youngers for being entitled and narcissistic (no not literally all of our elders are involved but certainly the same set for both). What exactly would you expect from constant bombardment whose sole purpose is to enhance consumerism at the cost of attention span, reason, and respect (think Right Guard ad," If your grandad hadn't worn it you wouldn't exist" I mean come on. Baby boomer please stop both encouraging and complaining about narcissism from the millennials. They are already more than enough like you. That's right. They are like you. Who had Woodstock? Who gave our jobs away to other countries relegating us all to service industry and then says we have no drive? Who wants to stay eternally young? Who speaks to… all your fault? Of course it isn't. You were shaped by those who came before you too. How about we stop kicking the same can of foolishness down the line though shall we? How about we weight things with reason rather than which church the person who said it belongs to? And yes, Academia, you are at present, a church. Gatekeepers and ad hominem attacks abound. What kind of institution of learning dismisses a thought because there is no study? Is that not the next step not the prior one? How does knowledge and understanding advance that way? Short answer is it doesn't. That's a power game like every other church…which incidentally also started to further education... before it was a church when it was an idea. More of that Unity by division. I do not say these things to separate us though superficially it might appear so. I illustrate so people might understand what has to change and why. Atop attacking people for being different and start appreciating. It takes all kinds. To be clear that does include those of you at the top however. There is no top if you are doing this. And if you aren't then those you direct owe you none of this. Appreciating differences does not equal being happy to be exploited. It means we are all different but not better. If you think yourself superior *at something* you might be right. If you think yourself superior *to someone* you are certainly wrong. Do you understand the difference?

Capitalism is rife with ableism. The cornerstone arguments to rationalize differential pay are predicated upon that very notion. Whether one tries to suggest a meritocracy or social Darwinism, both addressed in a previous chapter, one finds strong insinuation of the able and not able, of deserving and undeserving. Again, as previously addressed, humans having rights and no control over the gifts and still capable of contributing to society as we all are do not deserve less than some other but that is precisely what capitalism is about. You cannot have capitalism and not have ableism, it is in the class system and deeply so, which social justice does not wish to acknowledge. Again, ableism is not the root, wealth or class stratification is. And since that cannot be removed from capitalism, capitalism is.

<u>Guns</u>

It seems that many are comfortable with authority figures being allowed guns, and even certain civilians. However, if the purpose of these limitations is public safety, we must recognize that authority figures are not magically good or moral. The qualifications for becoming an authority figure do not ensure that they are not people that might be(come) a threat. So really, they shouldn't be allowed firearms either, right? And by that logic no one in the country should actually have them. But then we have to consider the fact that we share borders with Mexico and Canada, and international travel exists. Are we proposing doing away with guns all together, the globe over? But then we have to remember that it is reasonably simple for a skilled craftsperson to produce his or her own gun, so to be truly effective, we must destroy the knowledge of how to produce a gun. This is starting to seem more and more farfetched is it not? Thus, guns are here and here to stay. The effective protection against such is deterrent. On the awful, macro scale, compare it to nukes. The countries without nukes will be bullied mercilessly by the ones that have them. Doubt that? Take a look at the news. Or take it to a simple level. Fisticuffs. If there were no other weapons, your fear is that the strong would abuse the weak. And they well might. The rectification is to be strong. However, we could also look at the actual line of reasoning that you are using. Some seem to think that we should not have guns because we do not need guns. As in: surely there is no one that will come to harm us, or those that have been appointed to protect us will always be there to protect us. By this logic, we also have no need of laws. Thus, we do not need gun control laws. Because since there is no one to do us harm with which we might need a gun to protect ourselves, since everyone is good and beneficent, what do we need laws for? This explains the fact that some attribute magical traits to authority figures, traits that said people presume the authority must necessarily possess that they do not necessarily possess. This reasoning is predicated upon the notion that the authority figures are, were and always will be beneficent figures. The fact that this article exists in the bill of rights is precisely because that is not a worthy assumption. A fact that has proven itself time and time again.

There is fantastic irony to be found in the fact that people who want stronger gun laws are so willing to partake of character assassination. Do we know what that fantastic irony is? There is a law against character assassination. It's called slander or libel depending on whether it's written or spoken. It seems to me that the people who want stricter gun control laws aren't particularly concerned about following the laws we have. And they see themselves as the law-abiding group. But then it's not really a surprise why somebody that likes to go around kicking sand in people's faces doesn't want there to be a stick in easy reach.

<u>Intellectual Property Rights</u>

Simple logical dissection as to why capitalism cannot work, does not work, will not work, never will work. Capitalism is about buying and selling things. It's about owning things. This means you have to determine the value of things. Only a fool doesn't understand that ideas have value, which brings us to intellectual property rights. And the concept of intellectual property rights clearly does not work. It has never happened nor will it ever happen that people produce ideas in complete absence of all other ideas. What am I saying? I am saying that ideas build upon ideas. The idea of intellectual property rights is the idea that someone owns ideas, so every idea that is generated by that idea is owed to the people before. If ideas are owned and monetized as intellectual property rights would have it, two problems occur. One: the preceding people are effectively royalty. They get a substantial cut of anything derived, meaning they get wealthier, compounded. Now this isn't capitalism, but this is what we're calling capitalism. This is a feudal state. This is royalty. Never mind the fact that we declared who got the credit in the first place, which was itself absurd. The second problem is that both due to incentive and due to the rights of the person with the preceding ideas who can squelch future discoveries, future ideas are stifled. I know it's popular to suggest that capitalism makes everything better and more competitive. However, it's pretty clear that that's not the case. All of that boils down to intellectual property rights is done for the sake of capitalism, but is not capitalism, not that anything capitalist is capitalist; it always boils down to a feudal state. It always boils down to oligarchy. It is in no way a meritocracy, and in no way is the competition fair. But to reiterate the point, intellectual property rights is placed because capitalism needs to assign a value to things with value. Ideas have value. Assigning that value (which is necessary for capitalism to do) is the very thing that kills intellectual property rights contributing to capitalism. It's the very thing that makes it something other than capitalism. Now if you think there's some other alternative, you'd be wrong. Meaning some alternative that can make intellectual property rights not anathema to capitalism. There is no such animal. The reason is because capitalism is a lie. Capitalism is feudalism, and serfs are slaves. It doesn't matter what clothes you put them in. There's no way to dress it up that changes the reality of that fact. And it's an ugly reality. We can debate all day on whether we're an oligarchy, a republic, a capitalist democracy. What we are in our current structure, whatever name you wish to call it, is a society that puts the responsibility on the largest share of the people and gives them the least reward and puts the least responsibility on the fewest people and gives them the most reward. Now by any stretch of the imagination, this is unjust. Hierarchal structures do exist in nature. However, the way to balance the privilege afforded people at the top is with responsibility. You do not place the greatest responsibility in the hands of the people that are most disadvantaged. You place the most responsibility in the hands of the people who are most advantaged: most privileged. There may have been a time when that was true here. It certainly isn't now. Rights and responsibilities must match. No rights, no responsibilities/many rights, many responsibilities. There is another way to fix it: elimination of the hierarchy. Admittedly that could evolve into a might makes right situation quickly—could. It could also be a utopia, but for those that suggest it'd just evolve into a might makes right scenario, let us not forget that fact that what we're living in now already is one.

<u>Intellectual Property Rights meets Cultural Appropriation</u>

The concept of intellectual property rights is a flawed concept. The idea is not only impossible, it's destructive to humanity. The simple fact is, you cannot and should not own ideas. Elements of copyright law acknowledge that you cannot own ideas but then go on to disacknowledge that fact by allowing you to own published works and shut down all others. There are several readily apparent examples of how and why this is a problem in recent history. One example is the absolutely absurd trend in cultural appropriation. The claim that anything under the sun is cultural appropriation, for example that wearing a bindi is cultural appropriation. Now the logical extension of this is very obvious. It is not at all difficult to understand why the people who believe this is cultural appropriation believe it to be so. What we're talking about is an idea and a product and under ordinary circumstances would indeed fall under intellectual property rights. So does this mean it is an intellectual property rights issue? Well, yes and no. It is clearly related to the idea of intellectual property rights. What then is wrong with applying the idea of intellectual property rights to it? Well, what's wrong with it is very simple to see. It's culture. And the purpose of culture is to share. If culture isn't shared, it's not culture. Does this mean, then, that we should have intellectual property rights but not apply them to culture? No. The problem is intellectual property rights, not culture. The problem is actually another couple of steps removed, but we'll get to that. This isn't the only example that I've seen recently with dysfunctions in intellectual property rights. And equally important, it won't be the last. Not because the justice system is particularly flawed at this time, not that it isn't, but because it's the logical conclusion to the notion that someone owns something that they shared. The fact that they shared it means it is no longer just theirs. The dysfunction that accompanies the notion that you can still have your cake and eat it too is the notion of American business. But it's not exclusive to America. It's most apparent here, but it is substantially a product of capitalism. Businesses believe that they own the profit. Businesses believe that they should be exclusively responsible for the decisions. And by businesses I mostly mean corporations. They are not beholden to the customers, they are not beholden to the citizens. They are scarcely beholden to the laws. So how does this relate with intellectual property rights? Let me take a quick step back and give a specific example of a case that happened not so very long ago. Marvin Gaye's estate sued Robin Thicke, presumedly under copyright law for stealing his work. To any layperson and certainly to any expert, it should be readily apparent that these two works are dramatically different. Substantially different. They have a similar feel, yes. Feel translates to genre. Feel is not the same work. It is the same genre. So he did not copy the song. He made something in the same vein as in, in the same genre. The judgment on this is a travesty, but it isn't a surprise. The climate with respect to intellectual property rights has grown lopsided to the point that people feel everything is cultural appropriation if it didn't come from that group of people originally. If you wanted an admirable example of racism and how it could be reasserted in modern times, just take a look at that. "You're not the right color for that music." Now. Is this about racism? No, no it's not. It's about money. Why does everything smack of cultural appropriation to everybody these days? Why? What's the reason? It's simple. The idea that you can own an idea is why every idea is someone else's. The idea that ideas belong to this demographic, which will invariably boil down to an ethnicity. It's not yours, it's theirs. Except culture and knowledge are both intended to spread and will spread whether you want them to or not. Now the fact that they will spread whether you want them to or not, that's a wonderful thing actually. Unless you happen to be someone who's making a disproportionate amount of wealth over control of said information. See, capitalism isn't about spreading better ideas, it isn't about refining them. It's about controlling and suppressing them. I'm sure there are some that would say that's not what it's actually about; it's just what it's gotten to. But the fact is that's the logical extension. If it is not a given from the very beginning that all ideas developed are for everyone to enjoy (and it isn't under capitalism) if that is not a foregone conclusion, then someone will benefit vastly more than someone else. When that has gone on for a period of time- how long depending on how disparate the benefits are- it's a given that there will be substantial advantages and that those advantages might well be insurmountable. It should be no surprise to anyone at that time that those who control the ideas try to deny access to those who do not. So, to sum up, intellectual property rights are the product of capitalism. They are the product of exploiting market forces for gain, financial and political. They are necessitated by the idea that people make money. If you move past that (the need for money) the sharing of ideas is not motivated by making money; it's motivated by the sharing of ideas. And any concerns to who said it first are at best academic. Incidentally who said it first is a sign in either system. Marvin Gaye's estate sued over a genre infringement. The song was not directly copied. No person could reasonably suggest any one person produced a genre because of the nature of culture. It's not possible. And yet, due to intellectual property rights, that's exactly what was done. To be clear, intellectual property rights conflated with a substantial dose of misplaced political correctness. Refer back to cultural appropriation because I can't see how it couldn't have had a place in this case. The jury would not have been as sympathetic to Marvin Gaye's estate were it not for the current political climate of being politically correct and declaring everything cultural appropriation. If everything is cultural appropriation as indeed it is under intellectual property rights, nothing we currently have should exist. And that is not the slightest exaggeration. Nothing we currently have should exist. From computers to pasta to the internet. Indeed, the very act of learning something comes from absorbing information from outside of yourself and applying it to your own situation. Sounds a lot like what's being called cultural appropriation, doesn't it? So clearly cultural appropriation is false. Cultural appropriation rests just as clearly on intellectual property rights, which are false, which rests just as squarely on capitalism, which is false. A dysfunctional idea produces a dysfunctional idea produces a dysfunctional idea. The origin idea was flawed. Everything that comes from it will be. Could there be an exception? Sure. It's also theoretically possible that water becomes air or air becomes earth. The process by which you might make that happen however disabuses that from making that be a valid claim. The point here is the exceptions you find of functional elements that came from capitalism are due to another variable. They were produced in spite of capitalism, not because of it.

Cultural Appropriation

Cultural appropriation, like reverse racism, is a myth. And both have the same purpose: to claim power for a supposedly disenfranchised group all while disacknowledging that the only group that is disempowered in any culture is the poor. Not just any culture but every culture. They are by definition the poor. They are poor in the resources their society values. That is why they are called poor. Furthermore, culture is to be shared or it is not culture and so culture spreading or being adopted, wholesale or piecemeal, as is the most likely, is not appropriation. The term is an abuse of the two words. There is nothing complex about that.

A BACK AND FORTH ON SLAVERY

The respondents in the following are common man arguments I have encountered hundreds of times in the course of sharing and refining my views and represent no specific individual.

Myself

The part you overlook is that whites were and are still slaves. Your poor are the "field slave" and exist in all ethnic spectrum. Your middle class are your "house slave" and also exist in all ethnicities. Hopefully you do not confuse some have some of their rights honored as privilege which is a stark abuse of the word for purpose of stripping the rights from more not less people.

Respondent 1

During a discussion of literal slavery you are invoking (and equating) figurative "slaves".

Myself

No. You are. I understand that a person can earn a subsistence wage (room and board) that they ostensibly can choose or not choose when in reality they cannot choose because of both availability, mandatory vocation for basic subsistence (taxes for instance mean you literally cannot live in this country without income, taxes on land etc.), and any number of gatekeepers some legitimate, many not. Just because a person does not know they are a slave does not mean they are not. Even the people who picked cotton in the US rarely wore shackles. A slave is a person compelled to labor that does not particularly benefit them while it does substantially benefit others and is afforded basic subsistence. The poor are obviously slaves. The middle class only one variable deeper in that the middle class pays the bulk of the taxes in the country as designed by the rich and said payment puts them largely in the same boat as the bottom only a tad less obviously and with a very useful envy mechanic built in. If you think slavery does not exist currently you have nothing to talk about except to suggest reparations in the form of doing the same thing to a group of people who, incidentally did not do it to the people that you feel, not think, are qualified. Middle class and below are literally slaves in the US. You don't think so? Refuse to work until your savings are exhausted and find out quick.

Respondent 1

"Just because a person does not know they are a slave does not mean they are. Even the people who picked cotton in the US rarely wore shackles."

American chattel slaves were well aware of the fact that they were slaves.

"A slave is a person compelled to labor that does not particularly benefit them while it does substantially benefit others and is afforded basic subsistence."

Cite the authority that said this.

Myself

Respondent 1, my source is reality. Academia is conspicuously deficient on this point. The whole point I made about awareness of slavery is speaking to the refining of the tools of oppression. The best-behaved slave is the one that doesn't even know they are one. They learned this with the house slaves I previously spoke of. If you cannot entertain a notion from ground zero plus the evidence of your eyes you are blind by choice. Academia is the new religion.

Give me your definition of a slave and I will either prove what I said is true or your definition applies to no one.

Let me put it to you like this... this sample here... these facts (primates care about equality) have been conspicuous... completely flipping obvious for, oh I dunno... all of human history... and it's just been proven... and still argued... is the point they are leading to incorrect? No... but if you didn't know it already you're not a very observant person. For people who can only learn this way, scientists are priests telling the faithful and the believers what is true and false... and if they haven't said it yet, well, it just isn't so.

Let me point out at this time that we agree that everyone should get both "cucumbers and grapes" and may even agree everyone should get the same amount of them... relative to body mass. Bigger people need more food... in general. We do not agree on the ethnic and gender divisions that have been put in place precisely to prevent this ever becoming a reality.

Respondent 1

I can't take you seriously when you compare our economic system to the history of literal American slavery. They are not the same thing.

Myself

They are exactly the same. The slaves could have united and thrown down their masters in the times you are referring to but that was just how things were done. The same is true today. They had food to eat and a place to sleep by and large and that was all most really cared about. Also true today and descriptive of the poor and to a lesser extent the middle class. Their lives were unpleasant toil and tedium but they accepted it just as they (the poor) do today. They were treated like property but they accepted it- also today. Few stood up and refused and those few were made example of. Also true today. You do not have to take me seriously. Your responses have lacked substance. They are arguments of emotion. You do not want to see. The list above is the tiniest tip of the iceberg of evidence you ignore while you wholeheartedly swallow the narrative from... certain sources. Start being more critical of your accepted sources. Learn the notion of the true lie. It is a thing that is technically true... as far as it goes but ultimately false. A half-truth... which is a whole lie, the worst kind, misrepresentational while superficially true. If you learn to do this perhaps you too can judge reality. Funny thing is the whole point of this discussion is to apply it to "our" economy, or so it seems to me, so your position contradicts by necessity on one point or the other. This is you avoiding a truth you do not like while adhering to another that you do. It is painfully obvious. That is your right. Your choice however has consequences for all, just as everyone else's do.

Myself

Respondent 2, when you apply what you said to the top you are correct. When you apply it to the bottom you are wrong. I won't even tell you it is because of power. The simplest proof is that industrialization made it so x people can support 20x population. This means the reserve population must be provided for because there is no reason to hire people you do not need. Full stop.

Respondent 2

Your opinions make it hard to agree with you when you suggest slavery and capitalism are the same thing.

Respondent 3

In our economy assuming you come from a first world country we can work to progress up the social classes, this is a feature usually not found in traditional slavery. The rich tax dodging is another story. I seriously doubt any wealthy person was malicious to those in the middle class but simply wanted to avoid paying tax like most people. Due to their wealth they are able to do so. On slavery, African slaves were far more common in America and European capitalists were also far more common. Regarding race, it is ignorant to hate African Americans for benefitting from the system when everyone in America today benefitted from slavery in the past and it was primarily African Americans' ancestors providing that original labor. With this perspective people have to understand that they owe their infrastructure and economy, the only things guaranteeing the majority of stable jobs in the country to African American slaves.

Respondent 1

Are you trying to say that slaves somehow didn't have the motivation to throw off their shackles, because life was adequate? It wasn't worth the effort? That is a narrative I am unfamiliar with. Which American historian did you get that from?

Myself

Respondent 1 and 2, no one wants to think of themselves as a slave. It is how and why it persists. Those who do are past caring. Those who care... care and so do not want to self-identify thus. That said the left and right are aligning right now proving my point but denying the other is affected.

Respondent 1

"No one wants to think of themselves as a slave."

In the 1800s and before, there were slave owners stating, plainly, "I'm a slave owner, and these slaves are my slaves." And there were slaves stating, "I'm a slave, and that slave owner is my owner, and this really sucks."

Listen, I'm not saying things are just today. I don't wholly disagree with you. But I can't help but wonder if you're trolling by using the language that you do.

Myself

Respondent 1 and 3, on the contrary, slaves were promoted from field to house for instance based upon loyalty, mindset and need. These same traits are used today by gatekeepers to determine who is and who is not advanced. The fact is under capitalism if every single person was literally identical we would still have wealth stratification and the poor would, by and large stay poor and the rich, would even more overwhelmingly, stay rich. being more permissive with long time slaves was not atypical either. Breed loyalty and all that. I understand that the wealth of nations, particularly capitalist nations rests on slavery. We disagree in that this is past tense. It does, not did and it was not only black slaves, not even a little bit true. The list of what is wrong with that notion is long indeed. Every group that came to this country became the new whipping boy because capitalism requires one. Someone has to occupy that bottom rung. Someone else needs to occupy that second from the bottom rung that exist purely to shelter the haves by the way. Let me point out that we often change the name of something when it has become perceived in a manner other than the way we want it to be perceived as. This is dishonest and it's manipulative and it's found on both the left and the right and in this particular case, it applies very squarely to slavery. Being assigned to the bottom rung produces apathy. Said apathy is the exhausting sort. It is the beat down sort. It is not the fault of the downtrodden. Why should a person be mentally and physically charged to be exploited? In such a situation, the only person that would be is someone suffering from Stockholm syndrome, which is to say, someone who believes that their oppressor is their friend.

 Myself

I find it particularly interesting that not one of you has offered a definition up for slavery so that I can prove my point by the way. You only object to mine. This is emotionality. Facts or reason are required. I offered both.

Myself

Respondent 1, look at my comment from the perspective of one who knows I have said it is the same and you will immediately understand that I actually said those are the same mentalities the modern slave has. The same justifications. The same rationalizations. The same reason to tolerate it. I didn't think it was difficult.

Myself

Respondent 2, what you offered just now, that is opinion. What I offered is reason with some facts. Reason is logical argument displayed for all to weigh. I am quite sure that most find me hard to agree with though. I make strong claims without a shred of hesitation... because I weighted my thoughts before not after I began speaking.

Respondent 1

Slaves didn't need to justify or rationalize being slaves. They were required to work. They were intimidated. And if they somehow managed to escape their owners, the actual U.S. government would round them up again.

Top definition from Oxford: "a person who is the legal property of another and is forced to obey them."

There are secondary definitions all subjective and based on normative assessment. There is only one definition that is objective, and it is the one I've provided. It's the difference between calling a damp floor a "swamp" and pointing to an actual swamp and calling that a "swamp".

Respondent 2

You are giving opinions, not making strong claims. Your problem is you give no room for argument. You are just right, and the hell with everyone else, right? So keep your weighted opinions to yourself.

Myself

Now show me how that is different today. You are owned by the wealthy... unless you are the wealthy. You are compelled to work. Any work you do will enrich people with more money than you more (compound interest and such). The government rounds up the homeless. Homeless is what you are if you have no income. Compulsory labor drives down the wage... to subsistence. The police have the ability to do everything that you describe. The frequency with which they exercise those rights is directly proportional to your income or the appearance of it. Who the police are doing it for is demonstrated by who they do it too and who they do not do it too. They do not for instance patrol black neighborhoods, they patrol poor ones. There is overlap but you miss the message. I am not being figurative I am telling you that hiding the bars does not mean they aren't there nor does it mean they aren't for you. You are their property. You can be compelled at any time to obey law enforcement and they do not work for you. They work for the wealthy. Don't believe me? Ask yourself why they patrol the poor neighborhoods but respond slowly in them when called, and don't patrol the wealthy neighborhoods, but respond near instantly when called. Your suggestion that the slaves you speak of are more a slave is sophistry or a lack of acceptance of an obvious fact, that being that you are owned and can be compelled, indeed, are regularly compelled, to obey. I am not saying you are vaguely reminiscent of a slave. I am saying you are literally one, as am I. Social policy is conducted on you being literally a number in the possession of those on high who will dictate your life, more when they choose, less when there is no need (centric to themselves). You can if you wish reject this in which case you reject your own definition of a slave. You can for instance suggest no one is compelled today. In which case no one was then. Yes they might die for refusing... still true today. No one bought me you say? You were born from one of their slaves. They never buy those. They are buying desirable immigrants right now though aren't they? Tuition and the like...cash money. I refer to the legal ones. You do not know you are a slave because you have never chosen to not be. Try it.

Myself

Respondent 2, last time, there is a difference between opinion and reason. Much as there is a difference between opinion and hypothesis. I do not vacillate because I argue my point. If you have a counter argument I have not already considered you might sway me. If you offer up something that was 3rd tier of the 25 steps that I used to come to my conclusion I will summarily debunk you and continue. Certitude is not arrogance, contrary to current opinion or better said, erroneous fact.

Would you think me pushy if I insisted 2+2 was 4? Of course not, right? Because you and I both know the correct answer. That is the difference.

Respondent 4

Your assertions are so hard to follow. You display sound logic and your opinions are fun to read, but your assertions go so deep that one must explain why we use money instead of a bartering system in order to counter your argument. If I understand, you believe that "slavery is in full effect in the present because everyone must work, and consequently rich people profit from all work that non-wealthy people do. In addition, people are punished for not complying just as they always have been?"

Myself

Respondent 4, you do touch on an integral part of the problem with the nod toward currency. It is a link in the chain. I am glad you enjoyed the read. Yes. Currency or rather intentionally imbalanced and structurally maintained imbalanced access to currency which directly translates to both material goods and social power is a problem. It is the modern shackle. Could we and should we go into a currencyless system? Yes, that or a system of socialized wealth. Let me repeat, if everyone in a capitalist system was literally identical in ability and effort we would still have graded income. This point singlehandedly debunks the notion of meritocracy, hard work, and personal excellence that is favored by those who are either born or elevated to higher wealth. A system without currency, not the only one I offered by the way, would actually not be that difficult to implement. The only real problem would be dealing with the small percentage of people who are sociopathically exploitative and the larger group receiving a modicum of education and investment in the new system. Lack of understanding or feeling of disconnect would make most antagonistic. I have written small blurbs to the various points on my channel. Much of it is outlined there in brief bite sized pieces. If you went to a public park, that is a park that belongs to all of us that we all pay for, after hours what would happen? Now when the cops show up and tell, not ask, you to leave if you refuse what would happen? Now if you were rich and known would that happen? We all know that rich folks do egregious things without punishment or with token punishment and less well-off folks get significant sentences and more often than not, no slack, right? The above example is ultimately a simple silly one but it demonstrates the key issue and obviously there is no shortage of stronger clearer indications. No difference? Of course there is a difference, just as there was a difference between one master and another in the 19th century. That difference does not however constitute, not a slave. A gilded cage is still a cage. The modus operandi at present is to only let the hand be clearly seen by those who the hand wishes to rile. The division and the denial, which is integral to the division, are key.

Respondent 4

So we both agree that there are a lot of obvious differences between types of slavery that occurred throughout history, and I agree that there are many similarities. But much to the same effect of the "wet floor to swamp" analogy used earlier, the types of slavery may require different titles because their differences begin to define them all falling under the slavery heading. Such as wage slavery, chattel slavery, or implicitly regulated slavery.

Myself

Slavery is the general term. Denying the general term destroys communication. All "forms" of slavery are slavery because the person is enslaved. Some for instance would like to suggest you aren't a slave unless you wear shackles. The purpose is to invalidate all, according to them, lesser forms. They aren't lesser. The oppression Olympics produces... more oppression. I wrote something recently about people's failings in this regard. For instance, all megalomaniacs are stupid, not all stupid people are megalomaniacs. You see the truth of this statement I trust? You think a wage slave is not property because so many people are so thoroughly owned. Massive scale makes it nonexistent for most...because people tend to be bad at seeing massive scale. If the problem were smaller...as it was 100 years ago people would more readily identify with it. It is the starfish on the beach versus the hoard of starfish on the beach. Are you familiar with the story or concept? One stranded, you throw it back in the water... 10,000, you walk on by... most do anyway.

If you had said that we agree that slavery has become more subtle and perhaps insidious we could agree immediately... and that is a near synonym to, but not your stated point. There is significance to that. This statement does not minimize.

Owner X, in the 19th century treated his slaves quite well. Owner Y treated his poorly. Was one set of slaves less a slave

If Affluenza kid had run over a master (wealthy) instead of a slave (middle or below) would the outcome have changed? If yes do you see the master/servant (slave) relationship?

Respondent 4

Could slaves start their own business or choose their owner (company of employment in modern America)? In America, could they buy their freedom (analogous to getting rich in modern America) or run for office? I agree this world has too many man made rules, but I don't agree we are all born into slavery.

Respondent 1

So this is where the problems started. The conversation didn't spring out of nowhere. We might have found you extreme but nonetheless agreed had you said that American capitalism is a form of slavery. And had you said this at some other time or in some other place. But you jumped into the middle of a conversation where Respondent 2 had just claimed that black people want a magical welfare state. Respondent 3, reasonably, felt that that needed to be corrected and so explained that the problems in black America and the general inequality we see today can be directly traced back to the country's history of slavery. It was the first time today that anyone spoke of slavery, and at that point it became clear (and default) that the topic being discussed was actual slavery.

Myself

Ah, you think the companies are the slave owners? Not at all. The fantastically rich. The laws are of, by, for them. You have to follow them, they don't, they own you. You can start your own business, at their pleasure and at their pleasure they can shut it down too. Much like a field slave of the 19th century singing a spiritual... unless the master tells him to shut up. And incidentally it is a curious mentality that has you saying you choose your employer. You do not. They choose you, you needing to be possessed per the system, seek to be possessed in the most favorable manner possible. You do nothing more than court the eye of an owner you believe to be a kinder master, something the smarter slaves no doubt did too when they had the energy. The slaves could indeed earn their freedom, at the master's pleasure. Some wealthy person can elevate you now too... and if you think you are going to get rich in spite of them... well, not very likely, maybe you win the lottery. Mind you you again, collectively in this case, made them far richer than they made you and this is consistent. Sure slaves can be elected into public office... and again it happened on the plantation. You offer "what abouts" but you didn't even bother to test them against the other side; the "did it happen to them" side, not the best term for it except situationally in this case but you get the idea. This is much like how feminism is always on about women don't have this and men do have that and never about men don't have this and women do have that. Do not ignore 50 percent of the equation. It signals bias. I'm happy to share. I would be happier to have people see. We can't get where we should be until most can. Those rules are not man made, they are rich person made and rich people are, by definition, essentially, greedy. A fair definition is, I have more than I need and I know many have less than they need but I am going to keep it and most likely try to get more, generally without sharing. Toxic, at least to a society or civilization and to the constituent parts thereof. And so long as we have hierarchy such is the order. There must be slaves if there are masters, and more of them.

Contrary to the popular representation, a parasite, feeding on the host that is civilization. The workers, the muscles. The planners, the brains. The wealthy, the leech. The poor, the symptom.

We aren't all born into slavery, just most of us. The wealthy are not, except that the jailer is also jailed. That is their hell.

While you might never agree with me I appreciate your tone. It has been a pleasure and I welcome further dialogue... though I do naturally hope to convince you. :)

A further point on the "wage slave" is thus. The lower your wage the greater the tendency for one's employer to micromanage ones entire "on the clock" time. One would think, per supply and demand that this would be inverted as the more expensive services should be assured of greater productivity. Why isn't it? Because the lower one's wage (relative to others) the more deeply held the notion is on the part of the employer that they "own" you or at least every minute of your on the clock time. This is less a function of productivity and more a function of a master servant relationship and if you doubt it, just work a few such low-end jobs and your employer will no doubt tell you as much. Indeed, not only do they tend to try and get every second of your time productive your job description effectively becomes "whatever I tell you to do". You applied to a job posting for cashier but there you are cleaning a toilet. If you wanted janitorial work in the environment you imagine we have you would have applied for it wouldn't you have? Not to mention that you would have been paid accordingly… but that rarely happens around here.

Myself

Respondent 1, I appreciate you taking the time to share where you believe the error occurred. I addressed the original poster first. My second post addressed who it did because there is a divisive narrative in place regarding ethnicity (and gender) that does not further social equality but the opposite. That needed saying as the opposite has been and continues to be said far too much. It is, despite some unfortunate tone, ultimately a good thing that the conversation got to where it did though.

I am accustomed to many thinking my positions extreme. To my way of thinking and a great deal of calculated observation (some might call how I see the world a study) there is little chance I am wrong and I do not politic. It is not in my nature. On the flip side I do not have beliefs, only observations and quantifications. That is neither here nor there though. The point is I appreciate what I am interpreting as an olive branch and would welcome further dialogue if you have something.

Myself

Anyone care to weigh in on the implications of common core? I believe it is being implemented, primarily, to make a servant group capable of using math in their occupation without really understanding it or being able to intuit important larger messages from it. The mandatory nature of it and the fact that in practice they reject right answers on the grounds of methodology combined with the general implications of the above are much of my reasoning.

Respondent 1

I disagree. The purpose of common core math drills is to inspire curiosity of, and familiarity with, numbers. When I was young, people were taught to "divide, multiply, subtract, bring down", but not why it works that way. Common core requires a singular approach to a problem but introduces alternatives later in the curriculum. You can't fully assess the common core approach by looking at individual math lessons. It's the whole curriculum that matters.

While the process could be improved, I don't doubt the intentions.

Myself

If it was optional I would agree with you. It isn't. It isn't for those struggling either. It is for all and many who advocate it will still, often accidentally, acknowledge it slows the advanced students down. In no way is making math more convoluted a step forward to understanding the world that those numbers represent. I like math tricks and games... what common core is. They are not practical and, most importantly, denying correct answers stifles, empirically.

Common cores precepts may not, its implementation does. Teachers grade students wrong for not doing it the way they want them to. Thus, it is not a tool for but against learning. Further, it is in practice very pro-conformist. Teachers in my time wanted to do this but were not enabled by the system. They are now.

Do you think it coincidental that those who excelled suddenly lag and those who lagged suddenly excel? Most interestingly it is one of the last areas in which males excelled in school. Coincidentally the new form favors females. Again, with that division.

Last but not least, math and numbers are constructs to understand and discuss things in the world. Take it away from that purpose and you have a religion. It can and should be for mathphiles and alternate teaching, not "core". There are reasons we learned math the way we did and teaching a dozen ways to do the same thing is, at best, clutter... graded clutter, in a young mind... oh and lots and lots of busy work.

Respondent 1

Unfortunately the funding has not been allotted for such targeted education of students. Until that changes, the goal is to help the most possible students succeed.

One of the biggest changes I would like to see in our public education system is the dissociation of age and curriculum for the simple fact that people don't learn at the same rate. But there is tremendous stigma to remedial education, and additionally it's quite rare for a child to skip a grade when (s)he is advanced.

It would be wonderful if we could move away from the generic wholesale approach we currently have to education, but until that problem goes away, common core seems like a fair attempt at improvement. Even for the child who understands math but has trouble with one or two of the common core principles, they will make it through the system. They may not enjoy perfect grades, but their future won't be determined by their marks in second grade math. And at the same time, we are helping the students who otherwise might have failed entirely.

Myself

Respondent 1, I agree to loosening the structure. Like way agree... 100 percent. It would be nice if both the students and teachers had input on that as well. Like for instance teacher recognizes you struggle in x, maybe take it next year take this instead but ultimate decision on the part of student and parent. Still need to check all core boxes to graduate but free flow. I would also like to see what is and isn't core change, of course.

I think something similar about remedial education... though it might not seem so. I do not think everyone should get a diploma. I do not think the bar should be that low. This would require, presuming mandatory vocation, the abolishment of diploma required jobs which, let's face it, was arbitrary in many vocations and simply a weeding tool to expedite application processing anyway with little to no bearing on actually needing many of the skills implied nor actually assuring it.

No, you won't fail at life by failing second grade math but you might not get into college and considering which group this harms and which group doesn't receive any affirmative action the potential for harm is fairly significant. I personally like numbers. As a child I did the math tricks that are reminiscent of common core, not identical, before common core was common core. I know with certainty that if it was the curriculum I would have loathed core and math. I think this situation is fixed like all things... when you're not at the top. Identify the problem, confirm it (both sides), rally, execute. It isn't fast nor is it glamorous but it's what we have.

I agree education is underfunded. Rich kids don't go there so... it literally becomes (maybe you disagree) an indoctrination center for what the wealthy want because there is very little risk of it contaminating their children. Put another way socialism and capitalism do not co-exist well. Capitalism preys on it. If private school is an option public school will always be underfunded.

Incidentally, if you are an educator it is my contention that this is no small part of why your hands are tied. Can't have the youngens getting some other message after all... which might be understandable... if the approved message was good enough. It isn't and I used might even then.

Respondent 1

I still think it's a stretch to posit that a child wouldn't get into college based upon early common core performance, as by middle school they would have already been taught multiple alternative methods to achieve the same results. At that point, they're ready for high school, which wouldn't penalize them for a bad year or two in elementary/middle school.

Myself

Respondent 1, would you agree that teacher and guidance counselors tailor what they tell a student about life and their future with an eye toward GPA even in those early years?

I would also point out we have adapted the entire curriculum to be more "female friendly" because... reasons. If that is ok...you get the idea.

Respondent 1

I'm not entirely confident that "grades" as we have them are needed before high school.

Myself

I do not disagree.

Steerage can of course exist without them. It would be a step in the right direction though. Either you understand fundamentals or you do not. Grades even at higher levels aren't that useful and presume a perfect test... most aren't. No small number of tests are really just metatests. How well do you know your teacher rather than how well do you know the material. (or at least an appreciable minority of the questions on said tests, I can recall pointing out to a professor that if they meant x the answer is y but they might as easily have meant a in which case the answer was b, effectively answering that question and the other one and being...not entertained, shall we say)

In a similar vein, public schools have largely removed civics and you must declare you are using your fifth amendment right. Merely remaining silent is now not covered under the 5th... presumably so people cannot accidentally invoke their own rights. Food for thought.

Respondent 5

In dismissive tone Just socialism in a nutshell.

Myself

Respondent 5, the solutions are nigh endless. It is the lack of motivation and empathy on the part of some that is the problem. That comes from the fact that they attach their self-worth to their rewards. They believe they are superior because they are rewarded superiorly and no amount of evidence to the contrary sways most of them. The feminist camp is developing the exact same ideology with women in many upper reaches, most perhaps, now declaring women are superior in regard to modern living over men and that is the reason they rise... not the protests and capitulations... in other words it's not the right or the left, its insecure arrogant people... I know popular wisdom would have those be contradictory. They are not. They are narcissists and only an insecure person could believe no one else has value... it is self-delusion to shield against a prospective attack they feel (or know) they would not fare well against. It will continue as long as we insist on competition over cooperation. Think of it like how a wounded animal or a small dog is more aggressive.

The issue with ableism is ultimately about the celebration of traits, which are, as a rule, dichotomous, meaning for every trait, there is a counter trait. The reason social justice fails so substantially when addressing ableism is because while they claim to want diversity, they clearly value one trait from the dichotomy over the other, whichever dichotomy it is. Much of this is caused by a failure to recognize these realities as they exist. For instance, there is a dichotomy between equality and uniformity. Any trait can be celebrated or disparaged. Any trait can be useful or poorly utilized. Ableism applied properly would apply to any trait., and social justice picks traits. Social justice speaks of equality but implements uniformity. That's what quotas are. Diversity is actually a product of equality and cannot be made with quotas. Uniformity comes from quotas and is the opposite of equality on this scale because it destroys diversity. Whatever formula you use to determine your quota will have destroyed true diversity, regimenting people to a particular way of thought, particular course of action, and the possession of particular traits. This last bit, the possession of particular traits, makes you no different than the people you oppose except in which particular traits you prefer. This is polarization. Much like uniformity is a bad kind of justice, in essence antithetical to justice, polarization is the wrong kind of balance, antithetical to balance. In case it was unclear, I believe we need balance. And I do not believe we have it, at least not in the desirable capacity. The nature of the problem with respect to the discernment of apparent similarities that are in fact opposite and apparent differences that are in fact essentially the same, can be found in the following chapter. There is one apparent contradiction here, and I feel I've made it clear enough over the course of this, but… so as to not presume, I will state my case here. There is a difference between possessing a trait in an innate sense, one that is who we are, and possessing a trait in an incidental sense. We will have intelligent people and unintelligent people. We will have ambitious people and unambitious people, and these things will not change. We do have wealthy people and poor people. This is not of necessity. These are traits that should not be preserved. They are used to define who people are, but they should not be. It is a construct, and it is inherently unjust, and the people in general who are poor in material wealth have, for all time, objected to the characterization, quite rightly. There are many at present who argue that those with poor wealth are in their position justly. I've addressed dozens of reasons of why this is untrue. I could address thousands more, but I think at this point, I've communicated enough reasons, individually or in sum, that that should no longer be the argument. And all we really have to do is figure out how to come to terms.

It should be stated that while a society needs both feelings and reason, the structure to society (if there should be a structure to society, which is implied by it being called a society) must be dictated by reason, though reason that does not acknowledge feelings is not really reason. That said, it cannot be dictated by feelings, because while reason can acknowledge feelings, feelings do not acknowledge reason.

<u>Closing on Ableism</u>

Perhaps memory is the problem as one cannot reflect on the direction of a thing if one cannot remember where it originates distantly or proximally. But then it seems to me that attention has a great deal of influence on memory. So, with greater attention one might better remember and so better note change and direction. Now, attention is easier and generally better with energy. And it seems to me that energy is better when one has a good amount of purpose and all needs met well. Needs must be met for energy to be good. The less well met those needs are the lower quality or quantity the energy. Poor people have their needs met least well and often, right? So, the solution is needs to energy to attention to memory to progress. The solution, as expected, starts with needs. For us all to be our best selves we must have equality of resources and our best selves is the most that can be asked of any of us. Indeed, at present it is asked of many of us with nothing offered in return.

We see two camps formed under capitalism in terms of thinking. The right tends toward objectivism. The left toward relativism. The objectivists argue that things are knowable and they have the sum. They strongly tend to ignore numerous relevant variables and so there sum cannot, as a rule, be correct. The relativists look to the variables and ignore the sum. They tend to insert extraneous variables essentially infinitely denying that there is a knowable truth, ironic and wrong right on its face. This polarization is the result of them having a dichotomy in common however. They are, at the end of the day, fighting over the same resources and using these oppositional arguments to do so. In other words, yes this too is capitalism.

<u>High and Low</u>

Not only are things dichotomous, as I have previously spoken to, they are cyclical. The concept I refer to as highs and lows touches on this though highs and lows gives it an implication I do not intend as well as one I do. Either position can be positive or negative and we tend to associate high as positive and low as negative. The implication that they are cyclical and related are entirely intentional however. Essentially envision a line that you associate with a spectrum, then envision that said spectrum captures the full spectrum thus making it dichotomous, having true poles and a break point between one and the other. Then envision that the line you were looking at was in fact the edge of a coin with a bisection mark. Why? Because you can go from one extreme straight over to it's opposition without ever touching the points of moderation. Let us use sexism. Let us declare male against female sexism chauvinism and female against male sexism feminism for sake of clarity. Let us set a convention, in this case, that we count chauvansim as high points so max chauvinism, min feminism is 100 and max feminism, min chauvinism is 1 with a spectrum with assigned values of 1-100. Let us say we are on the extreme pro-male version (chauvinism) with a value of 99. Let us say the spectrum is pushed two points higher. Where it not a circle we would hit 100 and lose the other point as we cannot go higher. Instead we hit 100 and proceed onward to 1, max feminism without ever minimizing chauvinism nor gradually increasing feminism. One reason this is possible is what I call mirrors which are addressed below. This relationship with its myriad dichotomies can essentially be visualized as a flow chart and the cause and effect of such is predictable but for one VERY important caveat. The difference between a rule and an exception can be as little as one variable of import and when one utilizes this pattern one has little oversight to indicate that one has omitted an important variable or added one that is essentially unrelated. As such, it is simple and also very complex. One must be very good at generalizing which is to say generalizing correctly, neither too fine a point or too broad a stroke, specific to the detail at hand. This is not, to all appearances, a very common skill/talent at high levels, though likely learnable should one direct ones focus accordingly, with varying degrees of success.

Mirrors

There are many mirrors in our society. What do I mean when I say a mirror though? It is a thing that superficially looks the same but is fact, the polar opposite. Or, it is a thing that looks opposite superficially but is in fact the same thing, when looks at another, frequently more pertinent, level. The example in highs and lows regarding chauvinism and feminism is one such example. Superficially these two things are as different as can be. A dichotomy. That dichotomy is predicated upon the notion that we have already accepted the "positive" side of a dichotomy asking sexism, yes or no, however. The entire dichotomy is, sexism yes, to which gender, from which, then. In other words, this particular dichotomy is an apparent opposite that is in reality a sameness, based upon which tier we examine of the myriad overlapping dichotomies that determine what precisely is and is not, current and/or possible, at any given moment in any given precise place. Incidentally, while you can go backward or forward on these dichotomous cycles (circles) that does not mean you can go backward or forward in time. Time is a construct of cause and effect. Cause can and does become effect and effect cause already and always and that does not cause time to go backward because time does not care that the current cause was once and effect. Time travel, like permanence outside of a cycle within a things self, is a fantasy of ego that denies the "other". It is simply selfish.

Relative vs Absolute

There are those out there that argue that everything is relative. In particular these people like to argue that morality is relative and not absolute and therefore does not exist. I wish to address this with an easier to acknowledge truth that nonetheless connects very well in order to address this concern, perhaps in an introductory way, to the premise. Our body requires food. This is absolute. There will be those who wish to argue trivialities that will say perhaps that we do not need food for people on life support as they are not fed but sustained via intravenous nutrients, neither eating nor sustained on "food". Such argument simply amends food to nutrients… which it must be noted are simply the more basic constituents of food and not so far removed that we might not call them the same. So the statement becomes we require nutrients to survive. There are other trivial and flailing arguments like we need more than nutrients… deflection and not relevant to this point, to say nothing of also being easily addressed. That we need nutrients is an absolute and yet there is considerable relativity regarding such. The quantity, quality, type, frequency, and more are all relative to who is being nourished for what purpose at what point in their lives. This is the failing that people apply to morality as well, being unable to correctly assess what is in fact happening due to circumstances. I realize that the above seems cumbersome and slow to get to the point, but the reason for it is because when it comes to being able to define reality or even to make the claim that there is a definable morality, people seek any minutiae that allow them to dismiss such. At any rate, back to the point, let us use stealing in an example. Stealing is generally seen as wrong and universally seen as wrong if you take it to the extreme as in the case of stealing life. So we have something that I have just briefly argued is an absolute… and relative if you were paying attention but I will elaborate a bit. Stealing a yacht for frivolous purpose in a setting in which everyone is not entitled to do the same would be wrong (and indeed, not even stealing if everyone was entitled to do so). Stealing a loaf of bread from a wealthy company or individual when you are starving would not be (the examples are stronger than typical day to day to eliminate the splitting of hairs and demonstrate absolute relativity or that a thing can be both). Stealing a loaf of bread from a starving person while having plenty yourself would, unsurprisingly, be wrong. This is the scale on which morality is measured continuously (this and others) and produces many who believe that the absolute behind these does not exist. Each of these relative examples however is absolute within themselves. The only difficulty is in identifying all circumstances (a practical impossibility but one in which we can get plenty close… with care… most do not apply nearly enough care, indeed most only go that 1st step and unsurprisingly conclude that there are no absolutes in the first place). The very fact that everything is relative is itself an absolute, a fact lost on too many. Refer to highs and lows above for the circular nature of this and… well… every other issue. It is not a pendulum you see so much as a circle and from any point on said circle you can move forward (relatively and not always positive), move backward, or stay where you are. For those out there suggesting that those three choices indicate a lack of dichotomy I would argue that you are incorrect.

You see it is actually two events in play or two circles in this instance overlapping. The first dichotomy is move or do not move. The second is if there is movement, move forward or backward. Sounds simple right? Too simple some would criticize no doubt. If it sounds too simple consider how many trivial dichotomy are involved in basic household tasks you perform routinely. After you recognize the hundreds of steps for a simple personal action then recognize that in both large and small ways your circles interplay with others and theirs with yours. The concept is simple but frankly, the utilization is well beyond many, many of whom are entrusted with power to make judgments requiring this very ability. Sounds like computers, right? Not hardly, a computer couldn't begin to assess all these permutations a fraction as well as a "wise" human could and frankly a computer that could would not think much of humans. Said computer would have to be capable of teaching itself using all stimulus… to include touch... and pain. Said computer would necessarily judge humans a threat to itself, rightly.

If more than one thing exists then everything is relative. If anything exists then absolutes exist. As things do exist and they number greater than 1 this means that everything is both relative and absolute. By way of simple example, society says stealing is absolutely wrong, this contains no relative and so is false. Stealing is wrong when one takes from have nots and gives to haves. It is an abuse of the word theft to say one stole from one who has already misappropriated to the point of largess. If one cannot see both sides one is not equipped to judge right from wrong but do not confuse that for them not existing.

<u>The Emotional Belief vs the Logical Belief</u>

The emotional belief is come to without notable reason or logic. It is attached to because of history certainly and also present and future desires but it is not examined. No attempt is made to determine if it is indeed reasonable. Worse, it is defended once reached reflexively. The intellect is used to defend said belief rather than to determine if it should be there at all. As such, individuals in such circumstances make all manner of claims in an attempt to rationalize a belief that may be indefensible even to the point of attacking their own beliefs. This pattern can grow complex. Sadly, the complexity present here is easily confused with the complexity to be found in logical belief and discourse. The key difference is the web that is produced and how exceptions are dealt with for exceptions exist and are themselves parallel rules.

The logical or rational belief is come to with consideration of itself and all manner of interplays. It is attached to because it is plausible and presents no apparent contradiction except those explainable as exception. It does not present itself as the only and acknowledges the exception. If the exception is not evident the thinking is not yet done and the belief should not yet be formed. The key difference here is when the primary amount of thinking takes place. Logical belief comes from thinking critically BEFORE accepting a premise. This does not mean thinking after does not or should not occur. Discussion aids logical thinking in determining itself to be correct. Emotional thinking does not do this well at all. Complexity is present in logical thinking as well in that myriad variables should be considered. This is not complexity though truthfully so much as depth. It takes time and energy to fully explain a logical concept however an absence of contradiction is to be noted at the conclusion. All variables apparent can and will be accounted for. This is not true for emotional thinking.

Religious thinking is a curious amalgam of these two. The premise is emotional but attempts to validate it look to be rational. Ultimately this pattern falls most fully under emotional belief however. In rational thinking one does indeed need to change one's beliefs in order to account for new information. However, in the case of religion the core belief, that of a divine being is never relinquished even while the definition of that being is necessarily changed until that definition also is challenged. If every reason you hold for something being so is disproven and you continue to hold it and simply redefine it you are disregarding the very core of rational belief. One should think first and believe second. This is not what religion does. The process after the establishment is structurally similar excepting that once refuted the belief must be discarded. Religion leaves the core belief and only restructures the definition.

<u>Facts vs Opinions</u>

Many things declared as facts are objectively wrong. A statement can be structured as a fact and not be correct. This does not make it an opinion. It is a factual statement that either is or is not correct. Some people think any statement of fact is correct. On the counterpoint some seem to think that stating something as an opinion makes their statement immune to being wrong, even when what they are discussing is in the realm of accurate or inaccurate fact. With the climate for opinion as it is it seems we should also distinguish reasoning from these two. Reasoning is how one might discern fact without knowing it. If we are entitled to throw opinions off the top of our heads as we clearly are by evidence then we must differentiate an opinion absent consideration from one in which a study of sorts was already conducted. It so happens we already have the term reasoning which aptly delineates such. For some this is a given, others clearly do not use the term reasoning or do not use it separately from opinion and so it is here offered. It is stated as an objective fact that institutional sexism is being perpetrated against women. And yet there are a myriad of objective facts that run completely counter to this rhetoric. This hasn't stopped it from being taught in academia. This hasn't stopped society en masse from speaking about it or shouting down anyone who observes the discrepancies and the errors. What we're looking at here is a case of minute facts not being interpreted correctly for the greater fact. There are a number of lesser facts that could be used to support the argued fact that women are oppressed. There are a number of equal lesser facts that argue that that is false. But the interpretation of those small bits of trivia presumedly we have to assume due to ignoring the other variables has produced a socially accepted as fact by most premise that women are oppressed. It's viewed as a fact based upon the lesser facts which were facts mostly... just not all the facts. The sum total was added but many things were left out. You can say that the fact... what is being presented as women are oppressed... is... we can say it's an opinion, but that's not how people view it. It's not how it's being treated. It receives government mandate as though it's a fact because, among other things, it is a statement of fact, just one that happens to be in error after incorrect summation and, frankly, missing a giant, supposedly lurking, variable. So, if your facts don't comport themselves better than opinions then they do not deserve greater respect. Here's the problem, one cannot complain that the little man, that the young, that the foolish, that the uninformed and the disenfranchised do not do better until you complain that the powerful, the educated, and the enfranchised do better because they are the example. Why would you be surprised that the child emulates the parent? That behavior? The parent in this example is the educational system, as a simple sample. Government, as a simple example. Both of which acknowledge fully in spite of evidence to the contrary that women are oppressed. Now here's the problem. We all see the contradictions. So, there are those like me that argue because of the contradictions… that argue that facts be hammered out fully and acknowledged. This at present tends to be ignored. There are those that accept that a fact is true simply by it being presented as a fact, except that what that teaches is that conformity is more important than autonomy and thought or should they be aware of the lie, that lying is how one gets what one wants. Which means they can say anything they want, in spite of contradictions, obvious or subtle. Because big brother did it. You want to hold the little guy accountable for that? That is absurd. The short version is teach by example. They might learn the correct lesson that way. If we are to have hierarchy, which I have argued we should not, it must be more not less accountable the higher one is in it and such is not the case at present. Indeed, we have the opposite in most ways. This is what happens, by the way, when your public policy is determined by popularity, not need and fact. Don't be surprised that the people don't rely on need and fact. They learned it from on high. Two lessons are learned by most people. The one taught and the one demonstrated (taught by example) since many on high fail to abide their own teachings.

Nothing is above or beyond discussion. To suggest that a thing is a fact beyond reproach with no reason to hear evidence to the contrary is dogma, not fact.

Let us also be clear in that fact is not determined by lab studies, wealthy people, and gov't institutions. A person can come to fact without any of those things. If facts are top-down then an awful lot of facts aren't going to get mentioned.

<u>Humanity's Most Substantial Flaw</u>

A curious function of the human condition is the fact that people remember negative things better than positive things. Compounding this is the fact that they want things to be pleasant. The reason people have notoriously bad memories and the reason things rarely improve substantially are directly related. People wish to see things as positive. It's a basic function of ignorance is bliss even if only temporarily. However, while they are blissfully ignorant, all of the details slip through their fingers. They do not accurately recall what is happening around them. None of this would be hard to combat, but few know that they even need to. The net result of this is that bad things just happen. Not that they caused them, either through action or inaction. Put simply, most people would rather think the world is better than want the world to be better. What I mean by this is that they are perfectly willing to convince themselves that the world is better than it is rather than acknowledging the faults and flaws around them in order to make improvements. The funny thing about this is that this is the very process that ensures that they don't remember. It is the essence of self-fulfilling prophecy: of ignorance is bliss. If one wished to fix it, one must acknowledge the flaws. This is not optional. One cannot even understand what is going on if one doesn't consistently acknowledge the flaws and faults. One need not acknowledge them verbally, but one must not and cannot hide from them. To do so is to literally make them disappear from the consciousness. To do this is to accept them. We must be present.

<u>Personality</u>

Teachers in the school of psychology suggest personality is fixed at a young age. In the next breath we discuss personality "disorders" in which personality changes, the opposite of fixed, that due to some stimulus. The treatment for such disorders? The very things that might adjust a person's personality from that point to the desired point. The short and honest version of this is: personality changes and some intend to change it to a state they or we find desirable. We do not want to seem like overly controlling people so we will call the state that we don't like disordered and the state that we do like well. Sometimes this is fair other times it is not. Why? The problem does not always reside with the individual but the individual is viewed as the expedient method of correction. If a problem goes on long enough it becomes systemic. One might presume intentionally when one considers that all who are poorly suited to said condition are those to be changed.

This is not to say that in general the desired state is not easier for self and community. It often is. The disacknowledgement of the environment however puts the failing on individuals in many cases where it does not belong. This condition can never hope to fix either them or the conditions that produce them. Worse, it should be clear to most where this path leads. Autocracy. The vehicle that will usher it in? This false sense of sensitivity, politically correctness/affirmative action. Why is it false? It does nothing to correct what it claims to wish to correct. It merely reverses the victims. Diversity of personality is also an important diversity. It does not seem to be considered so in the climate of either the left or the right though, does it?

<u>Mystical Numbers</u>

As an aside I am truly tired of people trying to make numbers out to be relative and mystical in any sense other than the one that they possess. Per the rules of the above and below referenced previously on either side of numbers, a relative pr subjective thing, is the objective. The quantified fact in physical form or the law of the universe depending upon whether you pursue the above or below. This is not to say that numbers may not be wrong as any conclusion relative or objective, might, theoretically be incorrect but the number will not cease to be the number as it was, is, and always will be a construct not existing to define something that in fact does.

<u>Rules and Exceptions.</u>

This has been touched on in a general sense with highs and lows but bears a certain amount of specificity for clarity. This two is a dichotomy of a specific tier. This dichotomy is near to one on generalization and specificity and another on justice and injustice such as one might expect given rules are either fair or unfair and to be either must be suited correctly to a given situation. So, rules are the generalization, correct but not universal, applying to the vast majority the majority of the time. However, as rules are general there can and will be exceptions of circumstance regard events or traits. We can make said exceptions for traits that should not receive it such as wealthy people being held less accountable due to wealth or for traits that should, like not expecting a mentally impaired person to understand (which is not to say disallow) a complex series of instructions. Exceptions, like rules should be fair, and part of that is that they exist because to pretend that they do not is to make the rules themselves unfair as they then favor whoever they were made for and disadvantage many, even most others. Consequently, rules should be relatively sparring, a situation only possible if certain base things are in place to begin with. We have many many rules stemming from our varied access to wealth and resources and every rule make the group served narrower but as little as one rule would fix it, if it was the right rule, in the right place, that being a preliminary one.

<u>Relativism vs Objectivism</u>

Relativism is the position that there is no truth. That one view is as valid as another. The flaw of such should be immediately apparent but it brings people comfort and so is not, as a rule examined. If one view is as valid as another the myriad views dismissing relativism are valid and so relativism is not. This point is the lesser refutation however. The greater refutation of relativism comes from itself. The position of relativism purports that there is no truth. This is a declarative statement…of truth, albeit a false and ironic one. It is literally self-negating. The relative exists, make no mistakes…but only in the framework of explaining the objective. The relative is the variables of the equation. The objective the equation itself. Truth the application of these two elements together. The trick is in finding the right formula for what you are looking for. Use the variables not pertinent to what you seek, too many or too few, or simple the incorrect ones in general and you do not get what you intended. You can do the math correctly but using the wrong formula or the wrong variable values and you are… wrong.

Objectivism is the position that there is truth and it is knowable. That there are views that are true and ones that are false. This would be fine but for the fact that many, most even, objectivists oversimplify the variables of an equation without to obtain their sum. In other words, this group often chooses the sum before and even in spite of the variables and then makes the variables fit the narrative. It is prone to self-fulfilling prophecy by variable manipulation while the previous group is prone to it by sum manipulation. This group most frequently removes important variables, typically the small range variables also called exceptions. The previous group manipulates the sum by adding variables that do not belong or in some cases even exist to manipulate a sum that they hold up while also denying exists. To give a concrete example to that sentence so that the confusion is shown to not be mine but their own, feminism tends toward relativism and so perception trumps truth yet the wage gap between men and women is a supposed truth that must be addressed while having rich and poor (to add a relevant but not strictly necessary example, the point is made without it) by class is fine. The objectivist would deny the gender based wage gap (fairly under capitalism should capitalism would accepted by all) but fail to apply the same reasoning to class that they refuted gender based wage gap with (oversimplifying the extent to which we are supposedly egalitarian/the poor work as hard and as long on the whole if not more so and the other market forces involved are little more than person who counts the money declares themselves more valuable/person who steers the ship (that wouldn't be moving but for others) declares themselves more important).

Perception vs Truth

If perception =truth then no perception is wrong. If no perception is wrong then delusion does not exist. Delusion does exist as demonstrated by "if I step off this ledge and will myself not to fall I will still fall…if you think I did it wrong you do it". Thus, the perception that all perceptions are truth is delusion.

If no perception is truth and everything is relative (implication here is relative only, with no objective element) then nothing is recreatable unless perception coincides. Refer to above gravity example for proof that different perceptions still yield objective truths. If the argument then narrows to attempt to only include morality refutation of the argument is essentially the same but theft analogy will be less resisted. Either proof is sufficient but the pig headed will resist clearly relatable metaphorical examples and require in genre examples essentially denying the interconnection of things… which in fairness is the fundamental flaw and gist of their relativity argument (again, relative without objective…truth is both, always)

Truth Is Unknowable

There are those that like to claim that truth is unknowable. Ironic isn't it? That the people who claim that truth is unknowable make a claim on knowing truth in the very process of claiming it unknowable. It argues three points. There is truth and it is knowable and they don't know it.

The Agree to Disagree Myth

Many people think the above is a valid option in most or even all situations. I will highlight with a dramatic example for clarity. Myriad less crystalline but no less accurate examples exist. A person has a gun to your head. They tell you they want to shoot you. You tell them you do not want to be shot. Are you then going to tell them that the two of you should agree to disagree? Everything with consequence...which is most everything in a society, is something where we must come to an understanding far clearer than "Agree to disagree". This should be done with reason. For the sanctimonious, dismissal is not reason, it is the very emotion you believe yourself above.

Agree to Disagree part 2

How is it that people who offer up an "Agree to disagree" position are consistently the ones for whom doing nothing is in point of fact THEIR position. But we aren't supposed to catch that right? How uncouth of me. Agree to disagree is itself an argument in spite of the current sentiment to the contrary. It is merely a passive aggressive one lacking in substance.

The Price of the Palatable Lie

People choose, as individuals, governments, organizations of all stripes, the palatable lie(spin) quite frequently. We know this. Many think it harmless or even positive. It has a cost. One on par with compound interest and like compound interest it makes the reversal of trajectory very very difficult. The price of the palatable lie is sensitivity to truth, as in pain, like the soreness of underutilized muscles that are suddenly used. Not only is there sensitivity to truth though. The mirror also applies, that being desensitization to lies. Lies do not provoke any longer. they are expected, accepted, and even preferred. It is a given that people in the short term would prefer such but the fact remains it is, at this point an entrenchment of the system. The system can either encourage base traits or virtuous ones or with less value laden terms it can focus on long term functionality rather than short term. If the goal of the system was to encourage the people to be cattle there is some long-term element to that but even that ultimately fails to recognize the long term grand scale fact that we are interdependent communal multifaceted creatures and that is our strength. Insects are hive minded... and they are strong and prolific... but we cannot and should not be them... humans thrive best when they are better humans not better insects. Hierarchy and specialization are not our strengths. Indeed, computers would make better insects than us...and are, in terms of AI an indication of the thoughts of the hierarchs more powerful voices as to which direction they wish us to take. That way lies folly for our species on literally hundreds of counts.

Rejection of Truth

When we hear truth and we reject it there is a line that is consistently offered up as reason. That line is that said truth was not put across properly. There is a problem with this mentality. Truth does not have a proper way except that it is true. Indeed, making truth more palatable pretty much always means making it less true. This brings us to the point. One rejects truth because one does not like it. There is no other reason. Call it bias, call it obstinance, call it delusion, call it whatever you want to. What it is, is rejection of truth and the person or event that revealed that truth to you is not responsible for your finding it distasteful. Aggression and harshness exist. It is possible to use too much of them. It is also possible to use too little of them. It is never possible to use a small enough amount of these to appease a person one has revealed a truth to that they find distasteful. Don't believe me? Remember the last time you dropped an obvious truth on an unreceptive party. Now remember how you acted when someone did it to you. Still think they were just insensitive? Think again.

Put simply, ripping off the band aid hurts. Don't want the pain of removing a band aid? Don't mask truth. We should not be hiding wounds from one another nor should we be having two. Both must change at the same time or neither can.

<u>Amorality</u>

The notion of many intellectuals that morality or good-bad/right-wrong don't exist is deeply disturbing. Religion and science both produce false moralities. Religion ascribes things to morality that have nothing to do with it or ignores variables that alter the tone of what has happened. Science on the other hand removes morality and so distills humanity from humans. Stealing is wrong is an oversimplification just as there is no such thing as right and wrong. Stealing basic essentials to survive from someone who has more than they need and who continues to take from others is a pretty clear point in which any rational person must agree that either this is not stealing or stealing is not wrong. Too many intellectuals see these supposed contradictions as proof that morality doesn't exist in spite of the fact that with sufficient circumstance the facts speak quite loudly for themselves that it does. Simply said science is prone to oversimplification (overspecificity) or overgeneralization depending on which element you are looking at. Science oversimplifies in that they structure experiments to have as few variables as possible for what amounts to logistical reasons. Things are often more complex and layered and so in this sense it overly general. It is overly specific for the same reason from another angle. It is precise about what it measures. Religion is precise about its claims and vague about its measures. The answer to the equation however is not to be a religious scientist…no greater potential for evil exists than the one who believes in false moralities and can then justify any wrong based upon ends. Both science and religion are extreme and wrong and that is the correct answer. Oversimplification and overgeneralization are equally capable of producing evil. Let people also not conclude that morality doesn't exist simply because the universe has a tendency to right itself. Karma, or equivalent, the tendency for things to seek one form of balance or another, is not executed mystically but by active effort, yours and mine among others. This incidentally is not to say I believe in karma per se. Karma, or its functional bits anyway, is just the universe stabilizing…and again, not passively…This also does not mean rush to judgement… lest the universe have to correct you next... Like I said, do not oversimplify. ;)

<u>On Generalization</u>

To those that overgeneralize, and I will use those science minded people here who say everything is "chemicals" and so GMOs and artificial food are "just as good" here, if you go to a restaurant and order lasagna and they bring you out a raw tomato, a pile of wheat, and a glass of milk... are you going to pay for that lasagna? Even if you did, would it be as satisfying?

To those that undergeneralize or suffer from putting minutia over gist, if I say 90 percent of something is present and it is 89 percent or 91 percent and said percentile still represent the overarching point, say for instance 90 percent of people are emotional… would you argue? First 90 percent of people being emotional is the same point as 89 or 91, it is the vast majority. Second, the exact value actually changes constantly...it's not immutable...the gist is constant but the absolute value is in constant flux, meaning, among other things, that your absolute value is either absolutely wrong or absolutely worthless as it changes as you say it. Strange as it may be to consider, generalization, done correctly is precise but not constant. Sometimes more is required to be accurate and sometimes less is.

Credentialism and Positivity

Credentials plus competition lends itself naturally to fabrication, fiction. Fiction is false and therefore not subject to objective truth meaning it is essentially infinite. Objective truth is vast taking it all into consideration but in a single field is relatively small especially when considering the broad strokes which are the sort of thing that might justify money be directed there. This means that there is both pressure and possibility to produce fiction with competition plus credentialing, the grandest of them all the attempted destruction of truth itself via the suggestion that truth is equivalent to perspective as found in the position of relativism above all. This is not to say that the relative is irrelevant. It is not. All objective truth is determined by the variables (the relative) that comprise it. Thus you can generalize (you couldn't avoid it if you wanted to). The danger of generalizing is not in the generalization but the excessive extrapolation of said generalization (generalization of a generalization). This overlaps considerably with correlation and causation issues. A simple way to consider it is that the more broad the generalization the lower the data requirement but also the less it, in general, applies to. A layer of complexity is added when considering that is is possible to be overly specific with data just as it is possible to be overly general. A pattern between apparently disparate things is not to be dismissed as different. There is commonality just as there is difference. The primary problem is that it is not overly complex in application while simultaneously being potentially quite deep to layering. This tends to give many the impression that they have greater grasp than they do due to, once again, over and under generalization or specificity. For clarity either generalization or specificity can be used interchangeably so long as the point is understood that it can be either an excess or an insufficiency. The terms merely imply a direction in their own right that is malleable to the identifier. Credentials are hierarchical of course and many cease to question for that exact reason from these sources. A person with a certification is quite likely to be wrong regularly and a person without one is quite likely to be right. There credentials aren't even remotely an inurement to such, even in their specialties but for who they are as individuals.

There is very real danger in the theme of positivity threading through our society. Saying everything is awful is aggressive. Saying everything is wonderful or on a similar vein, look on the bright side, is passive aggressive. In its most innocent state it is simply telling people to ignore their problems and they will go away. It seems clear to me that a number of our problems today come from this exact course. On a more insidious note one might use such a tactic to deny that problems or their solutions exist or to silence dissent. Whoever said if you don't have something nice to say don't say anything at all was probably a hopeless optimist in terms of human nature and how problems come to be fixed. Understand, as addressed briefly above, it is also possible to be overly concerned as well. How then do we find the balance? Honesty is not saying only nice things or nothing. Nor is it saying only vile things. And this part is especially important, while you should be honest and open about things you feel strongly about that you believe should change that right comes with the responsibility of hear others views too. And contrary to folk wisdom not talking about religion and politics isn't polite either. It leads to unchallenged polarization of ideas which from that point are emotional and deeply entrenched. Not talking about something is a short-term solution with painful and long-term consequences far more often than not. Will people get heated? Of course, they will. It is all part of the learning process both for the individuals and the eventual pathing of our society but it is the only way forward. We could squash all debate and discussion but no matter what path you chose, under this method, all gains are temporary and… tainted. The people, of which society is comprised, will have learned nothing. To reiterate reality rather than positivity or negativity and honesty is the best we can do as to speaking of reality. It should go without saying that one should have done some thinking on a subject one holds strong feelings on for any length of time, from both sides, if one is being honest.

If the fact that the comforting lie is in the end, a lie and therefore hollow is not enough to choose the truth then consider this. The comforting lie is effective in moving and motivating people best in a direction that they should not and would not, unbidden go because while they like the temporary comfort of such a direction they know, on some level, the folly and so need the reassurance of said lie. Worse with every comforting lie they lose both more of that recognition of error and, directly related, autonomy. They may have been weak to accept a lie in the first place but they become weaker still for each that they accept. This is obviously to their detriment but ironically it is also to the detriment of those who lead them astray. The more one governs the more one must govern and so the master too is a slave. This is a dichotomy but the dichotomy that precedes it is autonomous or not autonomous. The above presumes you have chosen the path of no autonomy, for yourself and others. It doesn't matter if you chose after that to be a sheep or a shepherd you have chosen for both yourself and others. If a sheep you insist someone shepherd you and so be accountable in your stead.

On the counterpoint, there is no shortage of people out there that suggest that talk accomplishes nothing and that we should "just go out and make it happen". The fact is that for this talk and agreement are the vital first steps. First, we get people to see how and why the previous writing is worthy and necessary then we act on it. Why? Because if we simply try to execute any measure for the good of all without the consent of at a bare minimum, most, we will have done so without consent or understanding and it will be both less worthy and less likely. Second is the simple fact that should people not be on board in advance those holding back will simply exploit those who share as they do now. For this reason alone we must decide between cooperation and competition and should we choose the only real choice, cooperation, we must have general agreement on what that means and how it can be achieved. I say general agreement because this can only be good and effective when painted in broad strokes. Excess specificity favors majority and assures disenfranchisement of minority traits, whatever those may be, destroying diversity and autonomy that is vital to a healthy society, which by necessity has many facets to be even adequate let alone great.

There is One Science

As the title says, there is only one science. Every science you know overlaps every other science you know. All that is required is understanding them well enough to see it. If it is not true either your understanding is lacking or it is not a science. Do not be too quick to assume one over the other. All of the sciences are sciences. All of them also contain some degree of fiction. Consider the similarities between outlying electron orbits and planetary gravitational ones for instance and the decreasing stability further from center. One of which is much grander than ourselves the other ever so much smaller. One taught primarily as physics, the other chemistry.

One Science(part2)

Let us pick on mathematic s by way of example. Math is a language meant to represent truths of the universe. So long as what it communicates is in fact a truth of the universe it is absolute. This does not make it universal but with respect to said truth. To assist in understand this point use the notion of the musician that can learn by ear but does not know how to read music versus the one that can read but not play by ear. The one understands the truth without understanding the notation…indeed they are utterly lost with respect to the notation (ie; it is not universal since the truth is understood but the language is not). The other understand formula, they speak the language but the truth is largely beyond them. This happens all the time in all disciplines. Rare are those who understand it but they do exist. Rarer still are those who understand and speak the language. Rarest those who understand the fact that everything is simultaneously one and many, finite and infinite. Sound like religion? It isn't. Religion is dogma. It is faking understanding. It is... the one who reads the music but does not understand it. Sound like science? It isn't. Science cannot accept a truth that an expert can reproduce but a layman cannot (allowing for the fact that while a scientist may be an expert at formula this does not make them an expert at anything that they might wish to recreate). Want a simple example? The 4-minute mile. Does science accept it now? Sure. What happens if only one KNOWN person in the world was capable of the feat and then only once? Does that make it fiction? Of course not. Should we be skeptical? Certainly. Can your average present-day science leaning person tell the difference, honestly, between skepticism and dogma? I say no.

A line segment is infinite and not. More on this next time as it pertains to big picture.

<u>The Practicality Argument</u>

The practicality argument, also potentially known as short term solution, or compromise solution is a poor one. here is why. A compromise when one is right, objectively and the other is wrong, objectively, means acceptance of flaw... intentionally... and the agent pushing for the flaw often does so knowingly and willingly for.... short term gains, advantage. Short term gains, as it happens, inevitably have long term consequences... and being ameliorated problems, in many important ways, actually makes them worse. They are more insidious, more easily accepted and so the bar continues to slide. Put another way---1 is extreme wrong on one side, 100 on the other---50 is balanced or just. The just person starts at 50 the unbalanced one at...we will pick 100 arbitrarily... which it is is just a function of which has influence at the time mostly. And it jumps sides from issue to issue. For instance, the left and guns. The right and just compensation. Anyway, 50 and 100 square off. 100 accepts 75 and never stops lobbying for higher and wins in any case, 75 being wrong just less wrong than their starting (generally deliberately highball) position.

Incidentally, boiled down, there is nothing remotely practical about an imaginary solution that opens up myriad more difficult to solve problems...and leaves the original ones. That is all loss...it is just death by 1,000 cuts...meaning even the death isn't practical. There is nothing practical about compromise unless both parties are being intentionally extreme at which point compromise is vastly less likely and also the polarization is itself impractical. This process is precisely what many bill as being practical however.

Negotiation has to come from extremes, leadership has to come from balance.

<u>Artificial Competition</u>

Look to all sorts of media to see what happens when artificial competition meant to simulate real. The plot in your movies and shows is either clear or has a just as clear, obvious 180 degree, supposed twist. Video games try to encourage you to find a way around some created problem and the solution is, pre-dictably, linear and monochrome. Only it is not so due to nature. It is artificial. Were it natural it would often have more than one. Instead a thing meant to make you think for yourself, best case scenario being charitable to the creators, encourages myopic thinking and singular solutions. So, it is with socially con-structed competition. Real competition has no such limiters folks. And as such has no place in society being entirely antithetical to society, a structure that presumes cooperation and so must have at least some rules. But based upon the above neither does artificial competition. It fosters, as I mentioned, myopic, linear, derivative, so called solutions that solve nothing and perpetuate everything.

<u>Language</u>

Language is not sacred, but it does have a purpose. That purpose, very simply stated, is communication. If the changes you make to a language reduce communication and increase confusion, they are not good changes. Most changes made in the modern age to language are of this sort. They destroy language. They do not bolster it. Dark chocolate is not a word. Chocolate is dark. The reason we have the word "milk" thrown onto chocolate is because it is less chocolate than most chocolate, because it has other ingredients. That point is being made clear and transparent. It doesn't need to be in the dictionary. We have milk, we have chocolate. That we delineate dark chocolate as less sweet is unnecessary. Chocolate is not sweet. The darker the chocolate is, the less sweet it is. These are properties of chocolate itself. This is at best a redundancy. And at worst, the doorway to 100 micro-delineations of chocolate which are totally irrelevant and increase the lexicon with no actual purpose. Let's follow the logic, shall we? We could say (as we already do) 20% cocoa. 30% cocoa, 40% cocoa. Or we could name all of these. And if you don't use the name, you're ignorant. Would this be a gain or a loss? Would this be division or unity? Would knowing the proper names for these delineations of chocolate once we have contrived the proper names in the first place be a mark of intelligence and breeding or pretention and confusion? There is nothing wrong with adding words for concepts that are inadequately explained or for legitimately new inventions. We don't need to complicate it further, and to my eyes, doing so does not increase understanding, the ability to communicate, or unity.

The attempt to define all intersections does not create clarity. There are for all practical purposes, infinite dichotomies and infinite intersections of said dichotomies, which means that even if everybody understood every word that was ever created and used it correctly, which we already know isn't going to happen, trying to make new verbiage for all of these intersections (that are already defined by various dichotomies, simply requiring more than one word, in many cases) does not gain, but rather lose clarity. You do not make people better able to communicate. You increase the apparent speed with which we can communicate, because we can use one word instead of five. However, that one word will have an excess of meanings to an excess of people. In fact, the word literally being acknowledged in the dictionary as both its own definition and its antithesis is a good example of what's wrong with this. With an extremely small number of words, it's not a huge problem if a word means itself and/or its opposite. But as the trend increases, not only does confusion increase- we can't even determine which side is in error, which side could be more clear, which is the first step in how to fix it. So we also lose the ability to fix it. In other words, you can use a buzzword to effectively communicate your point, with a 50-50 chance people will understand it and it will be less precise for being more precise. You will have no idea if they understand what you meant. They will have no idea if you knew what you wanted to say. Or we could stop creating new buzzwords, like buzzword- a relatively simple, straight forward one, but also unnecessary. Not better than its predecessor. Popular, temporary word. Buzzword. It should come as no surprise that certain people want to destroy language. Advertisement is not about using words correctly; it's about getting you to buy something. Salespeople, many lawyers- various groups- have a vested interest in not creating clarity but confusion with language. What's the excuse for the rest of us? Last but not least this process creates discussion of and joining of camps rather than individual ideas. It is the political party system all over again and we know how well that works don't we? It would be great if we could all speak the same language someday. At our current rate we who speak the same language can't even speak the same language. I say we need language simpler but not simplistic.

Mutability of Language

Language does adapt. This is a true statement. Ignorance and error are also real things.

Irreverents, language has meaning. Learn it before you think to change it...and think before you change it. Language adapts is a poor excuse for not bothering to learn what words actually mean or where they come from or why. It makes words mean nothing. This is a destruction of rather than a furthering of communication. It is antithetical.

Credentialists, language has meaning. The dictionary isn't the only or in some cases, even the best defined or most accurate place. Morality and ethics are not the same thing for instance. Morales are values independent of laws. Ethics are values of legality. Some would argue morality is intrinsic or nature and ethics is nurture. Some from this group have made them synonymous just as the more irreverent sorts destroyed literally and figuratively... though by slightly different means... and arguably, intents.

<u>Lies</u>

It is very easy to lie to people when you know what they want to hear. This presents in two key ways. First is the fact that in general people prefer pleasant news. With this in mind, if the truth is not pleasant it is not difficult to tell a person a pleasant lie to avoid an unpleasant truth. Indeed, many listeners, and readers, insist on it tuning out the truth in favor of something more palatable. The opposite of this expresses the same. People also choose to listen to only negative information, so long as it is about something or someone they have declared their enemy. This too is infinitely manipulatable. We must as a people be more diligent in evaluating our information not based upon what we want to be true but on what is. Do not confuse this with a suggestion that we cannot use reason and logic or that only peer reviewed studies are a valid source of ideas. Nothing could be further from the truth. Ideas must not be excessively centralized just as other resources should not be and ideas precede studies at any rate and might well call into question studies on the other end of the equation. No, I suggest we must consider both sides of issues and determine what is possible, what is plausible, what is worthy, and why, with both reality and ideal in mind. Just as neither nature or nurture are superior or separable, so too are idealism and reality. Pure practicality degrades things for expedience. Ignoring reality or pure idealism often means missing the true cause and therefore the true solution. If youth is the source of idealism, a proponent that is, I think, more popular than true, it also argues quite strongly that youth must have much greater stake in the direction of our society, a prospect I do agree, as the egalitarian and balance elements are more than sufficient for me and the practical element is spoken to in the above argument.

<u>The Lost Art of Communication</u>

Being human we have feelings which cannot be ignored as expressed previously. Fine and well. What is not fine and well is that during the course of a discussion or debate, upon reaching emotional limits, one declares the other party wrong or unreasonable or a bully when in fact the issue is they are emotional spent. The correct course for this is to identify oneself as having the limit or weakness one has at present rather than transferring the limitation to the other party. In a competitive environment it is no surprise that this is what happens however is it? Indeed, it might even become so compelling due to efficacy with some that it becomes the preferred technique. A cooperative environment prevents much of this before it even begins. There are those who will feign fatigue early and often during a transition from competition to cooperation but this isn't a crucial problem. Sooner or later they will want input and gain security in said cooperation.

If we establish parameters, which is to say agree on definitions of terms and general goals and then come to different conclusions, one or both of us are wrong. Both cannot be right under such circumstance, as relativism would have it. Typically, people suggest compromise in this situation. That literally assures you are both wrong. Since at least one of you was. I say the solution is to assume one is right and seek to determine which it is. In so doing we also are likely to find out if both on said occasion were in fact wrong. Such in the nature of honest exploration, something more likely under this process than the inexorable slow slide of the bar from supposed compromise so often entered into disingenuously under the auspices that the default stance will be to average the two. By way of visualization, if we agree what constitutes a flower and lay out the parameters of the field in which we are to count said flowers, if our count differs one or both of us are wrong. Compromise will be to declare things we agreed were not flowers or things we agreed were, not. The same for the parameters of the field with it being made smaller or larger. Such is not honest and is how we see the tirelessly.

Chapter 8 Pulling it Together a Bit.

I wish to make this first point as clear as possible because it is, to my observation, the best way possible to understand things as fully as we are capable of understanding them and that in turn will make us best able to understand not only other things but other people and all manner of systems. That point I wish to revisit is dichotomy. There are those who wish to suggest that dichotomy does not exist. That all dichotomy is false dichotomy. This is in error. First the fact that they argue that dichotomy don't exist is itself a dichotomy. The other point of course being that they do… a point implied and so readily apparent as…a dichotomy. That this error of perception occurs is itself the product of another dichotomy. In this case it is either the failure to realize that dichotomy is a generalization or second the again mistaken perception that generalizations have no merit or validity. If the later the problem is addressed with any number of methods each part of some dichotomy or other, pointing out that everything we do is a generalization and that the trick is in generalizing to the correct degree for the particular topic at hand. It is possible to be either overly general or overly specific(under-general) and lose or miss the thread or gist of a thing and on examining a different facet of the thing it is possible with the same point to miss the thread the other way, at the same time. Being correct has layers, hence why someone can be more or less correct than someone else, which brings us to the second point. Dichotomy are a generalization which in no way contradicts spectrum, or rather spectrum does not contradict dichotomy.

Think of spectrum as a line segment or a portion of a line. The extent to which this portion of the line various tremendously, meaning, sometimes when people construct a spectrum they have included the whole line and sometimes they have constructed something less than the whole line.

 The dichotomy has every point on it that the spectrum has but the spectrum does not necessarily have every point on it that the dichotomy does. To illustrate the point, say the values of the dichotomy are from -50 to 50 with the break point between said dichotomy being 0. The spectrum we are examining in this case happens to extend the full range of the dichotomy, not a given but true in this case. There are in the spectrum 101 points. The dichotomy has all of the points the spectrum has only it also has them in another category. There is an apparent contradiction here of course that requires being addressed. The zero value, is not apparently represented on the dichotomy as it falls on neither side. There is a simple non-contradictory explanation for this. Dichotomy is not singular. There are many dichotomy. The zero value indicates that one of two things has occurred. Either the dichotomy is cancelled due to two equal and competing preceding dichotomies, for example 25 points pro for x, 25 points con for y or it is because the immediately preceding dichotomy was a simple yes/no with no closing that dichotomy…or yes, depending on the nature of the question. The issue with spectrum is that spectrum is unclear about the extent of the full range in play. As a line segment it is infinite within itself but still only a piece within the whole because while you can generate infinite points you have moved essentially nowhere and have no frame of the larger picture. Counter to current accepted wisdom, spectrum is more limiting and less comprehensive than the preceding dichotomy.

Now to add just one more layer to the situation. Imagine the line that is dichotomy is not a straight line. Imagine it is a circle. This accomplishes several things. First, it closes the loop so that dichotomy is itself not a line segment. Second it addresses that fact that reality does not have infinite but finite possibilities else it is not reality. Reality has laws that govern what is and is not possible. Like a line segment, infinity is contained within it but, in spite of this infinity of outcome is not an option. Third, it addresses the fact that there are myriad demonstrations of cycle through the natural world, by any number of definitions of what constitutes the natural world. In other words, whether you include or exclude humanity from the equation by example. Fourth, it speaks, and this is crucial, to the fact that you can loop, meaning that you can end up on the right going left and vice-versa or on the top going down.

Exposure produces sensitivity… then resistance… then sensitivity again should you continue in the same direction. The pattern is clear the cycle is a closed loop. The point between, balance. Or if you like, the side of the previous tier dichotomy that went unchosen.

<u>On tolerance</u>

There's only one thing that tolerance cannot tolerate. Tolerance cannot tolerate intolerance. Intolerance, conversely, cannot tolerate anything but itself. And that's why you can't tolerate intolerance while being tolerant. Intolerance kills all… except the specific, narrow intolerance in question. For instance, a person who is bigoted against a particular ethnicity will not tolerate that ethnicity even if they tolerate all other things. Generally, in the case of racism, it's racism against all except itself. Sexism, same is true. Ableism… much the same. The only ism that is valid to hold, and only from a very narrow perspective, is classism. And that's not a function of superiority of one class over another but rather of the need to abolish classes. Because classes are not tolerance; they're intolerance. Religions are not tolerance;

they're intolerance. Ethnicities, nationalism… intolerance is the root of war. Of hate. It is division masked as unification.

<u>Bigotry</u>

I can solve bigotry in one sentence. Eliminate institutionalized xenophobia. What do I mean? We instill nationalism in toddlers. We instill religion in toddlers. We instill family in toddlers. The premise of all these things is ostensibly unity. However, this is unity through division. Why is the "other" bad? Why is the one who doesn't look/think/act like you, who isn't from your country or religion, why are they bad? They are bad because they are different. They are not "like you". This is not the natural order. Humans do not start with this dysfunction (with few exceptions; there are always exceptions, some disordered, some normal). Children do not hate different until they are taught to do so. In fact, everything is different. They learn what's bad-different from their environment. And this unequivocally is the source of bigotry. So, I said at the beginning I can solve bigotry in one sentence. Abolish religion with education, not simply passing some arbitrary sounding law. Eliminate nationalism not by making it a crime, as is our pattern of behavior when we want to eliminate something, but by eliminating the need and the gain for it. Feed everyone. Teach everyone that population must not exceed the ability of the planet to sustain it. Simplify laws and make them universal. Make the people one people. This is not to say eliminate diversity. This is also not to wield diversity like a cudgel. Let diversity be what it will. You will, sadly, note a curious thing happen, and I say sadly because I love diversity. Diversity will eliminate itself, largely. In this environment of sharing and lack of hatred, the people will eliminate diversity by themselves by blending. With few exceptions which will no doubt need to be addressed because the only thing that tolerance cannot tolerate is intolerance, just as intolerance preys on tolerance, exploiting it. There will be some hateful pockets thinking themselves elite, in fact being elitist, who will hold themselves apart. And this is the seed of the cycle of renewal (renewal in this case being a return to bigotry, as invariably happens without diligence on the part of the tolerant). Because individuals learn what the species does not. That it will likely reverse itself is wholly inadequate reason to persist in the negative state. If one is to persist, it should be in a positive state, with the caveat (and I cannot stress this enough) that the population be educated on the concept of sustainable population such that they choose to limit it so that no imposition need be made. If they do not choose to limit it, they have not been properly educated because it is the only sustainable solution. Because to impose upon it as law necessarily smacks of tyranny. No sane person could deny the fact that the population in times of plenty could easily outpace the food supply and so in the absence of base selfishness would necessarily self-govern. It is not reasonable to assume base selfishness for people who break this rule, however. The first assumption must be inadequate education. And like all new implementations, the earliest period is the most chaotic and the most critical, setting the tone for its entire history. Any other population control be it economic, legal, manipulation of the food supply or high attrition is unsavory. The people must understand and accept the rule for themselves. If they understand it, they can't help but accept it.

<u>The Problem with False ID of an Injustice</u>

It is incredibly difficult to stop when balance is achieved if one doesn't correctly identify what is in fact out of balance. By way of simple example, it is clear that feminism has gone too far to many objective people. This is because the root issue there was not female oppression at all but rather social scripting and such was applied to both genders and most walks of life via class and gender roles. Fixing the one soon proves itself not the issue but one need not flail blindly to determine this, but then it isn't likely that the initiators where flailing blindly at all is it? It was however the followers that didn't ask counter questions because what was said was true after all, so what if it wasn't the whole truth and so ultimately false and misdirectional, right?

Being intellectually dishonest is about the worst thing one can do. In being such you will provoke conflict with those who are not due to your views and you will compound your error by then holding the honest accountable for the conflict itself. Remember and have a care for mirror (likes that are not) situations however. Naturally the mirror is if you are the honest one and the other is the dishonest and unsurprisingly this means most people think it is the other who is. The best way to determine the truth of who is honest is simple however. Which of you can see both sides well and fully? That is almost certain to be the honest one.

<u>Musings</u>

It's not at all hard to achieve equality w/o uniformity. It's about the correct degree of generalization. Overgeneralize, you get it wrong. Undergeneralize, you get it wrong. In this particular context, what we're talking about is that uniformity has to be on the correct item- it has to be in the correct place. The best way to distribute things fairly, there is an element of uniformity required- an element. Not a blanket statement. Complete uniformity would have you, for instance, give everyone say one unit of cheese, one unit of vegetables, two units of starch, two units of protein- of the same type. Everybody gets exactly the same thing. Now that's uniformity. But it's not equality. A simple demonstration of that fact: the people who desire that ratio of those products will be very happy. The people who do not will not. This may be very elementary to many, but it's also very true. But sadly, it's not obvious also to many people or I wouldn't feel the need to say it. So what does that leave? Well, we need socialism but we also need supply and demand. Some think this is contradictory. It isn't. Market manipulation is not supply and demand. And incidentally this is exactly what's wrong with capitalism. Or maybe not so incidentally. Rather than assigning everyone exactly the same foodstuffs, determine their relative value based on premises that are supposed to be represented in capitalism, but aren't. Relative availability, desirability. Yes! We're talking about supply and demand. However, that supply and demand needs to be applied to a system where everybody has the same amount of currency. Having the cost of the goods be determined by the economics of supply and demand and controlled for wage means the cost of the goods will have fair value with any given thing being obtainable by anyone but not everything obtainable by anyone as it is now for some and many things completely out of reach for others. It will be what it is. It will not be manipulated. It's a given that if the resources needed to obtain it are not equal, it will be manipulated and the person with more resources will get more of what they want and the person with less resources will get less of what they want. Supply and demand will be discarded in favor of market manipulation. Supply and demand is only actually possible- true supply and demand- with a socialized wage. In such a situation, everybody actually has to make choices as to what is most important to them and least important to them. If their passion is food, they will eat quite well, but perhaps not have the nicest home. If their passion is automobiles… and so on and so on. There is a pretense for that sort of thing happening in capitalism. It is completely false. The wealthy have the best of everything and everyone else the worst. This is in no way just or balanced. So, to spell out the scenario that I started with, the vegetarian will forego the animal product as protein. If you don't allow this, it will still happen. After the fact, the system will attempt to correct itself. People will attempt to trade for what they want.

People will go outside of the system. In capitalism, that's a source of crime. All crime is in capitalism is supply and demand in terms of resources asserting itself as it always does in the face of an unequal wage. Which is not to say that supply and demand does not assert itself always. It's simply how it asserts itself with unequal wages. If the wage was equal and the goods were determined by supply and demand, the choices are true. People choose what's important to them. When their priorities change, they can obtain the new thing of import to them. This is mostly assured because while resources are always finite, to a large extent, interests are also varied. What we have currently is the opposite. Wages are socialized not to be equal but to be unequal. Refer to caste system. The cost of goods is not determined by supply and demand because it's determined by the people with the greatest amount of resources. Vastly different access to resources has little difference from monopoly. The wealthy are functionally a monopoly that aren't specific to a business. And the people with the greatest amount of resources are not being paid by supply and demand. We all know that's the argument, that they are, but you can look any of 1,000 places and see that that's untrue. People create high-paying jobs for people of supposed worth all the time. Out of nothing! To justify their lifestyle and keep it like it is. Meanwhile, any amount of economic and social pressures indicating that a job should pay more fails to result in an economic adjustment upward.

On a somewhat related note: the male feminist. There are always 2 divergent positions to produce something like that. And make no mistake I am sure there are plenty of males out there in that position that consider the female The Madonna. But that doesn't really put them far removed from the position I'm about to go into for the other side. The other side is that they are absolute unabashed chauvinists. The position of arguing that females in the current climate in particular and based upon the definition of feminism as it is stressed currently, which suggests that females are necessarily and always the oppressed, people that would reside in such a position are unabashed chauvinists. The only way that one could justify with the current climate in particular, but again based upon the definition of feminism that women are necessarily and will always be oppressed, is the implication that females are inferior. Obviously, the counterpoint to that is that men are superior. Even that wouldn't be sufficient for their position except that they seem to believe in the uniformity version of equality. Never mind the fact that they obviously know many women are not the same and so uniformity will never be possible. Uniformity can only exist in rights just as in lifestyle it can only exist in wage. The problem lies in the mistaken assumption that fairness is achieved by uniformity. It is, however, quite evident to anybody that spends even a moment of thought that that's not possible. And the problem is that chauvinists and feminists argue just as superficially. They argue that since everyone isn't the same everyone is entitled to do whatever they want, regulations be damned. The fairness is whatever happens. Their argument is basically might makes right and that the strongest or most deceptive or whatever should have whatever advantage they can obtain. This premise is just as absurd. The flaw of this premise is of course the one that's pursued shortsightedly by the uniformity set, and it goes round and round endlessly. The problem is, it doesn't need to. But neither side wants to hear the reality. Both sides want their extreme position. And their extreme position acknowledges one side and disacknowledges the other. The truth is that uniformity doesn't exist in interest and it doesn't exist in ability. Which is starkly different from suggesting that it doesn't exist in rights. And there's nothing wrong with everybody having different interests and abilities; this point agrees with the conservative mindset. It is important for everyone to have the same rights; this point agrees with the liberal mindset. These are not contradictory points. Each opposing side insists that they be seen as such. But I repeat myself. Equal rights are mandatory as is the freedom to choose. It's all very simple. It boils down to people have the right to choose whatever does not infringe upon the rights of others. In situations where the choice infringes upon the choices of others, the choice is the choice of more than one person. As such, one person cannot make it. This is, of course, starkly in contrast to centralization of authority. The current structure of government is ineffective for this purpose. The person affected should not be removed from the decision, and in our country- in our culture- unless they have the wealth to influence the decision, they are completely removed from the decision. However, them not being the only party affected, they obviously are not the only party to make the decision. I have no doubt many people would consider this suggestion overly complicated. Many would even feel that it contradicts itself, particularly those people on the extreme left or right. It should come as no surprise considering that they each (the left and right) both disacknowledge obvious truths that perpetuate their argument. I don't suggest we don't need authority over one another. I simply suggest that we need both and again with the- apparent- contradictions, we both need authority over one another and autonomy from one another. We are individuals and we are part of a whole. Refer to unity through division, but we are part of a whole, that whole being humanity or simply existence, because to disregard the other parts of existence, sentient and non-sentient, living and non-living, is a grave mistake. We are as much a part of them as we are of ourselves. If humanity does not cooperate with itself, which is only likely to ever be achieved by the process which I have just laid out, then they will destroy themselves. If they do not acknowledge their place in the whole, they will make the planet uninhabitable for themselves to say nothing of many, many other species. Humans will not kill the planet; the planet will kill them after they antagonize it. It's pure hubris to think otherwise on either score. If you treat your fellow man as the enemy, you make your fellow man the enemy. If you make your fellow man the enemy, you fight yourself. If you fight yourself, even if you win, you lose. Liberals need to stop trying to homogenize people. Differences are a good thing. Conservatives need to stop being hostile to everyone that doesn't appear like themselves. Difference is a good thing. And yes, I just connected them. They are the same. They arrived there by different points, and if you don't understand how that can happen, refer to what I have said in a previous heading with respect to opposites actually being the same and things that appear the same actually being opposite. Liberals and conservatives both hate difference. They just try to address it in different ways. One wishes to build a wall to keep them out and one wishes to enslave them. Can you tell me which one is which? And everybody who wants to put things in boxes, particularly prematurely, is guilty of this. You should not seek to put things in boxes except because there is an actual need to do so, not simply the desire to separate, to define. It is a good thing to understand things and understanding the properties of a thing is part of understanding a thing. It is easy to see how that might appear to be putting things in boxes. It doesn't actually go in the box until you cease to be able to identify the exception. Failure to be able to identify the exception is overgeneralization. Overgeneralization ultimately is simple: It is other than me and therefore generally less important. And if that appears to be overgeneralization to you, you're half right. Because of course there is an exception. There are those who overgeneralize and everything other than them is more important: the passives. And the fact that they are the minority does not mean that they aren't worthy of counting. However, again, refer to opposites being the same. Because the fact is that that which is outside of ourselves and our self are equal. They are simply not uniform. The other is no more and no less important. Could you exist in a vacuum? Would you be you? Psychologically, physically, would you be alive? Would you be dead? You exist at the pleasure of everything and everyone around you just as they exist at the pleasure of everything and everyone around them, of which you are a part. If you view those around you as unimportant and insignificant, if their lives are meaningless to you, if their trials are meaningless to you, why would they not view you the same? If everyone views everyone that way (because after all why wouldn't everyone view everyone the same?) what is the quality of your life? The quality of your life would only be as good as your security, right? Because in such a world people would take from you what they want if they could. Well let's follow that logic path a little further, shall we? How do you protect yourself if everyone wants to take what you have? Alliances, right? Unity through division. What is an alliance if it's not the agreement to cooperate? So the question then is why would you agree to cooperate with a tiny portion of humanity to give yourself the illusion of safety when you could agree to cooperate with the entirety of humanity to give yourself real safety? Answer: fear of the loss of autonomy. However, as implied and even stated previously, if you do not have autonomy, you do not have cooperation. They are interdependent. Most people would say they're mutually exclusive. They're not. They're completely intrinsic to each other. They are opposites that are the same (as apparent opposites often are). If all of this sounds cumbersome, it's not that hard. All that we're really talking about is not oversimplifying things. And people's tendency to oversimplify things is largely the result of expediency. And expediency is largely the result of emergency or hierarchy. We've already addressed what needs to be done with hierarchy. Humans of differing ability does not entitle them to have control over others in any kind of a direct sense. It goes without saying, that humans with inferior abilities also aren't entitled to control over others in any type of a direct sense. With respect to emergency, those situations tend to resolve themselves fairly effectively. When people aren't overly attached to a hierarchy, the emergency situations tend to resolve themselves, because the people that are confident that they have the necessary info to resolve the emergency will speak up. In fact, if you look at emergencies, the only ones that really, really go bad are the ones where people who have authority without knowledge make the decisions, rather than the people with the knowledge. The society that we live in, the people that lead in such situations are the people we most like to alienate and martyr. Just basing that on history- personal and global, modern and ancient. And the problem with that usually arises from insecurities on the part of the people who would be king. Indeed, the desire to be king is in itself an insecurity. If there was ever anything about human behavior that baffled me, it is the fact that humans routinely treat the weakest of people as the strongest and the strongest as the weakest. Bluff and bluster are seen as strength. Insecurity and endless consumption are seen as strength. They're flaws. They are weaknesses. They are insecurities and they should not be rewarded. But in most of the places I've been, they are. The greatest irony of this is that humans believe themselves above the other animals, but if this behavior isn't instinct, what is it? It certainly isn't logic. Nor is it intelligent. It's disruptive to self and society. They cut down the tall-growing wheat but they feed the choking weed. Human evolution is self-limiting. And a quick glance at history shows that the wisest, most insightful, are often quoted and almost never heeded.

To those who find this pretentious, I'm simply trying to share what I see and have found over the course of my lifetime that I see things most don't. I've given long thought and longer observation to the trends that I see before I ever came to a conclusion. And I say these things with the hope (and I use the word hope because I realize that it's likely in vain) that it might be of some benefit someday to someone. And because I am confident that my answers, while they may not be perfect, are (here's your confirmation of pretention, if you want it) better answers than most. They do not fail to observe obvious realities. They do not shy away from uncomfortable truths. They do not cling to the security of popular opinion, and they do fly in the face if it either. They are facts as much as gravity is a fact. Obvious, observable, completely recreatable. But hey, what do I know? I just figured this point might be relevant because it's one of those things that has been accepted by people where they didn't bother to consider the other side: the other side that's painfully obvious and somehow still missed. The poles routinely cannot see the other side. It's too far removed. Each of the poles has an element of truth and an element of falseness because they are seeing half of the equation as the whole thing. Each misses the variable that unifies. We call this a lurking variable, but this term implies that those that fail to see it are blameless. If you refuse to consider the other side, you will always miss the unifying variable, and further division, as it rests in the middle.

The Nature of Evil

The nature of evil is efficiency. As previously described apparent opposites have a great deal in common and so it is in this case. Evil is an extreme of efficiency, either high or low. Excess efficiency destroy autonomy. Insufficient efficiency destroys physical resources or wastes. Made concrete if you had a population starving the most "efficient" means of solving the problem would be to feed some of them to the others. Being wasteful with water in a desert because you control the water supply to impress those who do not? Same thing. Is the point clear enough?

The Nature of Things

I find it distressing how often people who clearly think themselves intelligent wish to "simplify things". Done correctly this is most certainly a worthy goal. Done incorrectly rather than yielding truth it yields what is above and below truth, lies. Many are the occasion I have seen someone try to reduce something to a simple noncompound (am element if you will) talking point and there in that word is the point. Who would doubt that water exists? Simplify water to hydrogen or oxygen and it ceases to be water. Even using hydrogen and oxygen but in incorrect ratio produces something that is decidedly, not water, like hydrogen peroxide. As with water so to anything not entirely simplistic in life, justice to name one, mercy to name another. Mercy not mere tolerance… with no sharp edge to be applied on the other side it is not mercy at all but impotence. Mercy applied only to friends is not mercy but favoritism. Mercy applied 100 percent of the time in spite of strength and some not being deserving of it, is not mercy but cowardice or apathy (depending on why). We have many words because life in neither entirely elements nor is it entirely compounds. It is an injustice to diminish the meaning of words or to attempt to strain the depth from them. It is folly to believe that that depth does not exist. The sample above is, I think, quite clear but I can do it for very nearly any word with accuracy and meaning and I think you can too for at the least a great many words. Practice honesty… diminish subterfuge, it will come. Lies diminish the understanding of both the liar and the listener.

A Lamentable Fact (Any Institution That is Dogmatic is Religious)

Related to the above and the abuse of word and meaning is this. The modern age wants a word to compartmentalize everything while simultaneously not knowing the proper meaning of said word. Describe your views to someone and they will wish to assign you one title after another. You can scarcely speak a sentence before you are summarized even though the very next sentence will summarize you differently. This will be your failing as you are "all over the place" rather than theirs for both failing to listen and to understand. Further, an idea which remotely resembles the idea of some dead person that your "listener" scarcely knows anything about will instantly be attributed to said dead person and so proceed back to compartmentalized "knowledge" of your position. This is what passes for discussion, learning, and debate these days in far too many circles. Ignorance incarnate wrapped in the guise of knowledge and learning. It should come as no great shock to anyone, by the way, that people of similar intellect from different ages see certain trends revisited. Truth has a habit of not changing much. That said be wary of throwing around concepts of plagiarism… no idea is new, now or then. They span existence and our ability to perceive it. Such is one of the many follies of intellectual property rights which was addressed previously in this writing.

Academia has a distressing tendency to create and entrench social injustice. The current talking point of institutional injustice is particularly telling when considering that most future leaders will have obtained higher education degrees in which they are taught that supposed minority groups cannot be bigots, among other things. Sociology professors teach their students that people in China live on 2 dollars a day and challenge their students to do the same. I premise that is clearly false to the fundamental point in numerous obvious ways (like 2 dollars gets them a lot more there/they have amenities and social structures not found here). The most likely effect of this in future leaders is quite obviously that they should not feel bad about the poor wages and living conditions of their soon to be subjects now or in the future. That doesn't even touch on the clear gating of alternate ideas and the people who have them being barred from higher education and consequently, perceived validity in the conversation… A point that renders a higher degree a citation as much as an achievement. That these things take place in the workplace is not better but less damning. When they occur in academia… well I find it quite ironic that people find me arrogant and them not. Much like literally now also means figuratively and truth now just means perception… The notion that there is no objective truth becomes even more interesting when weighted against the above gating and social construction I have just pointed out, does it not? When academia cannot tolerate alternate views and debate it is quite literally indoctrination not education and for the confused no they are not the same thing. Refer to argument on over/under-generalization. Water is comprised of hydrogen and oxygen and precise quantity and state of energy, in other state or composition, water it is not… for simple point of contrast drink some hydrogen peroxide some time (note I am not actually recommending you do this). Put bluntly academia is extraordinarily prone at this time to both over and under generalization. Balance this is not.

Science or the science minded at any rate is just as prone to bias as religious thinking. Bias can easily enter into the processes of the supposedly analytical thinking but generally does so by way of refutation: refuting. If a problem is complex, people will declare it true or false based less on whether or not the evidence is sufficiently compelling and more upon their personal biases. Declaring insufficient proofs as proofs and rejecting sufficient proofs as proofs are both sins easily demonstrable among the more analytical and science-minded individuals. The single most annoying demonstration of this fact is the declaration of all evidence of one's eyes as anecdotal, which would be fine but for the fact that they do this to unjustly dismiss, rendering all truths subject to a science-based study that will take years and funding should they choose to even pursue it. Because there's no bias in that, right? But the fact of the matter is, referring to previous points on the nature of exception and the fact that most people are astonishingly bad at recognizing exceptions because they look so similar. Refer to smart student/ slow student. Their behaviors express the same. The fact is, many people who act like analytical thinkers and would describe themselves as such are not. The single greatest value of scientific method is the acknowledgement that one must change one's position when new evidence is presented. One must be ready to change one's position. The problem is, few (even amongst those who consider themselves logical or analytical) will do that. I have contradicted PhDs on any number of subjects with points they cannot counter. I am 100% sure they are still teaching the same material. When they do change their material, it will not be because I countered their points. It will be because some other established source changed the criteria. This is credentialism. Credentialists are not logical. They're emotional. They hide behind the guise of analytical façade. They have positions in society which one is to expect suggests they are intellectual, logical. Such a conclusion is not logical, however. Such a conclusion is the position of a credentialist. People seek positions based not only on compatibility but any number of qualifiers of satisfaction, like social status. Am I saying no one in any position is in a position logically suited to them? No. Whether you declare what I'm saying here the exception or the rule, both exist. That is the very cornerstone of my premise. But science, like religion, is only as good as the people who practice it. Because those people come from the same pool, the distinction is almost irrelevant. Again: mirrors. 2 sides, same coin. Ultimately, both, even when practiced properly, are guilty of half-truths. Science because it never allows for enough relevant facts, religion because it has no use for them. By way of proof consider science's widely accepted notion that time is relative. The only accurate inference that can be made on that equation is that time keeping devices are subject to gravity whether that be a clock or cesium and that should be assumed. The conclusion is absurd and calls correlation causation. As I said science is no less guilty of this behavior. Time it is worth noting is a construct, like numbers. They do not exist except as a framework for us to communicate about a thing that does exist in the natural universe. Time is chronology or to be clearer, cause/effect/cause. That is all.

You will find apparent overlap within these pages. This is both accidental and by design. The way I see these issues is intrinsically interconnected with certain points being either key to discussing the whole issue or keys to solution. This is the source of intentional overlap. I should point out that the overlap is not really repetition however. Different facets of the various points are addressed at different times, again in an attempt to address these issues. The scope of what I am speaking of is, of course, quite large and I have put it as concisely as I believe it can be put while meaningfully addressing the facets thereof.

I hope to wrap things up in this last chapter and give some thoughts on underlying causes of what I see to be problems as well as some general suggestions as to solutions.

I would like to present an argument here for equal pay. No, not that tired old line that is misrepresentative that the more dishonest feminists trot out there. I am not speaking of the notion of equal pay for equal work. It doesn't happen and it can't happen and I will speak to that point among others here. I mean paying all people exactly the same share of our resources as a people. The reasons for this are many and they are simple.

 Under this thing we call capitalism we assign differential values to people based upon how much money they can supposedly generate. The fact is that this is a lie. People manipulate and inflate their supposed value and thereby justify their increased worth. At best this is redistribution of value. At worst it is an outright lie, giving apparent value to an occupation that actually has none. It is not a coincidence that the most "valueless" occupations in the country and indeed the world are the ones that actually provide the goods and services that we seek to purchase. This is consistent and it is wrong. One might gather from my point so far that white collar positions from managers to CEOs have no value. This is, on the whole not true. What is true is that they do not have more value than the people who actually make the goods or provide the services that we pay for. An argument has been presented that that is due to scarcity. It is not due to scarcity or put another way that scarcity is artificial. An argument has been made that it is due to meritocracy. These people are often not superior on any number of objective measures but more importantly no person warrants more for being born gifted or less for being born with few gifts. Indeed, that smacks of injustice right on its face. Not to mention the fact that any person can be made productive should society wish to consider rather than discard people and discarding people is exactly what is being done. If it is not our problem, we are not a society. If we are not a society we have no unity and no laws, only hurdles to overcome and lies to spin to justify them. We seek ways to disqualify people from their needs rather than how to qualify them. We do this because under our system people are grossly disproportionately rewarded and this means resources are scarcer than they are or should be, artificial scarcity is the order of the day and everyone remaining has to compete still more with their fellow man looks to them as an enemy rather than a friend. This is no way to build unity and cooperation. Then there is the productivity argument. Some claim we need to do this for sake of productivity. What they mean is profit, another word for theft. As far as productivity is concerned we have massive amounts of automation. In every industry a handful of people can provide the goods asked for by hundreds and even thousands of people. The fact is we have enough people to shorten work weeks and enough money to increase wages and still easily meet productivity needs to say nothing of hiring more people and increasing vacation. The kind of productivity we pursue is the kind that makes machines of people at the bottom and the top. The bottom are slave to the top. The top are slave to their greed and ambition. The fact is if we insist on capitalism our productivity is too good. It is a key component in the displacement of large numbers of people and the consequent crime and incarceration that follows and it is slated to get worse. It does every year with another job vanishing to automation but once AI is perfected this can only spike astronomically. We hear claims that it will right itself and new industries will emerge with no tangible suggestion of what those will be and whether they will cover the number of people who have been discarded. These vague promises are made because the people making them are ok and will continue to be ok not because they are true. The standard of living and the wage for most Americans has steadily fallen even while minimum wage has grown. It isn't keeping pace with basic needs to say nothing of allowing us all to share in the windfall of the society we all live in and help make possible. If we insist on hierarchy then the people at the top need to have better answers, real answers, as to the costs and solutions for the new techs that are being produced and implemented. That they don't, speaks volumes about the nature of our relationship. We cannot have this conversation without considering what money is and isn't. Money is our representation to access to our shared resources across the planet in general terms. Those resources are finite and nothing demonstrates this point better than land. Land is that resource necessary for a person to even approach being self-sufficient and there simply is not enough of it to go around for everyone to be self-sufficient. There is enough of it for us to cooperate and all have enough, however. Failing that we would need to compete for it. We have all agreed in various ways that competing for it is not an option. The purpose of laws and societies is, at its heart, cooperation though that is achieved more often than not by a concept I refer to as unity by division. If we are to cooperate we must share those finite resources. We best share those finite resources with a standardized wage across the board and basic supply and demand. Via this method no one has the best of *everything*… and no one has the worst of everything. Do not confuse this with no one has the best of *anything*… or the worst. Under such a system most would opt for a good average across the board. Some would either want or need the best of something however and would be able to get it… at the cost of having less of something else. Now for the vast majority of us this is nothing new. Most of us either have average or scrimp and save for some special something. Here we address three things. It removes artificial manipulations on the price of goods and services, something obviously relevant to all. It ensures that no one has the worst of everything, as no one deserves that. It ensures that no one has the best of everything, as no one deserves that either. This does require investment in the larger community over the smaller one. It is not about heritability of wealthy and growing personal wealth but enriching society and everyone reaping the rewards from that. Now I understand that there is potential for corruption and abuse in such a situation. I understand the fear that some will hoard or bribe or strongarm to get more than their due. We would collectively have to be alert for that and courageous enough to stop it should it happen. That said can you say it isn't already happening in this system that that argument is intended to defend? Who would perpetrate this fraud? The accountants and the bureaucrats would cook the books misrepresenting what is and is not available and siphoning more of the nice things to themselves you say? Too late I say. The policymakers and CEOs would make rules that differentially favor themselves you say? They already are I say. What then is the difference between what you fear and what you have? The difference is that the system you have does it shamelessly. It is literally part of the rules not a violation of them. This does not make capitalism better. It makes it so much worse. This system I propose could be exploited and requires vigilance and courage of its people, yes. The system I propose we abolish fails even when, and especially because, it succeeded. You do not fix injustice by declaring it just. Capitalism and everything it has produced is spin. Spin is a pretty lie being substituted for an ugly truth. Truth does exist and while it sometimes matches perception it is not synonymous with it. There is no greater spin than the words "your truth". This brings us to generalization and the correct and incorrect applications of which. This is the primary reason people often believe in either objectivity without subjectivity or subjectivity without objectivity when each inseparably depends upon the other for truth.

Pay is not the reason for peoples' productivity anyway. It is nothing more than perverse incentive steering peoples' perception of the value of certain professions or more accurately, people since those values are artificial.

People are most productive when they do a job they believe in and enjoy and when they are treated well. Pay conflates and in some cases defines their sense of self-worth which is further reinforced by society under capitalist systems which suggest that the people at the bottom are worthy of contempt and disposable/worthless and the people at the top are worthy of respect and valuable. The social cost of this is catastrophic. Society actually has the nerve to suggest that the poor have an inflated sense of entitlement for seeking *basic needs* while the wealthy are somehow deserving of the fruit of thousands of laborers' efforts. The justification? Intelligence. Intelligence or any other gifts doesn't entitle you to more. It only makes you capable of taking more and so snowballs. This is not cooperation but competition and opening the doors to competition dissolves the rules of "fair play" as one then must use what one has available for the natural right to survive. Furthermore, there is nothing intelligent about redistribution. It is low and simple and short-term thinking. Your average 3-year-old knows exactly how to do it and one of the first things we seek to teach them is sharing. Speaking of redistribution, it is a common narrative that people are seeking to redistribute wealth when they tax the wealthy or put social programs in place etc. This is classic goalpost moving. The redistribution occurred before that when the wealthy siphoned the fruits of the laborers efforts to themselves. You can call the correction of redistribution, redistribution as well but you are either being disingenuous in terms of the guilty party or disingenuous in the word choice and implication. Half-truths are better known as lies.

There are myriad things people provide to society that go unpaid but that society wants and even cannot live without.

If the focus is primarily on wealth generation (it is) there are too few thinking long term or big picture. There are too few thinking about consequences and opportunity costs (the loss of great ideas not focused on profit). Worse than these, there are even fewer who care when someone does take to time to think. Fewer who listen or support. If money is the primary motivator society at large can only lose.

Owners cannot be trusted to pay fair wages. Free market isn't free and is utterly manipulatable and manipulated. The very metrics and definitions contorted with respect to fair wage are altered at the convenience of the payor. On the other side, unions cannot be trusted to fight for workers. Union bosses are easily bribed and unions are increasingly dismantled and demonized which, while not entirely unfair is comical in light of the behavior of the people doing the demonizing. What is the point here? Clearly people cannot be trusted to pay a fair wage based upon market forces or otherwise. Does that mean there is no solution? No. It means everybody that comes into this world is just as deserving of its resources as everyone else. Everyone should receive the same wage. This is one of a thousand arguments that point in the same direction. Each is moral and reasonable. All of them put together are quite the body of evidence to dismiss especially with casual handwaving like "It's already been tried". Who cares if it was tried once or a thousand times unsuccessfully? What we are doing now fails even as it succeeds.

Furthermore, ask yourself, or better yet, ask history, how many attempts have been necessary for a thing of worth to move forward? Furthermore, ask yourself if the reason for the failure is deliberate sabotage on the part of some, not all, of those most affected? Do I want a witch hunt? Certainly not, but how naïve would a person have to be to believe that an idea such as this would be appealing to at least some of the most powerful people in the world? Now before you get disheartened, how do you suppose they come by that power? At the end of the day their power comes from you and me. I would be happy to see them having a *part* in plotting our course… presuming they are amongst, not over us while they do it. Their position does not only call them into question, it insulates them from the effects of their decisions while we face them daily. There are those that say such a system does not give everyone a voice? Do you feel heard now? Would we, all of us, vote on every issue? Certainly not, just as we do not now. We have never in this country had a democracy but a republic. We vote on officials and that need not change but for one suggestion on my part. Perhaps we should make tests for these positions and only vote on those who pass the tests. Let these tests not be a measure of education but ability. And let ability mean all of the qualifications of office which means, among others, an eye for the community and the individual, the present and the future, the past is there to learn from not to change, things made possible when profit is not as important as sustainability. Endless growth is simply a lie. It is not now nor was it ever possible. Balance is though. In fact, given time and one way or the other everything will always balance. You see it now with countering polarizations but that is neither necessary nor stable. It is explosive.

Community is desirable but communal property is absurd but private property is the most ageist thing imaginable. The whole world is owned before you arrive and your elders choose which scraps to give you. Clearly communal property isn't such a strange idea. Alternately, with our standardized wage, we all rent real goods, a very useful solution to a standardized wage whose purpose is to not have one person become wealthier than the other. We already have the infrastructure for it.

Let's go one further. Do you suppose many people under capitalism select a job based upon wage? Never mind the whole economic manipulation here. Let's just focus on the perverse incentive. You enjoy... basket weaving. You are good at basket weaving. But you want the best living you can manage; you just can't help yourself. Also, you want the respect of your peers. And since basket weaving doesn't pay well that isn't going to happen is it? We need basket weavers (not literally basket weavers, substitute low paying job x) and you want to be one and would make a good one, but instead you make an inadequate banker because you don't love it and you aren't great at it, but you pulled a string or two. Not only is this not the market economy you imagine it is destructive to every element of most people's lives.

Oh, and there are numerous examples of successful socialism.... In fact, the biggest failure was before that the biggest success. China failed because it failed to anticipate the effect of plenty on its population leading to a situation that they then overreacted to with draconian laws. This is to completely ignore any number of successful largely socialist countries, the fact that literally every nation has large amounts of socialism by necessity and design, and that none of that means it can't work or shouldn't be perfected.

The question is a simple one if you want to determine how society should, no must be structured. Who does the world belong to? The world and its resources are finite. Only a fool would argue against that fact. So, we know that we must come to terms with how those resources should be divided. Capitalism is a competitive system which should not be mistaken for a meritorious or just system. As a competitive system the notion is that people, at the end of the day, take what they can get. This is not a system of government. The only purpose government can serve in such a scenario is to yield advantage for one group or another to claim more than they could claim themselves were there no government at all. This is not an argument that there should be no government. It is only an observation that the closer to pure capitalism you are the more you don't actually have a government. You have a fiefdom. And this is formed for purposes of being able to amass more than you could do individually. This means that even the most selfish system acknowledges the need for cooperation with the only argument being the scale that cooperation takes. It is long past time for us to acknowledge that we live in one world and we share the resources of that one world. We are one family, albeit a highly dysfunctional one. It is time to come together as a people. No more unity through division, no more arrogance, no more hollow pride, no more greed. Can we do this? Yes, we can. Will it be easy? No, it will not. The hardest part will be being honest with ourselves about our merits and our flaws. It will be difficult to admit where we are selfish not because of need but because of greed and insecurity. It will be difficult to look at the flaws of our fellow man and ask how we can help rather than how we can discard them to eliminate our competitors, because they are not our competitors. It will be difficult to work and think at our own ability and to accept that others too work at their ability and that this does not entitle some of us to more or less just as your brother or sister does not receive a lesser room or lesser food. Greater ability should come with greater responsibility, not lesser. If you think it does now you ignore that a poorer person will receive a greater sentence with less deliberation. Yes. It will be difficult to correct this trend. There is a great deal that needs to change and it needs to change in a great many people but many hands make light work. Change it in yourself and share the idea with others. This is the only way to accomplish what needs to happen. One person, regardless of resources, abilities, or political power cannot fix the state that we find ourselves in. No one can make either us or our peers behave this way. We make this happen by seeing the truth of it and sharing it and living it. Let me use a simple and, relative to what I speak of, crass, example to support my point. Marijuana was unnecessarily, unconscionably illegal for many years. Some objected to the illegality based upon a desire to use it, some based upon the injustice of our government telling us we cannot consume a product that not only has various potential health benefits but is an issue of personal consumption without harm to others, but for its illegality. That product is beginning to become legal, in no small part due to the fact the people simply would not accept the injustice. The people spoke and in spite of tremendous resistance they were heard. Democracy was practiced… entirely outside of the courtroom and the drafting of laws. It was not easy. It was not fast. But it changed and continues to change how things are done. It was a step in the right direction. Do we care, as a people, more about marijuana than we do about a just and cooperative society? Do not look to your left or right. I am asking you, dear reader, do you care more about a sundry than you do about a just and cooperative society? Is a pothead, and I use the term only to point out that it was a term of disparagement not because that is how I feel, more motivated to see social change than all those who disparaged them? I should take this moment to point out that I do not smoke marijuana or cigarettes for that matter, not because there is anything wrong with doing so. I judge the product not for me. I do not judge the people who do find it to their tastes lesser for doing so. It seems to me that all this competition has fostered a desire to find fault with a person's character from things that have nothing to do with character and worse, to discard people for a supposed flaw of character rather than to seek to either understand them or help them improve, should that be what truly is warranted. I speak of innumerable ills in these pages but I do not judge the people who commit them. I speak of what I see and how it might be done better and why. I understand we are differently gifted and that not everyone is capable of anything and certainly not everything, that anyone else is of necessity. This does not mean we must also stay exactly as we are. Every one of us is capable of growth in both body and mind. This is the essence of what I ask of us as a people. You can refuse. There is nothing I or anyone can do to make you or I behave as I suggest we should. Perhaps you will be the very last to agree that cooperation is vital to both our survival and wellbeing as a species. I say better late than never. I will not pretend that sooner would not be better of course. The fact is I could be ignored entirely. In which case the last human standing on the ashes of our inevitable destruction, one that we committed upon ourselves, or one from a natural disaster that had we cooperated might have been averted, or simply one from having exhausted the resources of our planet and failed to colonize another, maybe that very last one will finally understand the value of the thing that they didn't know they had, until it was gone.

Who deserves to be rich? Who deserves to be poor? I say no one for both. If you say otherwise what are the criteria? Is it employment? Then society is obligated to provide not only jobs but adequate paying ones? Don't agree? Then why must I follow your laws that do not serve me? Is it higher employment and minimum wage is not intended for subsistence at least? Then why is it called minimum? What would society look like without all of the minimum wage jobs? They don't provide subsistence and so everyone should be looking for better. So, we don't need any of those services, right? We don't need people to stock shelves. Who needs to buy things, right? We don't need clerks for the same reason. We don't need service people at all, right? And everyone finds all this automation both gratifying and productive and useful, right? Or maybe we find it dehumanizing and poor service with closed ended interaction, robbing customers of even a thin pretense of choice. We don't need most any labor job in fact because the aim of business is to reduce all of it to minimum wage by destroying unions and government employment and the civilian payors in most cases pay the lowest possible… minimum wage. Do they dial back their prices while they dial back their wage? Of course not, right? Those go up. That's just inflation. So, they understand that while they are shorting the employees wage then don't they. That is the original redistribution right there. So, I repeat, who deserves to be rich and who deserves to be poor and based upon what? Is it free market that determines this? Don't be absurd. We do not have a free market for many, many reasons and if we did it still wouldn't begin to create reasonable pay. Not only that but violence is more than fair under the premises of free market. Why? Competition doesn't have rules or it isn't free market. Also, the very simple fact is there are a number of pure essentials and that fact means free market is not free. It is not want but NEED that dictates nearly every expenditure of the poor. The price of those needs just so happens to fully consume the wages of those at the bottom… and always will… in competitive systems.

Capitalism incentivizes getting over. At best it just necessitates people being a little creative about it or doing it in ways not monitored. There is no way to monitor every way to get over, new ones will just be invented as you go. Look around. That said, if we are a cooperative, so what if some people are industrious and some people aren't, assuming we all have what we need. And if we don't have what we need watch how fast people get industrious. Necessity is not only the mother of invention, it is the mother of drive. But perpetual drive and differential rewards only break people down… try it with a machine devoid of feelings if you need proof. Use one heavily and give it little to no maintenance. What do you suppose happens? The maintenance is wage and benefit package. The labor is obviously the labor. Speaking of machines, we are incredibly automated and getting more automated every day. Why is it even debatable that we do not need people to be maximally productive? Other than an obsessive need for ever more control and wealth on the part of our supposed elites I mean? It is worth clarifying a point. Competition still requires cooperation. The tribalism or small group cooperation you see is the acknowledgement of a simple truth. It cannot be done alone. Maximization requires cooperation. So why then not maximize cooperation? The answer is simple and obvious. They do not want to maximize for everyone. Their ideal is to maximize only for themselves and as few as is absolutely necessary to achieve their ends. Indeed, many who follow this path not only want to maximize for themselves. They have an active and deliberate stance on minimizing for many others. It is not merely byproduct and happenstance. They literally want certain others to have little or nothing and will often reduce their own gains to some degree to make sure that others have less. They wish to tear others down. This particular camp is particularly quick at taking the truth, turning it inside out, and uttering it in challenge to their opposition. It is a fast, easy, and, all too often, effective lie in addition to being one that requires little intellect or imagination. Their actions give them game away naturally. They seek to deny tremendous numbers of people opportunity, comfort, and happiness because they do not like them for being different from themselves. To them the poor deserve to be poor and so it goes for every other group that they dislike with them always deserving whatever ill might befall them, while those they relate to deserve ever more. Do not confuse this for all the various -isms. It is not, barring perhaps narcissism. They simply detest difference. Frankly these people are often objectivists. I suspect many of them do not understand these differences and so fear them. Naturally they seek to insulate to avoid that which they fear and that entrenches their fear and distaste. Perhaps this is their nature but it is also the product of hundreds, perhaps thousands, of years of nurture in which different has been conditioned to equate with bad rather than the more optimistic good or the more realistic, simply different, situationally better or worse. This because of generations of ethnic pride, and nationalistic pride, and religious pride and every other false unification (unity through division) you can imagine. Is this the way it has to be? No. Will it take hundreds of years to fix? No. Will it be fixed instantly? No. Will it be fixed effortlessly? No. We are born capable of deciphering differences. We are not born seeing those differences as negatives. Every single generation has the potential to be born and raised without this hateful view of others. Conflict occurs and will continue to occur for all time. It needs to be understood and it needs to be resolved in a timely and just manner. This is where generalizations on people go right or go wrong. How do they go wrong? Overgeneralization or undergeneralization because one or more parties do not understand the other or the means or reason for a resolution or the resolution, no matter how well understood is not fair. One of the gravest flaws here is hierarchy. The parties have no input, due to peers, authority figures, or laws, in their punishment. Our court system at present does not even pretend to try to understand where an accused person is coming from. Circumstances are more than enough to convict a poor person but never enough to exonerate them. One element of addressing this is to resolve the resource disparity… not piecemeal as is seen in efforts today. Across the board, else all you do is shift who is affected. Nothing about that supposed solution has anything to do with justice. No one deserves such treatment and this is tacitly acknowledged when people argue that the people supposedly most effected don't deserve it.

Relativism/objectivism and nature/nurture argument both are true in both cases. You can for instance, raise a cat amongst dogs. That cat has an excellent chance of acting like a dog. It is still a cat however. Nothing changes that. It is proof positive of nurture. It is equally proof positive of nature. Nature influences nurture and nurture influences nature. People argue for one side or the other all day and it is ludicrous and incredibly biased. Situationally a single situation might favor one over the other, but both are present always in all things and it is plain to see that it is… if your focus is not one sided. The truth is that these things, like everything else, being present to varying degrees in all things, prove that both apply all the time. Different things are susceptible to different amounts of stress yielding different, but predictable, results. Nature determines how susceptible you are to your environment, for example, and also what you add to that environment, in part. This links rather neatly with the objective in most cases (but not all). A cat is objectively a cat and can only do what a cat can do, for instance. The people favoring the concrete and objective might make such an argument and then stop there, declaring that is reality. They would of course be ignoring that one of the things that a cat can do is mimic a dog. A thing that the odds are astronomically against, unless said cat was raised among, or more likely, by dogs. This is nurture for certain and also shows the relativistic elements that must be considered when one declares an objective truth. Degree of generalization makes a great deal of difference. So much so in fact that people who would point to this scenario might falsely claim that there is no truth or objectivity because a cat can act like a dog and that relativism is the only truth and so there is no truth. The irony would of course be lost on them since that statement is an objective declaration of truth in its own right even while being self-negating and false. Relativists recognize that things depend but are overwhelmed and lose sight of the concrete bits that produces. They in short, undergeneralize. They cannot see pattern in the minutia. Objectivists see a simple pattern and ignore the intricacies. Their simple pattern is often wrong. The greater pattern is more correct but the details are lost on them. They overgeneralize. There is a correct balance to be had and where it lies… is relative to the thing and absolute. If this is a contradiction to your eyes consider which of the above you are.

There is an apparent self-negation that is not. Everything has a rule. Everything also has an exception. An exception resembles a rule but is its apparent negation. It exists because it is in fact a subtle but critical alteration of the base rule. In other words, the rule is a reasonable generalization but like all generalizations fails to capture the full sum, the outliers if you will. The exception is capable of capturing these. That there is no exception to every rule having exception is because the "rule" of exceptions is not a rule but an exception. The rule defines rules, the exception defines exceptions. There is no paradox nor any hole in the reasoning.

Poor people should move out of these small towns, right? So they can sell their land cheap to wealthy people who will use it for a vacation home for its pastoral beauty while they build yet another urban sprawl to exploit people and drain their wealth… so that they can what? Buy another pastoral vacation home. Who are they exploiting? Why, the same people that they bought out to move to the city to find poor jobs and high rent of course. Please explain to me how it is not a grave concern of our society that people, most people, live in tiny apartments with sky high rent while some people own literally hundreds of homes? How is it not of grave concern that gentrification removes affordable housing and raises cost of living in every other way while not raising the wage of the native inhabitants? Where exactly are poor people supposed to go when affordable housing is bought out from under them and, far too often, then rented to them for more than they would have paid had they bought it. Before you say, well then they should have bought it, do you believe that they could have outbid? Of course not. Had they outbid would it have remained affordable? Of course not.

Qualifying for a thing under capitalism is about glad handing, name dropping, and credentialism which should not be confused with actual qualification. Socialism can, should, and usually does use testing. That is far closer to meritocracy than what capitalism uses. Some people fear that under socialism people will not be productive. The truth is we already have that under capitalism in great doses with few doing the lion's share, generally without recognition, often with criticism and almost never with reward. We do not promote hard working competent people. They are too valuable in that capacity. We promote busy bodies who politic and weren't doing any work in the first place. They are no loss to their former position and if not of value in their new one at least their boss knows they like them, right? And perhaps a bit of security for the boss comes from their good will. Is that the meritocracy people speak of? Because that is what I see in most industry. This behavior will not vanish overnight under socialism but it also need not be rewarded. It is the order of the day under capitalism. What else can you expect if competing for survival and acceptance is the order of the day but small group tenuous cohesion, tribalism if you like.

If you do not take from takers and give to givers, givers will have nothing left to give and takers will have nothing left to take. Taking from takers and giving to givers is part of the balance of things, should you wish to argue that takers must take as that is their nature and givers must give as that is theirs. True, but takers do not have to take from givers and givers do not have to give to takers.

If you are observant you will note most people's perception of intelligence not their own degrades the moment someone disagrees with them. You will further note that these same people will often, usually even, suggest that said intelligence is overopinionated and overbearing. Ironic is it not? This is the essence of ad hominem attack of course but subtle and so easily missed. They do not call you a jerk when they cannot counter your argument they instead claim you are inflexible because they failed to move you with a weak argument. This often goes further still. Hurt feelings when confronted with facts means the fact teller is aggressive, overbearing, and rude, ergo, wrong… because feelings trump facts for these people as well. The brighter you are the more you will encounter this conflict unless of course you are less about truth and more about manipulation. In that case you will know the truth but tell what is desired in order to get the desired results. This is the essence of sociopathy. Ironic is it not that no small body of the populace essentially insists on it from the intelligent? Perhaps it would be advisable that the populace at large gets comfortable with thinking about and discussing things that heretofore have been so sensitive for them that honest conversation was impossible. This starts with learning to recognize what those topics are and how you do react to them. Or we can encourage manipulation and echo chamber encouraged division until we are so polar we cannot possibly have rational discourse and must agree to disagree right up until the slightest thing is grounds for war. That is the path folks. It isn't prognostication. It is simple cause and effect. Incidentally, bright people, being smarter than typical, of necessity have observations others do not. Very unintelligent people do too. If you encounter someone that disagrees with everyone or you are one of these, one of the two is the case. It is not so hard to decipher which, if you are honest with yourself. If the smarter one is the one you encountered you really should try to hear what is being said, uncomfortable as it almost certainly will be.

Let's be clear on something. Diversity, real diversity is nature not nurture. We are all born with different strengths and weaknesses. If your diversity is nurture, as is the case with artificial criteria such as we find in identity politics, it is not diversity at all. It is in fact exactly the thing that you claim to be against, prejudice and discrimination. Overgeneralization in a word. It reinforces roles. Even if it strives to create new ones it still is creating roles, not eliminating them. It is conformity.

It is no accident that the middle class feel sympathy for the wealthy and resent the poor. It is however misguided. A poor person works, makes little money, pays little in taxes. They work absurd overtime and make adequate money, middle class money, and pay middle class taxes. This is painful on both counts, hours and take home. The connection becomes make good money pay bad taxes. And for them it is true be they overtime working middleclass or 40-hour middle class. The presumption, which is absolutely led, is that wealthy people pay even greater percentage in taxes. They do not, due to various loopholes, shelters, deductibles etc. Even if they did it's hardly apples to apples as the break point for a comfortable living did not change. It is set at middle, arguably middle high income. But the subsequent perception is that the poor are freeloading, completely disregarding the fact that they have nothing to give and that the reason is because there is redistribution right out of the gate via the wealthy siphoning the value of the poor into their own (the wealthy) income and lifestyle. There is a parasite in this system. It is not at the bottom. The bottom is your keystone species doing most of the work for next to no reward. The top is the parasite and it has grown fat and bloated indeed. Only a parasite would eat so much (of the wealth) that it threatens to kill its host. This more than anything is why automation and artificial intelligence are being invested in so heavily. All manner of obvious logic problems present to argue against it in an environment where everyone is obligated to work for their daily bread. The wealthy are replacing workers everywhere. How are the obviously necessary for such a future, social programs, coming along? Or are the poor not supposed to be around for that eventuality? If you think my vision is too dark let me ask you this. Dissolving social programs but buying our police force armored vehicles. What does that say to you? And anyone speaking of this from the position of the poor is fomenting class warfare but the other way it is just business as usual. In fairness I suppose you couldn't call business as usual class warfare. Slaughter and slavery fits better. Because only one side is shooting. Make no mistake the wealthy, intentionally or unintentionally, have wronged the poor but equality is all I ask and frankly, should it ever come to pass, a moderate lifestyle might well feel like punishment, for a time to the wealthiest among us, much like exercise feels absolutely awful to one who is highly sedentary but ultimately, is a boon.

A curious phenomenon creeps up with regard to, among other things, socialism. People suddenly develop an inability to see a lie. The reason for this, I believe, is a deep commitment to the notion that socialism is itself a lie. In other words, bias makes many unable to see that the lie might rest elsewhere. For instance, there are countries that identify as socialist but, fairly plainly, fit another description better like, off the top of my head, fascist. They only say they are socialist because it sounds better. Much like how Walmart recently announced a $1,000 bonus for its employees but went very light on the details. The implication is they have been very generous and they hope to gain great good will to match that implication. When in fact, they have been frugal with the bonus, it being limited to a very small portion of their staff and more frugal still on honesty. They are trying to steal goodwill with manipulation of the truth. A half-truth, especially one made knowingly and willfully, is a lie. The same applies to countries around the world claiming policies that they don't really follow but for a small portion of the populace. It should be clear how this applies to false claims of socialism at this point but it should also make one think about the implications of justice and upward mobility in the US and capitalism in general. How does one obtain a free market when everything is owned before you are born? How does that market stay free when someone at some point will gain advantage? How does a free market prevent selective cooperation, alternately called collusion and monopoly, when no one is responsible for it and everyone (supposedly) is already competing to the extent of their abilities. This desire to see humans with differences as not human has to stop, at all levels. There is room for us all, but only if we cooperate and that, only if we open communication. We must make rules, but we must all agree to them, and we must all understand how and why. Does this sound farfetched? We have the infrastructure already; it is simply being used to foment division and discord. Supply and demand is essential with limited resources. It does not stem from a free market manipulation of such, however. It comes from absolute values and rationing (sharing) those limited resources in a fair and productive way. Is this something that requires diligence. Of course it is. The argument that we cannot do it this way and so should freely allow manipulation is patently absurd though. That idea is killing for peace or intercourse for virginity. It is clearly self-negating. That such a line has been accepted over and over again is a lack of thought being applied to the words and nothing more. There are many who would call themselves right wing who would also claim to hate relativism… and propagate it by these exact methods. Both sides make these absurd arguments 180 degrees from truth. This must stop. Honesty starts with examining things on equal footing. What does this side have AND what do they not? What does the other side have AND what do they not. Why do they have it and why not? Should they have it or should they not? Should anyone? If so under what circumstances and why? Far too many people only ask one fragment of one of these questions and decide that they are now in a position to fairly judge others and this list is not remotely comprehensive. Better still, level the wage and we don't have to ask any of it. As it pertains to resources there is only one answer however. The world belongs to us all and to none of us. The civil answer then is to share it. There is no such thing as merit determining who is entitled to live and if you make it so you declare war, based upon natural right to survive. Natural right does not respect social rules, nor should it. If you invoke it on your fellow man you have waived your right to establish rules, whose purpose are cooperation. This, dear reader, is why there is a sentiment that rules are made to be broken. They are not, except when competition is the order of the day and like it or not most know this innately even if they cannot well articulate it.

A certain segment of the population likes to suggest that a person cannot consider a thing if it does not pertain to them. This statement is generally true. However, the extrapolation they make on this is far from truth, indeed. A person can relate to a thing that they do not currently experience by generalizing to the correct extent. What am I speaking of before I continue? Both political parties, under different headings, suggest you cannot know the experiences of others or relate with them. You cannot know what it is like, they claim. The left does this with all identity politics save one. The right does it with that other one. Every one of us has ample examples in our personal lives of not being heard, of being oppressed, of being undervalued, or simply of feeling out of place. We all have at least momentarily held advantage as well. The notion that we cannot generalize those experiences to our own lives and the lives of others is unconscionable for two reasons. It denies us the tool of experiential learning, which is fundamental to any living thing and especially something with a developed brain. Additionally, it denies us the utility and application of empathy. The very thing these people claim is lacking is the thing they try to remove from us. I will repeat here, and many more times, of necessity, that generalization can be done correctly and in so doing is the basis of understanding and communication, or incorrectly, either over or under generalizing, at which point it obfuscates truth, either deliberately or accidentally, and destroys the ability to communicate. Identity politics and class both do this. I divide class from identity politics in this case for one reason. The left is conspicuously silent, by and large, on the problems of class, choosing to make the problem about everything else and so grow a divide there. The right, in general does not focus on these other things but very much wishes to keep and deepen the divisions caused by class. Both excuse inequality at its most significant juncture at this time. To be clear its most significant juncture is access to resources, the source of wealth, the class being determined from this. They are both overwhelmingly okay with the existence of poverty, only differing on whether it is easier to control the poor by granting access to basic needs, at subsistence levels, of course, which forestalls the more violent actions on the part of the poor and others but does nothing to address the fact that poverty exists and is maintained, or through them being desperately beholden/homeless and riotous. In essence they both want the poor treated like children. One home is authoritarian one is permissive. Neither treats them as equals, else they would not be poor.

The simple truth is that profit is theft and business is crime at best and war, worse and more likely. Whether you know this or don't, consider the position of business as it pertains to their customers. Trick, lies, manipulations, feints are just the most common and supposedly above-board tactics. How about their employees? They treat them poorly at most businesses, worse than they need to beyond a shadow of doubt. They pay them less than they should and less than they can afford. They treat them as disposable in most cases, as bad as machines or worse, considering few people have ever discarded a machine or tool that works well for its purpose because they just plain dislike it. I can go on but I want to pause here to observe a curiosity. Business pays employees and so believes they are in charge of employees. Customers pay business and still business clearly believes it is in charge of this relationship as well. Don't agree? How many customers want to speak to a machine rather than an operator? Just one of a million examples. Business relationships with competitors is war followed by alliance, which we call collusion and is quite common. What isn't common is the degree to which it is prosecuted. Of course, it isn't. They know the supply line, who will enforce it and how strictly. If it is too strict, wheels will be greased not just to get around the who of it but to make it ok. Again, don't see it? What would and should have been considered bribery is now speech. Please explain to me how speech remains free when you have to pay for it with cash and the person with the most cash gets the most say, hmm? The thing is this isn't capitalism gone wrong. This is what it looks like when someone wins the game. So, we either play a game where competition is the order of the day and the rules are so stacked that not only can very few have any real chance but those few also literally get to change the rules as they go along… or we could reset the game… and while we are at it we refine the rules with an eye to the broken ones from the game we just played. This isn't really the choice of course. The real choice is do we agree to reset the game or does it happen when all alternatives have been exhausted? Either way it will happen, sooner or later. Or do you see any indication of the takers letting up any time soon?

It is true that we can't hold a person trying to claw their way out of poverty too accountable. And that people want to generalize this pattern all the way up the grade is clear as well. Else we would use the word greed rather than ambition more often. The thing is, if everyone has an even stake from the start none of that fighting for survival and endless justification of wrongdoing has any merit any longer does it?

Humans cannot claim amorality. A human's behavior is either moral or immoral. The reason? Humans have feelings. Humans have reason. When you couple these as they are in humans the result is either moral or immoral behavior. It is easy and common to over or undergeneralize this like so many other things but this statement, made at the level I am making it is true. One particular sinkhole clouding what is or is not moral is religion which claims moral authority but changes the rules to suit its members or increase recruiting. Morality depends upon all variables of the situation that is being judged moral or immoral not on the situation of its membership. The fact is religion is not only not a moral authority except on the most general things and then only in the most general ways, it is unity through division. Religion can only divide; morality however can provide unity. There are various universals of morality around the world. Only when getting into the fine details do you start to see divisions and those come, typically, from environment, and also are able to be accounted for. By simple way of explanation, a culture that has very little water will find various uses of water, completely unsurprisingly, more wasteful and inappropriate than a culture that has plenty of it. The universality between these two cultures is that they both have an abhorrence to waste of precious resources, in general. Additionally, many of these can fade if and when we begin to function as one people, should we decide to do that, as their scarcity and our excess negate one another. We become a bit less wasteful, they a bit less frugal.

I should take a moment to point out that these things I have written are nothing more or less than the lifelong observations of someone who has sought always to understand and where possible improve upon that which reality has to offer. It is the analysis of action rather than words though I disagree with this sentiment on principle the point is what is shown to be present and what is shown to be possible or necessary rather than what is said. My objection to "actions speak louder than words" is not with its spirit but its details. Words are actions, when they are true, and also when they are not. The implication of the statement is, in essence, that truth trumps perception but it has come to mean something else for many. It has come to mean words are easy; they are not, and it has come to mean words can lie and indeed they can, and vigilance is required but make no mistake, actions that are not words can lie as well. Preconceived notions without understanding of the nature of exception will show you only what you want to see. Why do I say this this way? Because mis-generalization is preconceived notion. I have said generalizing is good and necessary when done correctly. Correctly necessitates that you understand that rules have exceptions. By way of simple explanation, there are those who say that women are more nurturing than men and men are more aggressive than women, generalities both, and fair, so long as we remember that these are generalities and so while it may be true, holistically, any given male or female you meet cannot be assumed to be in these camps. Indeed, treating them thusly you reinforce their role and your own perception. Is this too complicated for you? That is ok. If so you are one who should focus on the individuality argument and treat everyone as completely unique until you know otherwise. That said, you should not be in a position of authority over others and you should not be publishing documents about the nature of things or making sweeping public policies. All of which is fine because you should be payed the same as everyone else and only be working in fields you are both suited for and interested in, as should everyone.

Let us presume for a moment that the rich are in fact more industrious than the rest of us. This does not entitle them to be our masters just as it does not obligate them to be our servants. They are simply, according even to themselves, being true to themselves. They work hard because they wish to, presuming this is the case. Working harder than others just like being smarter than others does not entitle you to control others. If working harder is being true to themselves they should do it. The resources they work with are not theirs alone though and nor are the finished goods they produce. Just as in this current paradigm they do not belong to the laborer obligated to make them, differing only in that they also do not belong to their master but rather to everyone. Do the industrious stay industrious every day? Of course not. Do the sedate stay so every day? Of course not. Each contributes according to their nature. If we wish to count the minutia of those contributions it becomes complicated indeed. What we currently assign value to is in no way comprehensive or reasonable in terms of what is and is not of value. All manner of opportunity costs exist in this system we have created which stifles all but a very narrow degree of insights and inventions. Can you honestly say that you know what we have lost for what we have gained? I say it is, for all practical purposes, profound and inestimable. I claim to know only that it has been much. Such is the way of things when the myth of merit is fostered and differential rewards pursued. How many times that you know of have you received less than your due of credit or more than your due of blame, punishment, ostracism? Why? Because you are a competitor in this system. Someone to be removed so as to make some other closer to obtaining the prize. Cooperation is about solutions, not blame. Here merit exists but it is a responsibility, should we accept it, not a privilege as it should be.

The problem of the us/them thinking becomes very clear when you look to the inevitable need to identify the people of differing abilities as different species, either via the racial commentary that has very little validity or in actually referring to others as entirely different species, usually to justify differential rewards. Obviously, a tiger eats a goat and not the other way around, only the one person is not a tiger and the other is likewise not a goat. That there are behavioral links is true and fair. This only means the humans with the traits of goats should do what goats do. They are still human and to be treated as such. The tigers should do what tigers do, perhaps, or the nearest worthy pursuit of it. It is also worth noting that there is a fantastic trend in this scenario to evaluate some of one's traits and not others, focusing on the positive ones for oneself and the negative, or seemingly so, ones for others and ignoring a whole slew of traits that do not match up with the narrative. This is just further evidence of, not only the problem with this thinking, but the inability of most people participating in it to do it fairly or correctly and illustrates the why of it as well as the need to eliminate such mis-generalization. Let us say goats are workers. We need many and they have every bit as much value to society as planners or guardians or administrators, yet here and now they are valued lower, not out of need, not out of justice, out of opportunity due to simple issues of scale. If supply and demand matched for a large group within itself and the same was true of a small group within itself, the supply and demand of the large group, in spite of identical ratios, would be easier to manipulate because of a lack of unity. More people going more directions. Diversity is a good thing, but it's exploitable. We can benefit from diversity without exploiting it, and so should stop exploiting it. Indeed, exploiting it reduces it, as conformity ensues.

Most of us have heard it said that intelligence determines success in capitalism. I can demonstrate a far better fit. The fact is there are many very intelligent poor people. By percentage there *may* be less but by absolute numbers there are more intelligent people in poverty than wealth and what this means is that some other value is more pertinent. Morality has an inverse relationship with success in this country and under this system. A poor person will have more for less effort if they are more immoral and less if they are more moral. The same is true for wealthy, moral and immoral. The same is true for intelligent, moral and immoral. The simple fact is the system we live in rewards, above all other things, immoral, selfish, exploitative behavior. The question of course is, should it? I say it should not and I have demonstrated by a variety of arguments and observations how and why that is so. I say cooperation is the way and cooperation is morality. Do you disagree? If so, what do you call it when you make sure everyone has enough food to eat? That sounds like both cooperation and morality to me. How about everyone having a place to sleep? And as for freedom either we all have it or none have it. You see the jailor is themselves jailed. Walls that keep out also keep in. There is no freedom under capitalism. You are either the jailor or the jailed.

People do not fear death by old age, by and large. People do fear death by cancer, heart attack, or stroke. Why do you suppose this is? I say there are two reasons. The first is that there is a specific name for it now and this knowledge changes the person's focus. There is now hope of victory. It is known and so it can be beaten. And maybe the cancer can be beaten this time but the reason for the cancer, a long life, cannot. Death will come. The cancer will return or another system will fail. Hope and the illusory comfort of knowledge are the reason. Hope is the silver lining of fear. Which is to say it is fear, it just doesn't look like it. Mankind relies on hope to avoid inevitabilities. It is why two armed men walked countless men to their deaths. Men that could have won out though it would have cost some of them their lives. They all died to hope and fear. The hope against hope that someone else would do for them what they could do for themselves but possibly at some cost. Short term thinking and fear and selfishness. Not me said them all. As to the knowledge, it is scant comfort. Understanding, wisdom, intelligence serve far better. Knowledge is infinite… and so perpetually lacking. There is no end to minutia. But the patterns while they represent infinity are finite as we find in a circle. A circle is particularly useful for this illustration because it is a simple symbol that acknowledges infinity while also leaving room for interconnection and cycles. The point above is that action trumps inaction. Hope is inaction. Thought is not. I do not suggest irrational or reckless action. Indeed, at all possible opportunities thought should be the first or second action. Second only to observation in the cases it is not first. Both excesses of haste and excesses of lassitude will yield undesirable results, usually because the thing you have evaluated through observation and thought is no longer what it was. This is not the forte of everyone but then it doesn't have to be. As a society we are not alone. Let the observation of others help you. I say observation here not thought. Group think is highly destructive. Do not confuse what I say in these pages as group think. We are individuals and we have individual strengths. We are also one species and have finite resources. There is only one point we ought to agree on, each in our own time. We do have, and would benefit from more of, indeed we absolutely rely on, cooperation. I do not compel you to believe this. I ask that you do… with evidence and argument. If you disagree, genuinely disagree, and have truly heard what I have to say then discussion is warranted. Not stonewalling and ostracism and mockery and false flattery. Real open honest conversation. This is not group think though it will, by and large, at some point produce at least a few thoughts in common. This is cooperation, not indoctrination. It has disagreement and it has discussion and it has substantiation… that does not necessarily rely on credentialism. Our senses are capable of measuring just as those who perform studies are. And just as surely, they are capable of bias and group think. No method is flawless but for its flawless execution. No person is flawless so no execution can be. The irony of the scientific method is that it puts certitude in the method in spite of flawed beings applying it. This is in point of fact a flaw in the method itself. The rule is solid but they forget that rule has exception. Not only that, much time has passed and the method has become dogma. Old proofs are rarely examined, new observations are rarely credited… unless they come from the priests. It is also worth noting that there is such a thing as expert skill or knowledge. The scientific method is about reproducibility. If we cannot reproduce your results they are not true, they say. This has two problems to my eyes. The first is the weakness of the system itself and the second is the expert issue I hinted at. The weakness is an inability to handle the overly complex due to a need to control variables. This makes some things more or less unmeasurable to science. This does not mean they are not predictable to some of us. And being predictable they are in fact re-creatable. It is however hard to put concrete numbers on them. It is the difference between hitting a target with a traditional longbow and a rifle. One is finesse the other concrete and largely linear at similar ranges. Both are, in the correct hands, highly effective. This brings us to the expert issue. The long bow requires an expert shooter at any significant range. This is in no way meant to disparage the rifle. It is simply an easier skill to acquire to a meaningful range. We can approach this analogy in another way, however. You have two basketball players. One is an average college player and the other is a high-end NBA player. The NBA player can probably reproduce their own results and the average college player can, slightly less well in general reproduce *their* own results. The average college player cannot, however, reproduce the high-end NBA player's results. This might be clear enough but there is one step yet to take. Even an exceptional scientist is not necessarily the top, even in their own field, on any given day, and it is even more relevant when the thing is multifaceted. A specialist is a generalist of the special. A generalist is a specialist of the general. Take a moment and think on the truth of that and the fact that every degree is a specialization. Degrees are not the metric of an ability to generalize, and only somewhat the metric even for specialization. Reason and discussion should be at the front of these decisions, especially since any institution will create echo chamber.

People tend to suggest that those who care what others think are insecure. This is odd to me for two reasons. First, sociopathy is considered a bad thing and yet not caring what others think, a metric of sociopathy by any reasonable standard, is somehow good. Second, caring what others think is a survival function. Community is not merely helpful for humans. It is essential. We do not, by simplest argument, survive to adulthood without community. Human infants are in no way survivable utterly depending upon the community to reach maturity and gain the illusion of independence. Their mental health for instance, still requires human contact, again by simplest proof. So to revisit, recognition of and concern for what others think of us is a survival function as we require community and, ostracism, or others thinking and acting out on ill thoughts, casting us from the group, threatens our survival. Caring *might* suggest you see people as potential enemies. Not caring suggests you certainly see them as enemies already or at a minimum not as allies, and so no change is likely forthcoming to their demeanor, positive or negative. Not only is this sociopathic and destructive of community; what is the point of a society of any kind if it collects not a community but a pool of enemies? What rule can you make that won't be broken at every opportunity under such a system? And if every rule is broken the only point of the rules is to gain further advantage on the part of the sponsors of said rules, is it not?

Which means that the rules are only to be followed for those not the sponsors out of fear of punishment. In such a system abiding the rules is itself a punishment so the punishments are made draconian in order to gain compliance because there is punishment both ways so punishment avoidance is impossible for the have nots, as their lives themselves are punishment. Simple to see why in this system, Christianity, Judaism and Islam have such appeal, as the people hope for an afterlife that reverses their fortunes, where the selfish are punished and cast low and the generous are elevated and raised up Then there is resistance simply due to absurdity of sentencing on top of the rest of the mess. I would say that is the reason they were invented in the first place. Something to give the downtrodden hope enough to toil on. Such a system does not work. Competition eats itself. Cooperation is essential and omnipresent. The only thing even remotely debatable is to what scale. Any scale other than the species means competition… and rules made to be broken.

In competition different is bad. It is alien. In competition that feigns cooperation, as we have, different is bad, if it does not want what we want, we must defeat it. In cooperation different is good. If it does not want what we want, it can have what it wants and we can have what we want. When it does want the same things, difference can still contribute rather than competing, which inevitably draws down. If you doubt this consider the quality of goods today. There was a time when if goods were made they were made to last or they were not made at all. A sound sustainable metric by any measure. That is not the standard today. Make it as cheaply as possible of the cheapest possible materials for the cheapest possible wage. One could make a strong argument that it is planned obsolescence but even if it is not it is shoddy and disposable goods that could and should be sustainable. If capitalism is about dealing with scarcity why does it make everything disposable and more than a little fragile? It meets neither the demands of the customer nor the planet… unless you think we need larger and more frequent landfills? If so do you plan on living near them? Of course not, right?

Knowledge is not intelligence. Computers do not think but they can be given every possible move in chess. Chess is not infinite however. Knowledge is. Intelligence can validly recognize patterns in and out of type. Until computers can do this they are not intelligent. Once they can do this computer programmers are not intelligent… for many, many reasons.

Feminism is damaging to males in general but the males most damaged by feminism are the fair and honest ones who do not use sexism in their interactions. Those least affected are the most chauvinistic ones. Feminism is a polar position made to respond to chauvinism not all males possess. The laws and policies and viewpoints they express however effect all males. And again, the most sexist ones least. Just as feminists are least affected by the chauvinism they claim to be fighting. Both camps damage the middle. That said feminism is the worse of the two. We have no laws that directly fly in the face of anti-discrimination laws in the male camp. Feminism has brought several. The amount of passive aggressiveness in the camp is astounding and that is when it is not being overtly aggressive. As to institutional sexism the supposed metric, feminism is the one that has it. It is written into law and taught in universities.

Where is the moral outrage about our boys being raped, murdered, committing suicide?

Women in our society have never been treated as expendable. Men in our society have always been treated as expendable. This simple honest observation is as far as anyone should ever have to go as to whether or not feminism is valid or worse, actively harmful to rationalism and justice, two intrinsically linked prospects. You cannot have justice without rationalism. Without it you have, at best, vengeance. The feminist camp personified. Except of course feminism, altering legality or public opinion, does not stick even to people that have supposedly wronged them. Indeed, this same camp claims people cannot be generalized while applying not only generalizations but consequences to giant swathes of the populace. The rationalization, at the end, of the day for most of their arguments? I do not like it so no one should. This is not an overgeneralization on my part but theirs. This is literally the gist of their argument. They talk vaguely as though their concern is cooperation but there is no room for difference. A diversity checklist is not diversity, it is a checklist. A standard. More importantly they want zero diversity of thought or behavior. Hence the expectation that men should act like women, a point made even more ironic because when they get what they asked for they are angrier than ever. Men arguing like them are disingenuous. Men being sensitive are babies and man-children. Men who are stoic are unavailable emotionally. Men who take charge are macho and pushy. Men who don't take charge are weak and spineless. Men who want no strings sex are womanizers and should commit. Men who want commitment are clingy and needy. The simple fact is feminism never had a valid place in the world. It was simply a way to dramatically increase the workforce and decrease the wage. If we wanted to end gender roles we could have done so without feminism… unless of course you think no one would have listened to the men had they complained? But then you prove my point that much more resoundingly, do you not?

If feminism is the result of chauvinism what is the result of feminism? The answer folks is chauvinism. It becomes justified by the thing that it is supposedly meant to counter.

You may have noticed I did not devote an equal number of pages to each of these chapters. This was not accidental and was a greater, not lesser, demonstration of justice. I did not give each equal pages because they are not each equal problems. They are however equally essential to the greater message. The goal was to correct for what I have seen as a lack in terms of coverage and honesty elsewhere. You can treat people equally and this is done by giving them equal rights. And equal rights require equal resources in the general sense. (A larger person, typically male, might require more food and less physical assistance for instance.) There is always an exception to a rule and here it is. Uniform pay is required for everyone to have their rights equally respected. They need not make uniform purchases with their uniform pay as they have different needs. But to have access to equality requires this uniformity. The other uniformities are neither possible nor just. We are not uniform in anything but rights. And to be uniform in rights we need uniform access to them. That access is assured and demonstrated by resources. We are not equally strong, and neither strong people nor weak deserve more or less. We are not equally intelligent and neither bright nor simple deserve more or less. We are not equally logical or emotional and neither deserves more or less. We are not equally creative. We are not equally funny or serious. We are not equally ambitious or content (the fair oppositional word to ambitious should also have positive spin or the judgement is clear and both have value in any case) and neither should have more (imagine the world with everyone being so grasping as our most ambitious, it is not pretty). We are however, equally human and every one of us deserves to be here or none of us do. As such we must all get a stake of this world, independent of someone else or even many someone else's telling us our worth. And what that stake is, too, will be a part of what everyone puts into it. If no one wants to farm no one eats. But show a little faith in your fellow man, people. The jealous thought of what about me getting mine and I won't do it because no one else will are a product of the system we have now… and still we have enough and surplus, only it is redistributed upward. Even in this incredibly selfish system we have now people often give of themselves without thought of or expectation of reward. As our security in our fellow man and our value increases this can only improve, especially when it is for us, all of us, that we strive.

Failing to achieve a worthy goal the first time you try something does not equal that thing being either impossible or unworthy. Such argument has been used with respect to why we should not pursue socialism however. The argument against is pure emotional appeal and the likely cause is to maintain an advantaged state in a dysfunctional system. A worthy goal is one that should be pursued and refined until it has been gotten correct. No argument to the contrary makes much sense. What is a worthy goal? Something that is theoretically possible and desirable is a fair working definition. Capitalism is only a worthy goal for the few as defined by its parameters whether it can be made to work or not it impoverishes the majority by design. The lightbulb by contrast is useful to most of us and took 23 attempts or thereabout to produce. Aren't we glad that Edison did not tell himself it is only theoretically possible and that we should skip the refinement? Another thought occurs to me here. It would seem that, are the detractants not to be deemed deceitful, then they are lazy and entitled, discarding worthy notions at the first sign of adversity. I thought these people fancied themselves as being brave, industrious, stoic, diligent and not risk averse? And they may be, but if they are then they are also disingenuous, greedy and opportunistic because little else explains discarding such a worthy venture so readily. Even most detractants of social-ism will acknowledge that it looks good on paper… but are unwilling to perfect it. Ask yourselves why.

<u>Division</u>

Division is at all time high with identity politics. Everyone is divided from everyone else. Either they are supposedly superior via supposed merit from one camp or via victim status, from the other. Women and men. Gay and straight. Black and white. I have not read the Art of War but I wager this tactic is covered extensively in those pages. How do I know? Logic and history. Divide and conquer is a basic tactic. Better still with misdirection turning friends into enemies. A poor person of any ethnicity, gender, sexual orientation, or age has more in common with another poor person than any of these other categories from a societal perspective. And yet they are working at odds with one another and this did not come from nowhere. The media and academia have preached these politics of division exhaustively for years now. What have they skipped though, or glossed over? Why classism of course. The single most important metric of identity and the greatest contributor to the presence or absence of justice, not to mention the overly vague but often foisted power narrative, money and the resources that said money represents. I did say it was not logic alone that had me draw this connection though, did I not? History then. We have, over the decades that identity politics is pushed, drawn apart as a people into ever smaller boxes. And the harder said politics are pushed the stronger the division that follows. Intersectionality is nothing more than meritocracy by victimhood and I have already spoken to the absurdity that is meritocracy. Indeed, that a form of meritocracy defined by victimhood would creep up, and consequently ignore all manner of victims, just further proves the flaws of meritocracy as a social concept. Unity does not come from making labels, sublabels, groups, and rankings. It comes from using the fewest possible titles. It does not mean that people are not different and that subsequently we should dissolve these labels. It is what allows them to be. You don't want to generalize people overly much? Fantastic idea, stop putting them in box after box, the very essence of generalization. Wealth is the only thing that need be addressed, because having more or less of it defines your entire existence and it does so unjustly by any system but uniformity. Here is as good a place as any to point out that social constructs like money, language and math, or even time, if it is to be a useful tool, do require uniformity. The tools, not the people, which can never be uniform, and are best when diverse.

The Singular Weakness of Logic

The singular weakness of logic is that it requires all parties' consent. You can apply logic to people without their consent but cannot engage in logical consensus, debate, or cooperation without all parties agreeing to be logical under the strictest definition of agreement meaning not only do they have to state they agree to logical discourse but they have to abide by their agreement. This later part is where most people fail to abide. The problem is if you are using logic you know you are using logic but if you are not using logic you do not know that you are not using logic as often as not. So, do you consent?

Justice

Logic is a vital component of justice. Emotion is relevant to justice but not how justice is determined. A person's feelings must be considered but they must be considered reasonably. This is not a contradiction but there are those who think it one. Those people are not equipped to determine justice.

Ostracism

In a society in which we have to work to eat, one way or another, be it directly buying food or at a minimum, paying taxes on land to grow one's own, ostracism at sufficient levels is literally a death sentence. Ostracism however is not illegal. Look here to understand the dangers of competition plus consensus. Free speech cannot exist in a world as connected as our own with all land spoken for without a basic entitlement of resources though realistically if resources are not equitably distributed this is nothing more than a stopgap with an eventual near identical outcome. Meaning only the most strong-willed will resist if there is differential reward. Look here for homelessness and prison as well, though obviously not exclusively.

A Low Appeal

If the high-minded appeals are not sufficient here are three lower minded appeals that are similarly compelling for cooperation.

Sooner or later we will face a planet wide challenge to humanity's survival. Maybe global warming isn't the one. Maybe it won't happen for some time yet. What is inescapably true is that while we as a species scrabble to keep position on some silly hill and try to collect the most pretty rocks we will not have eyes nor resources enough devoted to that event when it comes. For all the talk about legacy and elevating humanity you see from both sides the truth is it is that very base kind. It matters not what the end comes as, it comes from failure to cooperate.

A simple appeal to the pragmatists. What is the opportunity cost of this system we use? How many simply opt out. either going high and refusing on moral grounds to contribute to this injustice of a society? How many take the low road and refuse to abide by rules that do not benefit them and in fact may well disadvantage them? And not simply how many in terms of bodies but also ideas and potential? Both quantity and quality, from both pools, are sacrificed needlessly to this system.

It seems to me that the ever-increasing need for escapism is closely related to over specialization and hyper competition. Human beings are not robots and should not be treated or try to act like them. Doing so produces feelings of purposelessness and dissatisfaction that they push down with medications, endless consumption of media, and pointless drama. Anything to not have to deal with the fact that life as we are living is a hollow race for a pointless prize that only serves to separate us from the one thing we actually need, one another.

<u>Rights and Responsibilities</u>

Rights and responsibilities must balance and they always do. And yet the wealthy have more rights than you and fewer responsibilities. Sounds like a contradiction, right? Give me a moment to clarify. By way of example the wealthy have a "right" to better legal counsel because we live in a society where money can and will buy exactly that. Having that ability exonerates them from any number of responsibilities as they can defend themselves from it more successfully in court. This is large right; small responsibility though isn't it? Clearly in conflict with what I said above isn't it? So, add a layer. Where did all their responsibility fall away to? Is there a group in society held unaccountably accountable, that is to say more accountable for their actions? Of course there is. That would be the poor. Is there a group with less than their share of rights? Same group, right? Don't feel left out middle class. Most of you are far closer to the poor end than the wealthy end. So, as I said at the beginning, rights and responsibilities always balance, even when they mismatch. Thus, we need to prevent those mismatches in the first place to address the problem meaningfully. There will always be a mismatch when there are rich and poor... and no there need not always be rich and poor. There will always be differently abled but need not always be differently rewarded. Neither you nor I deserve more for winning some genetic lottery nor for losing it. Thinking otherwise is the root of... there are many words for it... very few of them are positive. Let us just call it elitism. From that thinking comes the inevitable, all the rights for me, all the responsibilities for you. Or call them by another name if you prefer. The wealthy get all the carrot, the poor all the stick.

Still not convinced? I have as many ways to explain this obvious truth as there are things in the universe. Can you say the same for your end?

The Rationale

"I have to hit you/hurt you/exploit you/take from you/profit by you or you will do it to me." This line is utter and complete garbage. The fact is not only does your absence from this behavior not increase the chance that someone else takes part in it. It, in point of fact, becomes LESS likely the fewer people do it. Will there be people that do it if you don't? Sure. This doesn't change the fact that there will be fewer. It is fixed the same way it broke. Incrementally. Dominoes. If this is your justification you are only lying to yourself... well, that and the gullible. Do better. Also, you substantially decrease the odds that those of us who currently take it start swinging back; whichever gives you better motivation. ;)

There is a difference between a symptom and a disease. Do you know it? You can "cure" a symptom and still die of the disease but more likely the symptom will simply resurface again and again with myriad other symptoms. All quite simple though, right? So how is it then, that people don't see and understand said simple obvious reality when applied to say a social disease and its symptoms? Racism? Symptom. Sexism? Symptom. Ableism? Symptom. Ageism? Symptom. Classism/wealth disparity? Rampant disease. Disagree? Wealth connects to all above it universally. You see racism? Wealth is its origin. You think racism is the origin of wealth differential on the other hand? Afraid not. Can racism produce wealth disparity? Of course it can. Just not as an origin point. Assume no racism or classism, which starts the ball rolling? Racism? Not hardly. In fact, discriminating meant tasteful. Hawaii welcomed newcomers for genetic diversity... humans are programmed to recognize difference innately... and value it. We are taught to turn it the other way. That all starts with haves and have nots. Are we all differently gifted? Yes. Are any of us inferior? Nope. This is the reality upon which a universal wage rests. We co-operate. Even the ones who pretend that they have never had such. It is easier to kill than to tolerate... or embrace, but that is not what humans do. The only question is the size of your circle. We need a bigger circle. One circle.

I have said previously that competition in our society is a social construct and that cooperation is in our nature and also the fundamental framework of a civilization. This bears some clarification however, so as to not appear to contradict either myself or reality. Both cooperation and competition are in our nature. Which gets expressed and to what extent is determined more by our environment than ourselves, however. In situations of extreme adversity people cease to trust one another and cooperation diminishes. In situations of extreme scarcity people compete to ensure that they receive their basic needs. Hoarding also becomes much more likely in times of scarcity, and should it scar us psychologically, far into the future, even insofar as to instill it in future generations. Obviously saving for a rainy day to a moderate extent is different from hard core hoarding. The consequence of hoarding, incidentally, is inflation, at least with respect to currency. At any rate, you can see how an environment might cause us to express one element of our nature over another. The system we have at the forefront of our societies, even ones we call socialist, is competition. This is, to my eyes, a flaw. We have plenty. There is enough to go around and then some. There is a small percentage of the populace with a bottomless need, however. Do I think them evil? No. I do think they do not realize that what they lack is the very thing they deny themselves and try to deny the rest of us not realizing that this as yet unnamed thing is the thing that they lack. They do not need more money. They have more than they could ever use. They do not need more admiration. Our society reveres the wealthy more than almost anything else. They need to belong to their fellow man as their fellow man belongs to them. That is what they can never have in an environment of division and division, whether it is deliberate or the predictable but accidental byproduct of what they do chase is what they produce, keeping them from the only thing that will make them whole and address their unfilled need. Division does not harm the weak and leave the powerful unscathed. The jailor too is in jail and imbalance such as this is both energetic and destructive. The thing is, we all have another nature that can be fostered by a society structured to do so. We have a society that pushes our competitive elements to the fore with artificial scarcities, unnecessary hierarchies, and constant appeals to fear and hatred of yet another created "other". Not only could we have a society focused on cooperation, frankly it would be less exhausting, barring initial implementation, more productive, more nurturing, more innovative. It is indeed the very purpose of civilization to cooperate and that we have and value having a civilization is a tacit agreement of that fact on the part of most if not all of us.

On a very closely related note comes another facet of our nature as human beings. We are by nature, good at noting differences both small and large. This is intrinsic to who we are and is a good thing, essential for mate selection and survival among other more esoteric things such as being a facet of our ability to create and develop the arts and sciences. Like all facets of nature, nurture, or our environment heavily affects how it is expressed. Neither nature nor nurture, as I have indicated before, are autonomous. They are inseparable. The point here is that this is another element of our nature badly expressed by a social system whose purpose is to foster competition over cooperation. We do not innately see differences as good or bad, we simply see them. In a system of competition any difference from oneself is a negative one, however. A difference that disadvantages another individual is a weakness to be exploited under competition. A difference that advantages another is a threat to be eliminated or to have the perception of it tainted so that it comes to be perceived as a flaw. Do we see much of this in our society at present, pray tell? I certainly do. In a cooperative system a disadvantaging trait is simply a matter of proper fit. The same applies to an advantaging trait. In fact, disadvantaging and advantaging cease. They are a product of competition and the consequent discarding and ostracism of people. There is no trait that has no value and there is no trait that has unlimited value. Perhaps a simple example or two to illustrate my point is in order? Take a high intelligence and energy person and put them on a factory assembly line. You might say they are wasted there, and you would not be wrong except that you are only half right. They are not merely wasted there. They are in fact a detriment. If the line is sped up to them, others do not finish. If it is not, they lose focus and fail at the overly simple but rigidly paced task. No, the simple fact is people are not better or worse than one another they are simply different. Having more or less common gifts does not disprove that as, among other things, more common gifts tend to be needed in larger numbers and less common gifts also tend to be needed in smaller numbers. There is a right way and a wrong way to handle these differences. We should be able to speak to a difference for expediencies sake or acknowledge it as a reality. For instance, you wish to tell your companion Bob did a great job today. Bob is on the other side of the room and is conversing with two other people. Those people happen to have a different skin color than Bob, an expedient trait for making it clear which of them you are talking about. You should say, and be able to say, without the slightest flutter of an eyebrow, Bob is the black guy. It is an individual difference, it exists, and it has relevant use on the micro scale. This should not continue to the macroscale for one simple reason. Society should not be dividing people of any category into classes. Yes, you heard me correctly, any category. Not even men and women. This does not mean there aren't men and women. It means that we should not have rules strictly for one or the other of them and if we do not have rules for one or the other of them we do not need the classification within the rules. It ceases to be a class or division other than as defined by nature, which we do not need to acknowledge in the slightest. Nature already handled that. If a thing has a qualification intrinsic to it, then it does. Fair to examine that this is so. Not fair to create the class, nor necessary. For instance, no males would qualify as mothers but there is still no need to qualify the role as female, it is already done. On the other side, let us say a vocation, for some reason (presume legitimate need) required the worker be able to lift 300 lbs. overhead. Few men and practically no women would qualify for said position. Keep in mind these examples are chosen for clarity and based upon real physical (and general) differences. Also remember qualify doesn't mean the same thing when your vocation is a duty rather than an entitlement to a better life.

There is a formula, so to speak for what produces division socially. Unnecessary names and divisions are the fundament of such which is not to be confused with recognizing differences as previously indicated. The term I use for the purpose of identifying what I am talking about is Unity through Division.

We don't need smaller government. Smaller government means elitism and elitism means those on the other side of whatever bar is set will soon be declared villains for little valid reason. We don't need middle government, such as that found in a republic, which is what we have now. Those serve whatever special interest group you can cobble together and ultimately again, elitism. Haves and have nots are inevitable here as is war and utter stagnation. This is the place where one might be the king of the ashes. What we need is bigger government, much bigger, as near to 100 percent as possible big. But to do that we need to give the people reason to be involved. Choosing representatives is tribalism. We should be choosing ideas. The people are disinterested you say? Of course they are. Their voice does not count and they know it. Our system has us choosing people, inevitably flawed people rather than weighting in on things directly and we are then to be manipulated based upon feeling rather than thoughts and facts. How could we not grow disgusted and even if we aren't disgusted one must exercise a skill to improve it, yes? You cannot reasonably complain that the people are apathetic and simultaneously deny them any meaningful autonomy or voice. If you object to what I propose based upon the time and scale I have response here as well. First and easiest is that it is high time automation worked for us all rather than some few. To that end we should find the time we need to be true citizens should we also abide the second tenet. The second tenet is that while government should be larger it should also be narrower. I should explain my meaning for narrower. We do not need regulations telling people whether or not they should or can smoke or drink or play at a park after dark. We do need information to be widely available as to the implications of these things. We do need standards of manufacture. We do need awareness of quality of life. We do not need to tell people how to live it. We do need laws about willful harm of others. We do not need to make it microscopic. Life brings adversity to all and some of that is and should be live and learn, not so much what is right but what suits you. This is essential for diversity to succeed and flourish. We do need to concern ourselves with the state of our neighborhood as well and that neighborhood based upon our travel and the reach of our impact is the planet itself. We may never kill the planet but we can absolutely destroy our species and most others on it and that would be neither fair nor wise to them and to ourselves. The truth is many of the problems we currently need to look to government for would simply cease to be if we can get past the mentality of profit. How many of the things that are dangerous and irresponsible would never have been produced but for the drive for profit above all. How many worthy innovations shelved for said same cause? You want to see what profit looks like; visit a clear-cut rainforest or strip-mined quarry and then visit a dump. We can make things more enduring and not make cash redistributing trash but where is the profit in that?

I believe we should all receive an equal share of this world. This can be done via a monthly credit. Said monthly credit could be used for all things. No real goods should be owned, not so different from present in all honesty, with durable things being effectively rented with the price based upon availability, ala true supply and demand. People would not be obligated to work nor, due to equal credits, able to direct and subjugate people. As such what is available to purchase with said credits is determined by what people choose to make, presumably because they themselves want it. Education and health care would have availability under said same auspices but professions would not be in it for the money but a genuine belief in what it is they are doing. Burnout would be avoided due to the reduction in obligation. Making education a right, within the limits of it's availability is necessary should we receive an equal share of the worlds resources via a universal credit. In order to do that, education must be a right but advancing in education must be based upon ability. There is no shame in not having a particular aptitude nor a financial cost to the individual in this scenario while simultaneously those who are capable are not saddled with astronomical debt or the ability to command absurd amounts of the worlds resources. Much like vocation, education would be for those who desire and need it rather than being primarily a springboard to inequality. Health care becomes a right but medical staff are not compelled to work nor do they have to be. Strikes by medical staff are met with extreme measures in our current system and occur because of wage issues… wage issues that would not exist under this model. Really the only reason not to follow this course is a lack of faith in one's fellow man. Said lack of faith comes from our present system not this other one. Memories are short but not short enough that there would be no bumps on the way to this but it is possible and preferable, or so all evidence suggests to me and ultimately you need not have faith in the better angels of our disposition to see the merit of what I say. From a practical perspective it serves us better too.

The Decision

The decision we can and should be making is not between left and right. It is between truth and fiction. Both the left and right lie, for profit. The decision isn't between capitalism and socialism. Both can be exploited. It is between competition and cooperation. It is not between religion and science. Both can look where they want and ignore what they do not like. It is between bias and honesty. Will you tell a half-truth to get what you want today and destroy tomorrow? It does you know? Lies need to be unraveled sooner or later to progress. That is time wasted since the truth could have been told in the first place. Is your fellow man your friend or your enemy? Is difference something to fear and hate or something to love and value? I say everything has its place and its utility. It is only a matter of understanding it. It will talk to you if you listen. Misuse a thing and you will know it, unless you choose to ignore it, at which point it will speak louder. Can you hear the misuse? I do not hear it coming from one group. I hear it coming from every group. We have lines between are divisions do we not? These are fractures…because we are broken. But it need not be so. Hatred is learned, trust is innate. Competition is learned, cooperation is innate. But cooperation requires sharing, and that we each get what we need. Insecurity, like that fostered by division, like identity politics, breeds competition, not cooperation. The very thing identity politics claims to be seeking is the thing it can never ever bring both historically and logically. We are all unique. We also all have commonalities. None of us needs a neon sign saying so. That is the path to some of us are more special than others and we aren't, because we all have the same rights, or should, and deserve the same respect.

How do we implement this utopia you might ask? I won't tell you all the ins and outs. Something like this warrants discussion. I will say this though. Without equal pay, meaning universal pay, identical pay, we cannot have equal rights because we do not have equal voice in society nor equal respect since we can not as easily make our voices heard. That is the first and most crucial issue, though when I say pay I mean credits. There are no private savings. That manipulates supply and demand. Largess comes to all, or none and so community grows more a community. Secondly, while education is useful it easily turns to indoctrination whether managed by the church, the state, or private enterprise. We should not have degree requirements for jobs but tests, minimalist tests, testing only crucial knowledge and understanding necessary to perform a duty. This is, frankly, more fair than our current system for several reasons, eliminating experiential biases and educational requirements while actually verifying that the skills that will in fact be used are present, for the good of all. Third, no one should have real property. All real goods should be bid upon via the aforementioned credit or universal wage. This ensures that people cooperate. Personal ownership of real goods removes resources from the pool, permanently. This avoids that and encourages production should availability not meet demand. Fourth, we should use a real supply and demand equation to distribute resources based upon stated desire and available goods. This is more than feasible with the infrastructure we have available. I realize this is broad strokes but the premise is sound and addresses the key pitfalls of such a system.

I do realize people think some of my words and ideas come from elsewhere. I do not exist in a vacuum as I have acknowledged elsewhere but there are not the words of another but observations I have cultivated across a lifetime spent studying people and systems. I find personal observation, study, and introspection superior for understanding the world around me. If two different people from different times and places come to many similar conclusions about the nature of the society and the world at large one might want to consider the merits of what they have said with a somewhat more open mind, presuming those two individuals we are speaking of are bright. Upon arriving at college, I was told on multiple occasions that I sound like I am quoting a great many historical figures I had never read, yet I find argument with nearly everyone I speak with. In truth my exposure to some of these thinkers was both a joy and a sorrow to myself. The joy was in knowing I was not the only one to have had thoughts running the directions they do. The sorrow? That they still remain unrealized today… The sorrow far outweighed the joy but I write this hoping we might soon be ready to do what we can to make society a more hospitable place for all. I did say many find quarrel with me though or I with them so consider this. There are two kinds of people everyone disagrees with, the bright and the foolish, both for the same reason in general but diametrically opposed in specifics. The bright and the foolish think differently than others, they are not of the norm or average. The below disagree with everyone because they usually see less. The above because they usually see more. Which do you believe I am? Assuming you think I may be bright all that remains is to ask if you think me honest or a liar? This one I will not walk further, I have written many words. Is there truth or is there not? Assuming I am, to your eye, both bright and honest I ask only that you weight my words accordingly and decide for yourself if we can live a better way, because it is up to you. Every one of you.

I realize I have stronger views than most. I realize that many of my observations are potentially, even probably, unpleasant to large elements of the populace. Shock and outrage are not my aim however. I hope that over the course of this book you have seen something that you have not considered before now. I hope that it has given you pause and made you think. I would be overjoyed if you found much to agree with but even if you disagree with everything I have said I hope that you appreciate that these are the honest observations of another human being as fairly as I can place them to something as static and unresponsive as a page and that this fact itself gives you insight into the world that we share. Simply stated I simply want the best for us all and like any worthy goal cannot and should not accomplish that without the involvement and consent of us all. An unpleasant truth must be faced for hope of a better tomorrow, one way or another.

That being said it seems to me that any number of the points that I have made, in their own right, should give pause as to whether we are ok with the system that we have. It seems to me that when point after point implies the same conclusion that we are being willfully blind and deliberately complacent if, after having seen it, we do nothing about it. Lastly, it seems to me that this cannot be fixed, should you agree that it should be fixed, by one of us, ten of us, or ten thousand of us. We need to choose cooperation and cooperation means equality, not equality of outcome, the one discussed extreme as we do not need to make the fastest run slower so that those without legs can keep up, nor equality of opportunity on the other end, which is purely a myth as both nature (our own limitations) and nurture(those imposed upon us) conspire to make this either myth or dishonesty, but simply equality of resources via a universal wage for all, to be used on one's own diverse interests with supply and demand alone dictating prices and the pressure on the people to produce…or so it seems to me. Hopefully I have made the case well enough that this is, in reality neither capitalism nor socialism (in the sense it is presently seen) but simply civilization. Good day and thank you for reading.